REEDS MARINA GUIDE 2020

The source directory for all sail & power boat owners

© Adlard Coles Nautical 2019

Adlard Coles Nautical,
50 Bedford Square,
London, WC1B 3DP
Tel: 01865 411010
e-mail: info@reedsalmanacs.co.uk
www.reedsalmanacs.co.uk

Cover photo: ancora Marina, Germany, member of TransEurope Marinas
www.transeuropemarinas.com

Section 1

The Marinas and Services Section has been fully updated for the 2019 season. These useful pages provide chartlets and facility details for some 200 marinas around the shores of the UK and Ireland, including the Channel Islands, the perfect complement to any Reeds Nautical Almanac.

Section 2

The Marine Supplies & Services section lists more than 1000 services at coastal and other locations around the British Isles. It provides a quick and easy reference to manufacturers and retailers of equipment, services and supplies both nationally and locally together with emergency services.

Advertisement Sales
Enquiries about advertising space should be addressed to:
adlardcoles@bloomsbury.com

Printed by Bell and Bain Ltd, Glagow

Section 1
Marinas and Services Section

M000169996

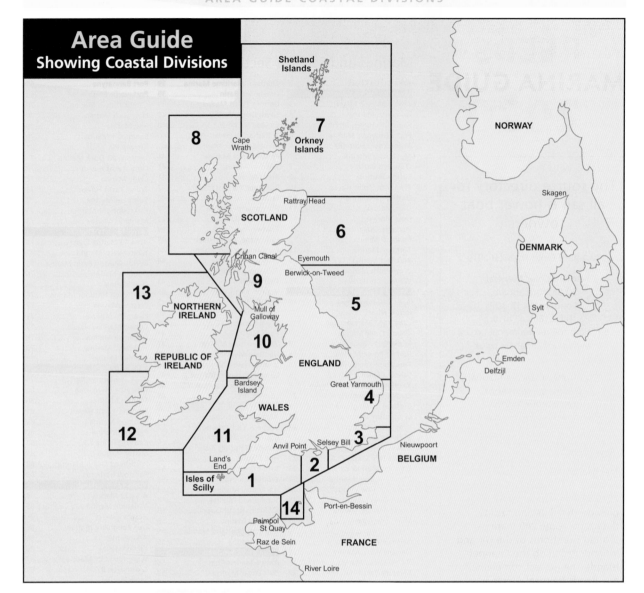

Area Guide
Showing Coastal Divisions

Area 1 .....**South West England**.. Isles of Scilly to Anvil Point

Area 2 .....**Central Southern England**...Anvil Point to Selsey Bill

Area 3 .....**South East England** .... Selsey Bill to North Foreland

Area 4 .....**East England** .... North Foreland to Great Yarmouth

Area 5 .....**North East England**... Great Yarmouth to Berwick-upon-Tweed

Area 6 .....**South East Scotland**.. Eyemouth to Rattray Head

Area 7 .....**North East Scotland**..................Rattray Head to Cape Wrath including Orkney & Shetland Is

Area 8 .....**North West Scotland** ....Cape Wrath to Crinan Canal

Area 9 .....**South West Scotland** ....Crinan Canal to Mull of Galloway

Area 10 ...**North West England** .... Isle of Man & N Wales, Mull of Galloway to Bardsey Is

Area 11 ...**South Wales & Bristol Channel**.. Bardsey Island to Land's End

Area 12 ...**South Ireland** ....Malahide, clockwise to Liscannor Bay

Area 13 ...**North Ireland**...Liscannor Bay, clockwise to Lambay Island

Area 14 ...**Channel Islands**.. Guernsey and Jersey

SOUTH WEST ENGLAND – Isles of Scilly to Anvil Point

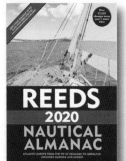
Key to Marina Plans symbols

Bottled gas	Parking
Chandler	Pub/Restaurant
Disabled facilities	Pump out
Electrical supply	Rigging service
Electrical repairs	Sail repairs
Engine repairs	Shipwright
First Aid	Shop/Supermarket
Fresh Water	Showers
Fuel - Diesel	Slipway
Fuel - Petrol	Toilets
Hardstanding/boatyard	Telephone
Internet Café	Trolleys
Laundry facilities	Visitors berths
Lift-out facilities	Wi-Fi

Area 1 - South West England

MARINAS
Telephone Numbers
VHF Channel
Access Times

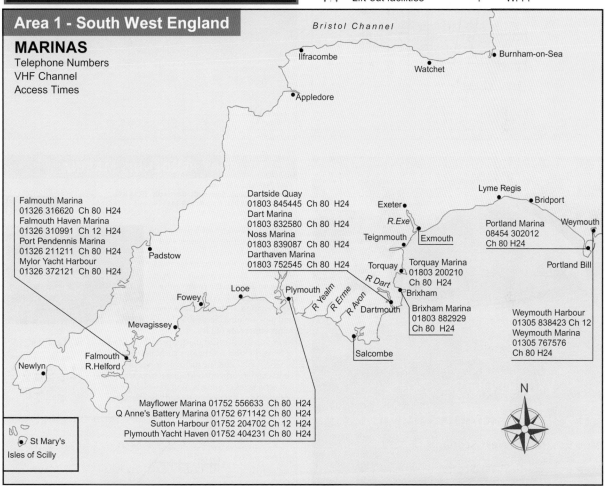

Bristol Channel

Ilfracombe

Watchet

Burnham-on-Sea

Appledore

Falmouth Marina
01326 316620 Ch 80 H24
Falmouth Haven Marina
01326 310991 Ch 12 H24
Port Pendennis Marina
01326 211211 Ch 80 H24
Mylor Yacht Harbour
01326 372121 Ch 80 H24

Dartside Quay
01803 845445 Ch 80 H24
Dart Marina
01803 832580 Ch 80 H24
Noss Marina
01803 839087 Ch 80 H24
Darthaven Marina
01803 752545 Ch 80 H24

Exeter
R.Exe
Teignmouth
Exmouth

Lyme Regis
Bridport

Portland Marina
08454 302012
Ch 80 H24

Weymouth

Padstow

Torquay
R Dart
Brixham
Dartmouth

Torquay Marina
01803 200210
Ch 80 H24

Brixham Marina
01803 882929
Ch 80 H24

Portland Bill

Fowey
Looe
Plymouth
R Yealm
R Erme
R Avon

Salcombe

Weymouth Harbour
01305 838423 Ch 12
Weymouth Marina
01305 767576
Ch 80 H24

Mevagissey

Newlyn
Falmouth
R.Helford

Mayflower Marina 01752 556633 Ch 80 H24
Q Anne's Battery Marina 01752 671142 Ch 80 H24
Sutton Harbour 01752 204702 Ch 12 H24
Plymouth Yacht Haven 01752 404231 Ch 80 H24

N

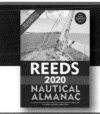

St Mary's
Isles of Scilly

FALMOUTH MARINA

Falmouth Marina
North Parade, Falmouth, Cornwall, TR11 2TD
Tel: 01326 316620 Fax: 01326 313939
Email: falmouth@premiermarinas.com
www.premiermarinas.com

⚓⚓⚓

VHF	Ch 80
ACCESS	H24

Falmouth Marina lies tucked away in sheltered waters at the southern end of the Fal Estuary. Welcoming to both visiting and residential yachts, its comprehensive facilities include a restaurant, convenience store and hairdresser, while just a 20-minute walk away is Falmouth's town centre where you will find no shortage of shops and eating places. Comprising more than 70 sq miles of navigable water, the Fal Estuary is an intriguing cruising area full of hidden creeks and inlets.

FACILITIES AT A GLANCE

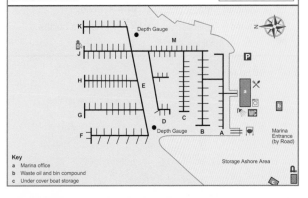

Key
a   Marina office
b   Waste oil and bin compound
c   Under cover boat storage

FALMOUTH HAVEN MARINA

Falmouth Haven Marina
44 Arwenack Street
Tel: 01326 310991
Email: welcome@falmouthhaven.co.uk

VHF	Ch 12
ACCESS	H24

Run by Falmouth Harbour Commissioners (FHC), Falmouth Haven Marina has become increasingly popular since its opening in 1982, enjoying close proximity to the amenities and entertainments of Falmouth town centre. Sheltered by a breakwater, Falmouth Haven caters for 50 boats and offers petrol and diesel supplies as well as good shower and laundry facilities.

Falmouth Harbour is considered by some to be the cruising capital of Cornwall and its deep water combined with easily navigable entrance – even in the severest conditions – makes it a favoured destination for visiting yachtsmen.

FACILITIES AT A GLANCE

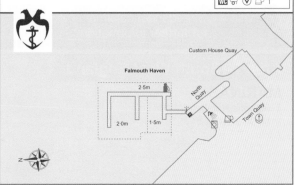

PORT PENDENNIS MARINA

Port Pendennis Marina
Challenger Quay, Falmouth, Cornwall, TR11 3YL
Tel: 01326 211211 Fax: 01326 311116
www.portpendennis.com

VHF	Ch 80
ACCESS	H24

Easily identified by the tower of the National Maritime Museum, Port Pendennis Marina is a convenient arrival or departure point for trans-Atlantic or Mediterranean voyages. Lying adjacent to the town centre, Port Pendennis is divided into an outer marina, with full tidal access, and inner marina, accessible three hours either side of HW. Among its impressive array of marine services is Pendennis Shipyard, one of Britain's most prestigious yacht builders, while other amenities on site include car hire, tennis courts and a yachtsman's lounge, from where you can send faxes or e-mails. Within walking distance of the marina are beautiful sandy beaches, an indoor swimming pool complex and castle.

FACILITIES AT A GLANCE

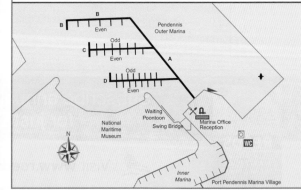

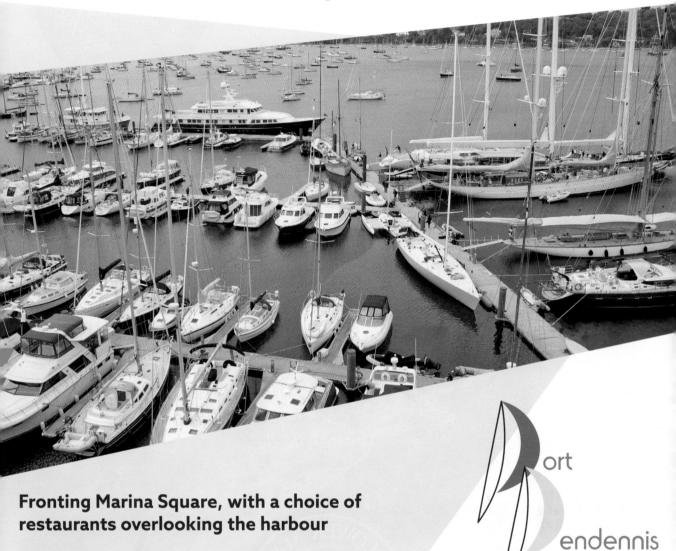

1

MYLOR YACHT HARBOUR

Mylor Yacht Harbour Marina
Mylor, Falmouth, Cornwall, TR11 5UF
Tel: 01326 372121
Email: enquiries@mylor.com

VHF	Ch M, 80
ACCESS	H24

Nestled on the western shore of the beautiful Fal Estuary, Mylor Yacht Harbour's stunning marina has 180 berths and is surrounded by 240 swinging moorings. A large dedicated visitor pontoon, easy H24 access and excellent shore-side facilities set within an Area of Outstanding Natural Beauty combine to make Mylor a must-visit cruising destination.

The historic site was founded in 1805 as the Navy's smallest dockyard but is now a thriving yacht harbour and full service boatyard. Superb on site café, restaurant and yacht club all overlook the harbour and scenic coastal footpaths run from the top of the gangway. Falmouth is just 10 minutes away.

FACILITIES AT A GLANCE

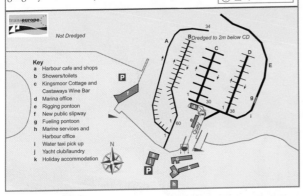

Key
- a Harbour cafe and shops
- b Showers/toilets
- c Kingsmoor Cottage and Castaways Wine Bar
- d Marina office
- e Rigging pontoon
- f New public slipway
- g Fueling pontoon
- h Marine services and Harbour office
- i Water taxi pick up
- j Yacht club/laundry
- k Holiday accommodation

MAYFLOWER MARINA

Mayflower Marina
Richmond Walk, Plymouth, PL1 4LS
Tel: 01752 556633
Email: info@mayflowermarina.co.uk

VHF	Ch 80
ACCESS	H24

Sitting on the famous Plymouth Hoe, with the Devon coast to the left and the Cornish coast to the right, Mayflower Marina is a friendly, well-run marina. Facilities include 24 hour access to fuel, gas and a launderette, full repair and maintenance services as well as an on site bar and brasserie. The marina is located only a short distance from Plymouth's town centre, where there are regular train services to and from several major towns and cities.

FACILITIES AT A GLANCE

Key
- a Marina office
- b Brokerage, chandlery
- c Cafe
- d Bar
- e Brasserie
- f Berth holders toilets and showers
- g Ocean Court Flats

NB Arrows denote direction of numbers low to high. Even numbers on port side, odd to starboard

Northern approach
Breakwater
Southern approach

QUEEN ANNE'S BATTERY

Queen Anne's Battery
Plymouth, Devon, PL4 OLP
Tel: 01752 671142
Email: qab@mdlmarinas.co.uk   www.queenannesbattery.co.uk

VHF	Ch 80
ACCESS	H24

Plymouth, a vibrant and fast growing city, is home to Queen Anne's Battery, a 235 resident berth marina with outstanding facilities for yachtsmen and motor cruisers alike. Located just south of Sutton Harbour, QAB promises a welcoming stay with alongside pontoon berthing protected by the surrounding breakwater. While on the city's doorstep, the marina is a short walk away from the historical Barbican, providing peace and tranquility to visitors.

The marina is often frequented by crowds of people marveling the many prestigious international yacht and powerboat races Plymouth Sound facilitates.

QAB is an exposed treasure along a beautiful historic coastline, at times resembling a mini 'Cowes' with its vibrancy.

FACILITIES AT A GLANCE

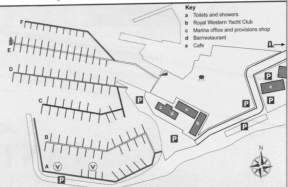

Key
- a Toilets and showers
- b Royal Western Yacht Club
- c Marina office and provisions shop
- d Bar/restaurant
- e Cafe

Because it's not always plain sailing

Call us for a quotation
+ 44 (0)1752 223656

The unique Pantaenius Yacht Scheme offers some of the broadest insurance cover available. Why not join the 100,000 boat owners worldwide who enjoy the peace of mind a Pantaenius policy provides.

PANTAENIUS
Sail & Motor Yacht Insurance

Plymouth · pantaenius.co.uk

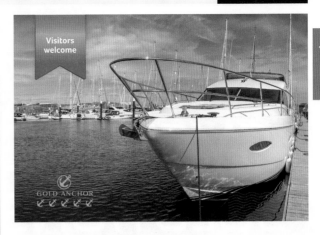

PLYMOUTH YACHT HAVEN

Plymouth Yacht Haven Ltd
Shaw Way, Mount Batten, Plymouth, PL9 9XH
Tel: 01752 404231 www.yachthavens.com
Email: enquiries@plymouthyachthaven.com

VHF	Ch 80
ACCESS	H24

Situated minutes from Plymouth sound, Plymouth Yacht Haven enjoys a tranquil setting, yet is just a five minute water taxi ride from the bustling barbican with all its restaurants and attractions. The Yacht Haven offers excellent protection from the prevailing SW winds and is within easy reach of some of the most fantastic cruising grounds.

This 450-berth marina can accommodate vessels up to 45m in length and 7m in draught. Members of staff are on site 24/7 to welcome you as a visitor and to serve diesel. With an on site 75T travel hoist and storage, a restaurant, chandlery, and extensive range of marine service, Plymouth Yacht Haven has plenty to offer both on and off the water.

FACILITIES AT A GLANCE

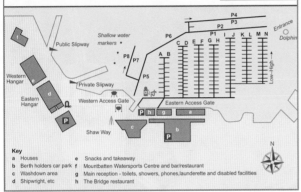

Key
a Houses
b Berth holders car park
c Washdown area
d Shipwright, etc
e Snacks and takeaway
f Mountbatten Watersports Centre and bar/restaurant
g Main reception - toilets, showers, phones,launderette and disabled facilities
h The Bridge restaurant

SUTTON HARBOUR

Sutton Harbour
The Jetty, Sutton Harbour, Plymouth, PL4 0DW
Tel: 01752 204702 Fax: 01752 204693
Email: marina@sutton-harbour.co.uk
www.suttonharbourmarina.com

VHF	Ch 12
ACCESS	H24

Sutton Harbour Marina, located in the heart of Plymouth's historic Barbican area and a short stroll from the city centre, offers 5-star facilities in a sheltered location, surrounded by boutique waterfront bars and restau a minimum 3.5m depth, the harbour has 24hr lock access on request with free flow approx 3hrs either side of high tide. The marina of choice for international yacht races such as The Transat and Fastnet. Visitors are invited to come and enjoy the unrivalled shelter, facilities, atmosphere and location that Sutton harbour offers.

FACILITIES AT A GLANCE

Key
a Fish market
b National Marine Aquarium
c Customs House
d The Cove
e Marina office
f Lock tower

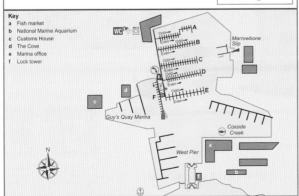

Guy's Quay Marina

Marrowbone Slip

Coxside Creek

West Pier

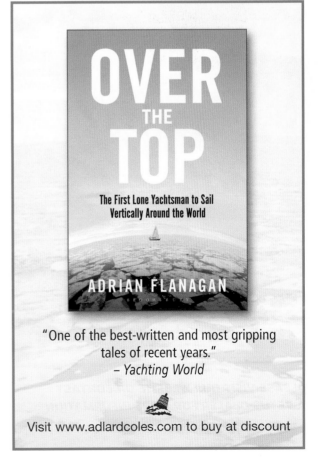

DARTHAVEN MARINA

Darthaven Marina
Brixham Road, Kingswear, Devon, TQ6 0SG
Tel: 01803 752242
Email: admin@darthaven.co.uk
www.darthaven.co.uk

VHF Ch 80
ACCESS H24

Darthaven Marina is a family run business situated in the village of Kingswear on the east side of the River Dart. Within half a mile from Start Bay and the mouth of the river, it is the first marina you come to from seaward and is accessible at all states of the tide. Darthaven prides itself on being more than just a marina, offering a high standard of marine services with both electronic and engineering experts plus wood and GRP repairs on site. A shop, post office and three pubs are within a walking distance of the marina, while a frequent ferry service takes passengers across the river to Dartmouth.

FACILITIES AT A GLANCE

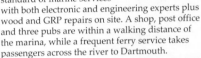

Key
a Main office
   Chandlery
   Electricians
b Shipwrights
c Engineers
d Yacht taxi pontoon
e Berthing office
f Welding workshop

DART MARINA

Dart Marina
Sandquay Road, Dartmouth, Devon, TQ6 9PH
Tel: 01803 837161 Fax: 01803 835040
Email: yachtharbour@dartmarina.com
www.dartmarinayachtharbour.com

VHF Ch 80
ACCESS H24

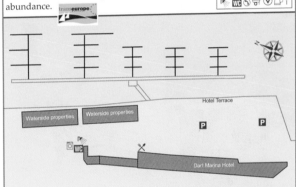

Dart Marina Yacht Harbour, in one of the most stunning locations on the UK coastline, is a peaceful spot for simply sitting on deck relaxing and perfectly positioned for day sailing or more ambitious cruising. With visitor berths, 110 annual berths, all accessible at any tide, the Yacht Harbour is sought after for its intimate atmosphere and stylish setting.

Professional, knowledgeable and helpful, the marina team is on-site all year round and there are impeccable facilities including showers, bathrooms and laundry.

In Dartmouth there are restaurants, bistros, cafes, delis, independent shops, galleries, a cinema, chandlers, antique and lifestyle shops in abundance.

FACILITIES AT A GLANCE

NOSS MARINA

Noss Marina
Bridge Road, Kingswear, Devon, TQ6 0EA
Tel: 01803 839087 Fax: 01803 835620
Email: info@nossmarina.co.uk
www.nossmarina.co.uk

VHF Ch 80
ACCESS H24

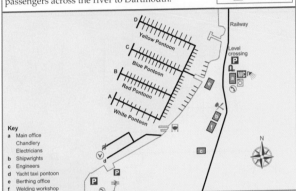

Upstream of Dartmouth on the east shore of the River Dart is Noss Marina. Enjoying a peaceful rural setting, this marina is well suited to those who prefer a quieter atmosphere. Besides 180 fully serviced berths, 50 fore-and-aft moorings in the middle reaches of the river are also run by the marina, with mooring holders entitled to use all the facilities available to berth holders. During summer, a passenger ferry service runs regularly between Noss-on-Dart and Dartmouth, while a grocery service to your boat can be provided on request.

FACILITIES AT A GLANCE

Key
a Marina office
b Amenities

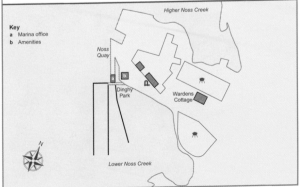

DARTSIDE QUAY

Dartside Quay
Galmpton Creek, Brixham, Devon, TQ5 0EH
Tel: 01803 845445
Email: dartsidequay@mdlmarinas.co.uk
www.dartsidequay.co.uk

VHF Ch 80
ACCESS HW±2

Located at the head of Galmpton Creek, Dartside Quay lies three miles upriver from Dartmouth. In a sheltered position and with beautiful views across to Dittisham, it offers extensive boatyard facilities. The seven-acre dry boat storage area has space for over 300 boats and is serviced by a 65-ton hoist operating from a purpose-built dock, plus a 20-ton trailer hoist operating on a slipway. There are also a number of overnight/monthly pontoons available (dries out) in the summer months. You will also find various specialist marine tenants on site able to assist with boat repairs and maintenance.

FACILITIES AT A GLANCE

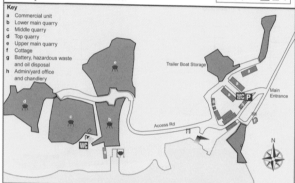

Key
a   Commercial unit
b   Lower main quarry
c   Middle quarry
d   Top quarry
e   Upper main quarry
f   Cottage
g   Battery, hazardous waste and oil disposal
h   Admin/yard office and chandlery

BRIXHAM MARINA

Brixham Marina
Berry Head Road, Brixham, Devon, TQ5 9BW
Tel: 01803 882929
Email: brixham@mdlmarinas.co.uk
www.brixhammarina.co.uk

VHF Ch 80
ACCESS H24

Home to one of Britain's largest fishing fleets, Brixham Harbour is located on the southern shore of Torbay, which is well sheltered from westerly winds and where tidal streams are weak. Brixham Marina, housed in a separate basin to the work boats, provides easy access in all weather conditions and at all states of the tide. Provisions and diesel are available and there is a bar and restaurant, ideal for when you've worked up an appetite out on the water.

Local attractions include a walk out to Berry Head Nature Reserve and a visit to the replica of Sir Francis Drake's *Golden Hind*.

FACILITIES AT A GLANCE

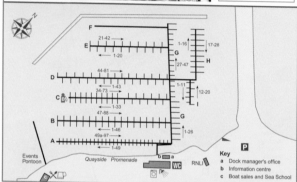

Key
a   Dock manager's office
b   Information centre
c   Boat sales and Sea School

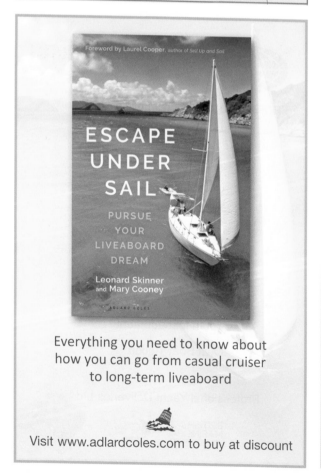

ESCAPE UNDER SAIL

Foreword by Laurel Cooper, author of *Sail Up and Sail*

PURSUE YOUR LIVEABOARD DREAM

Leonard Skinner and Mary Cooney

ADLARD COLES

Everything you need to know about how you can go from casual cruiser to long-term liveaboard

Visit www.adlardcoles.com to buy at discount

TORQUAY MARINA

Torquay Marina
Torquay, Devon, TQ2 5EQ
Tel: 01803 200210
Email: torquaymarina@mdlmarinas.co.uk
www.torquaymarina.co.uk

VHF Ch 80
ACCESS H24

Tucked away in the north east corner of Torbay, Torquay Marina is well sheltered from the prevailing SW'ly winds, providing safe entry in all conditions and at any state of the tide. Located in the centre of Torquay, the marina boasts a brand new stand-up paddleboarding/watersports centre and artisan café, and also offers

easy access to the town's numerous shops, bars and restaurants.

Torquay is ideally situated for either exploring Tor Bay itself, with its many delightful anchorages, or else for heading west to experience several other scenic harbours such as Dartmouth and Salcombe. It also provides a good starting point for crossing to Brittany, Normandy or the Channel Islands.

FACILITIES AT A GLANCE

Key
a   Dock manager's office
b   Dockmaster offices
c   Restaurant, cafe and newsagents

1

PORTLAND MARINA

Portland Marina
Osprey Quay, Portland, Dorset, DT5 1DX
Tel: 08345 430 2012
www.deanreddyhoff.co.uk
Email: berths@portlandmarina.co.uk

⚓⚓⚓⚓

VHF	Ch 80
ACCESS	H24

Portland Marina is an ideal location for both annual berthing and weekend stopovers. The marina offers first class facilities including washrooms, on-site bar and restaurant, lift out and storage up to 50T, dry stacking up to 9m, 24-hour manned security, fuel berth, sewage pump out, extensive car parking and a full range of marine services including a chandlery.

The marina is within walking distance of local pubs and restaurants on Portland with Weymouth's bustling town centre and mainline railway station just a short bus or ferry ride away.

FACILITIES AT A GLANCE

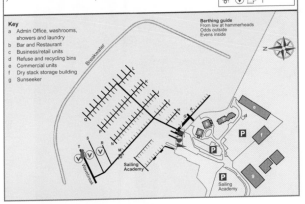

Key
a Admin Office, washrooms, showers and laundry
b Bar and Restaurant
c Business/retail units
d Refuse and recycling bins
e Commercial units
f Dry stack storage building
g Sunseeker

Berthing guide
From low at hammerheads
Odds outside
Evens inside

WEYMOUTH HARBOUR

Harbour Office
13 Custom House Quay, Weymouth, Dorset, DT4 8BG
Tel: 01305 838386
Email: weymouthharbour@dorset.gov.uk
www.weymouth-harbour.co.uk

VHF	Ch 12
ACCESS	H24

Weymouth Harbour, situated on the Jurassic Coast, lays NE of Portland in the protected waters of Weymouth Bay. Located in the heart of the old town and accessible at any state of tide, the Georgian harbour has numerous overnight berths. Pontoons on both quays have electricity and fresh water, as well as modern shower facilities. Restaurants and shops abound within walking distance and visitors are also welcome in the Royal Dorset YC and Weymouth SC, both situated on the quayside.

Vessels are advised to call *Weymouth Harbour* on Ch12 on approach, and vessels over 15m are recommended to give prior notification of intended arrival.

FACILITIES AT A GLANCE

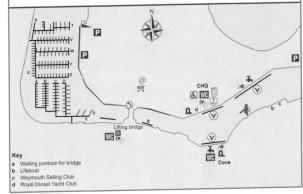

Key
a Waiting pontoon for bridge
b Lifeboat
c Weymouth Sailing Club
d Royal Dorset Yacht Club

WEYMOUTH MARINA

Weymouth Marina
70 Commercial Road, Dorset, DT4 8NA
Tel: 01305 767576 Fax: 01305 767575
www.weymouth-marina.co.uk
Email: sales@weymouth-marina.co.uk

VHF	Ch 80
ACCESS	H24

With more than 280 permanent and visitors' berths, Weymouth is a modern, purpose-built marina ideally situated for yachtsmen cruising between the West Country and the Solent. It is also conveniently placed for sailing to France or the Channel Islands. Accessed via the town's historic lifting bridge, which opens every even hour 0800–2000 (plus 2100 Jun–Aug), the marina is dredged to 2.5m below chart datum. It provides easy access to the town centre, with its abundance of shops, pubs and restaurants, as well as to the traditional seafront where an impressive sandy beach is overlooked by an esplanade of hotels.

FACILITIES AT A GLANCE

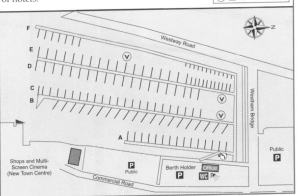

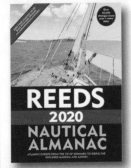

Reeds PDF ebooks

In response to popular demand, all the Reeds Almanacs are now available as searchable, highlightable PDF ebooks. (All ebooks incorporate the Marina Guide.)

Visit www.reedsnauticalalmanac.co.uk for further information

Key to Marina Plans symbols

Bottled gas		Parking
Chandler		Pub/Restaurant
Disabled facilities		Pump out
Electrical supply		Rigging service
Electrical repairs		Sail repairs
Engine repairs		Shipwright
First Aid		Shop/Supermarket
Fresh Water		Showers
Fuel - Diesel		Slipway
Fuel - Petrol		Toilets
Hardstanding/boatyard		Telephone
Internet Café		Trolleys
Laundry facilities		Visitors berths
Lift-out facilities		Wi-Fi

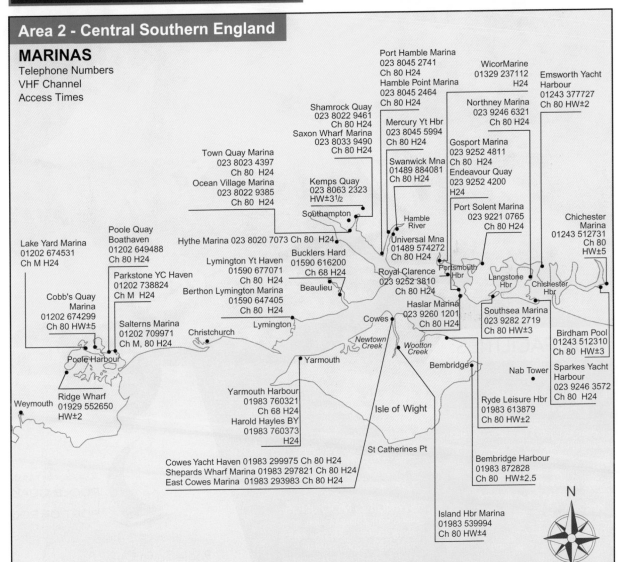

Area 2 - Central Southern England

MARINAS
Telephone Numbers
VHF Channel
Access Times

Port Hamble Marina
023 8045 2741
Ch 80 H24
Hamble Point Marina
023 8045 2464
Ch 80 H24

WicorMarine
01329 237112
H24

Emsworth Yacht Harbour
01243 377727
Ch 80 HW±2

Shamrock Quay
023 8022 9461
Ch 80 H24
Saxon Wharf Marina
023 8033 9490
Ch 80 H24

Mercury Yt Hbr
023 8045 5994
Ch 80 H24

Northney Marina
023 9246 6321
Ch 80 H24

Town Quay Marina
023 8023 4397
Ch 80 H24
Ocean Village Marina
023 8022 9385
Ch 80 H24

Kemps Quay
023 8063 2323
HW±3½

Swanwick Mna
01489 884081
Ch 80 H24

Gosport Marina
023 9252 4811
Ch 80 H24
Endeavour Quay
023 9252 4200
H24

Chichester Marina
01243 512731
Ch 80 HW±5

Southampton

Hamble River

Port Solent Marina
023 9221 0765
Ch 80 H24

Lake Yard Marina
01202 674531
Ch M H24

Poole Quay
Boathaven
01202 649488
Ch 80 H24

Hythe Marina 023 8020 7073 Ch 80 H24

Bucklers Hard
01590 616200
Ch 68 H24

Universal Mna
01489 574272
Ch 80 H24

Portsmouth Hbr

Langstone Hbr

Chichester Hbr

Parkstone YC Haven
01202 738824
Ch M H24

Lymington Yt Haven
01590 677071
Ch 80 H24
Berthon Lymington Marina
01590 647405
Ch 80 H24

Beaulieu

Royal Clarence
023 9252 3810
Ch 80 H24

Cobb's Quay
Marina
01202 674299
Ch 80 HW±5

Salterns Marina
01202 709971
Ch M, 80 H24

Christchurch

Lymington

Cowes

Haslar Marina
023 9260 1201
Ch 80 H24

Southsea Marina
023 9282 2719
Ch 80 HW±3

Birdham Pool
01243 512310
Ch 80 HW±3

Poole Harbour

Newtown Creek

Wootton Creek

Nab Tower

Sparkes Yacht Harbour
023 9246 3572
Ch 80 H24

Weymouth

Ridge Wharf
01929 552650
HW±2

Yarmouth

Bembridge

Yarmouth Harbour
01983 760321
Ch 68 H24
Harold Hayles BY
01983 760373
H24

Isle of Wight

Ryde Leisure Hbr
01983 613879
Ch 80 HW±2

St Catherines Pt

Cowes Yacht Haven 01983 299975 Ch 80 H24
Shepards Wharf Marina 01983 297821 Ch 80 H24
East Cowes Marina 01983 293983 Ch 80 H24

Bembridge Harbour
01983 872828
Ch 80   HW±2.5

Island Hbr Marina
01983 539994
Ch 80 HW±4

N

Poole....

The next page in your adventure

- The Jurassic Coast
- Brownsea Island
- Dining out
- Enterainment
- Fireworks

Plus much more!

OUR FACILITIES:

PERMANENT BERTHS
It's in a private position that makes the most of the views and gorgeous sunsets, yet it's still close to Poole's historic quay, old town and vibrant shopping centre.

- 75 permanent berths
- Superyacht berths
- Floating docks for jet skis and RIBs up to 6.1m
- 24 hour security
- Deep water: 2.5 - 6m
- Water taxi service, parking

VISITOR MARINA
Use your boat as a holiday home; entertain family, friends, colleagues or customers onboard; sail the stunning Jurassic Coast.

Enjoy all the attractions of Poole, Bournemouth and beautiful Dorset. A warm welcome always awaits!

- 125 visitor berths all year for vessels up to 70m in length and up to 4.5m draft
- Swinging moorings

SWINGING MOORINGS
Relax with a glass of wine, on a sunny afternoon, on your own swinging mooring in Poole Harbour overlooking Brownsea Island. Away from the madding crowd, these offer you ultimate privacy, peace & tranquillity.

Marina of the Year 2017
UK Coastal
Under 250 Berths
WINNER
GJWinsurance

Marina of the Year 2016
UK Coastal
Under 250 Berths
WINNER
GJWinsurance

POOLE QUAY
Boat Haven
PORT OF POOLE
Marina

Poole Town Quay, Poole,
Dorset BH15 1HJ t: 01202 649488

poolequayboathaven.co.uk
VHF Channel 80 call sign "Poole Quay Boat Haven"

2

RIDGE WHARF YACHT CENTRE

Ridge Wharf Yacht Centre
Ridge, Wareham, Dorset, BH20 5BG
Tel: 01929 552650 Fax: 01929 554434
Email: office@ridgewharf.co.uk www.ridgewharf.co.uk

VHF
ACCESS HW±2

On the south bank of the River Frome, which acts as the boundary to the North of the Isle of Purbeck, is Ridge Wharf Yacht Centre. Access for a 1.5m draught is between one and two hours either side of HW, with berths drying out to soft mud. The Yacht Centre cannot be contacted on VHF, so it is best to phone up ahead of time to inquire about berthing availability.

A trip upstream to the ancient market town of Wareham is well worth while, although owners of deep-draughted yachts may prefer to go by dinghy. Tucked between the Rivers Frome and Trent, it is packed full of cafés, restaurants and shops.

FACILITIES AT A GLANCE

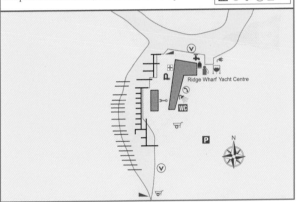

LAKE YARD MARINA

Lake Yard Marina
Lake Drive, Hamworthy, Poole, Dorset BH15 4DT
Tel: 01202 674531
Email: office@lakeyard.com www.lakeyard.com

VHF Ch M
ACCESS H24

Lake Yard is situated towards the NW end of Poole Harbour, just beyond the SHM No 73. The entrance can be easily identified by 2FR (vert) and 2FG (vert) lights. Enjoying 24 hour access, the marina has no designated visitors' berths, but will accommodate visiting yachtsmen if resident berth holders are away. Its on site facilities include full maintenance and repair services as well as hard standing and a 50 ton boat hoist, although for the nearest fuel go to Corralls (Tel 01202 674551), opposite the Town Quay. Lake Yard's Waterfront Club, offering spectacular views across the harbour, opens seven days a week for lunchtime and evening meals.

FACILITIES AT A GLANCE

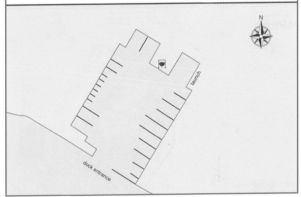

COBB'S QUAY MARINA

Cobb's Quay Marina
Hamworthy, Poole, Dorset, BH15 4EL
Tel: 01202 674299
Email: cobbsquay@mdlmarinas.co.uk
www.cobbsquaymarina.co.uk

VHF Ch 80
ACCESS H24

Lying on the west side of Holes Bay in Poole Harbour, Cobb's Quay is accessed via two lifting bridges. The hourly lifting schedule which runs from 0530 to 2330 (except for weekday rush hours) makes the entrance into Holes Bay accessible 24/7. With fully serviced pontoons for yachts up to 20m LOA, visitors can enjoy the facilities including the highly reputable Cobb's YC. The marina also offers a convenient 240-berth dry stack area for motorboats up to 10m. With increased security and lower maintenance costs, the service includes unlimited launching on demand. There is also a 40-ton hoist, fully serviced boatyard and on-site self-storage. Poole Harbour is the second largest natural harbour in the world and is rich in wildlife, water sports and secret hideaways.

FACILITIES AT A GLANCE

Key
a Dock manager's office
b Information point
c Yacht club
d Convenience store

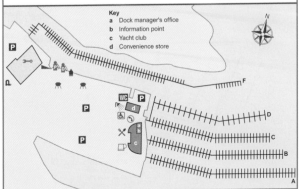

POOLE QUAY BOAT HAVEN

Poole Quay Boat Haven
Poole Town Quay, Poole, Dorset, BH15 1HJ
Tel: 01202 649488 Fax: 01202 785619
Email: info@poolequayboathaven.co.uk

VHF Ch 80
ACCESS H24

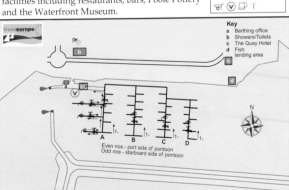

Once inside the Poole Harbour entrance small yachts heading for Poole Quay Boat Haven should use the Boat Channel running parallel south of the dredged Middle Ship Channel, which is primarily used by ferries sailing to and from the Hamworthy terminal. The marina can be accessed via the Little Channel and is easily identified by the large breakwater alongside the Quay. With deep water at all states of the tide the marina has berthing available for 125 yachts up to 60m, but due to its central location the marina can get busy so it is best to reserve a berth.

There is easy access to all of Poole Quay's facilities including restaurants, bars, Poole Pottery and the Waterfront Museum.

FACILITIES AT A GLANCE

Key
a Berthing office
b Showers/Toilets
c The Quay Hotel
d Fish landing area

Even nos - port side of pontoon
Odd nos - starboard side of pontoon

PORT OF POOLE MARINA

Port of Poole Marina
Poole Town Quay, Poole, Dorset, BH15 1HJ
Tel: 01202 649488 Fax: 01202 785619
Email: info@poolequaybathaven.co.uk

VHF Ch 80
ACCESS H24

Beware of the chain ferry operating at the entrance to Poole harbour. Once inside small yachts heading for the marina should use the Boat Channel running parallel south of the Middle Ship Channel. The marina is to the east of the main ferry terminals and can be identified by a large floating breakwater at the entrance.

The marina has deep water at all tides and berthing for 60 permanent vessels. It is also used as an overflow for visitors from Poole Quay Boat Haven, subject to availability.

A water taxi is available during daylight hours to access the quay for restaurants and shops, also accessible with a 10–15min walk round the quays.

FACILITIES AT A GLANCE

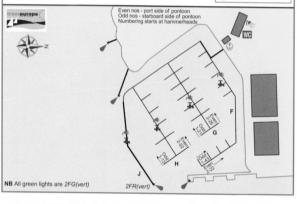

Even nos - port side of pontoon
Odd nos - starboard side of pontoon
Numbering starts at hammerheads

NB All green lights are 2FG(vert)   2FR(vert)

PARKSTONE YACHT HAVEN

Parkstone Yacht Club
Pearce Avenue, Parkstone, Poole, Dorset, BH14 8EH
Tel: 01202 738824 Fax: 01202 716394
Email: office@parkstoneyc.co.uk

VHF Ch M
ACCESS H24

Situated on the north side of Poole Harbour between Salterns Marina and Poole Quay Boat Haven, Parkstone Yacht Haven can be entered at all states of the tides. Its approach channel has been dredged to 2.0m and is clearly marked by buoys. Run by the Parkstone Yacht Club, the Haven provides 200 deep water berths for members and visitors' berths. Other services include a new office facility with laundry and WCs, bar, restaurant, shower/changing rooms and wi-fi. With a busy sailing programme for over 2,500 members, the Yacht Club plays host to a variety of events including Poole Week, which is held towards the end of August. Please phone for availability.

FACILITIES AT A GLANCE

Western Point

Parkstone Yacht Club

1.5m

2.0m   F

2.0m   E

Elm Park

SALTERNS MARINA

Salterns Marina
40 Salterns Way, Lilliput, Poole
Dorset, BH14 8JR
Tel: 01202 709971 Fax: 01202 700398
Email: marina@salterns.co.uk www.salterns.co.uk

VHF Ch M, 80
ACCESS H24

Holding the Five Gold Anchor award, Salterns Marina provides a service which is second to none. Located off the North Channel, it is approached from the No 31 SHM and benefits from deep water at all states of the tide. Facilities include 220 alongside pontoon berths as well as 75 swinging moorings with a free launch service. However, with very few designated visitors' berths, it is best to contact the marina ahead of time for availability.

Fuel, diesel and gas can all be obtained 24/7 and the well-stocked chandlery, incorporating a coffee shop, stays open seven days a week.

FACILITIES AT A GLANCE

Key
a Marina office
   Reception
   Chandlery
   Salterns Brokerage
   Coffee shop
   Toilets/Showers
   Marine Sales
   Laundry
   Sales offices

Private Houses
Private Flats
Hotel Car Park
Tender Pool

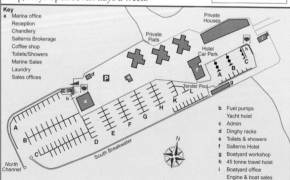

b Fuel pumps
   Yacht hoist
c Admin
d Dinghy racks
e Toilets & showers
f Salterns Hotel
g Boatyard workshop
h 45 tonne travel hoist
i Boatyard office
   Engine & boat sales

North Channel

South Breakwater

YARMOUTH HBR/HAROLD HAYLES BY

Yarmouth Harbour
Yarmouth, Isle of Wight, PO41 0NT
Tel: 01983 760321 Fax: 01983 761192
info@yarmouth-harbour.co.uk
www.yarmouth-harbour.co.uk

VHF Ch 68
ACCESS H24

Harold Hayles Ltd
The Quay, Yarmouth, Isle of Wight, PO41 0RS
Tel: 01983 760373 Fax: 01983 760666
Email: info@haroldhayles.co.uk
www.haroldhayles.co.uk

VHF
ACCESS H24

The most western harbour on the Isle of Wight, Yarmouth is not only a convenient passage stopover but a very desirable destination in its own right, with virtually all weather and tidal access, although strong N to NE'ly winds can produce a considerable swell. The HM launch patrols the harbour entrance and will direct visiting yachtsmen to a walkashore or standalone pontoon berths; call *Yarmouth Harbour* on Ch 68 prior to entering the harbour. The pretty harbour and town offer plenty of fine restaurants and amenities.

Walkashore pontoon moorings are also available from the Harold Hayles and River Yar BYs in the SW corner of the harbour, the latter S of the bridge. Pre-booking is preferred for both individuals or rallies.

FACILITIES AT A GLANCE

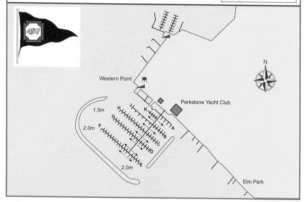

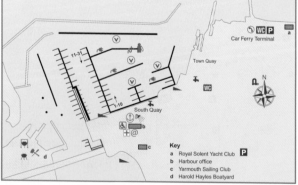

Car Ferry Terminal

Town Quay

11-31

1-10

South Quay

Key
a Royal Solent Yacht Club
b Harbour office
c Yarmouth Sailing Club
d Harold Hayles Boatyard

2

LYMINGTON YACHT HAVEN

Lymington Yacht Haven
King's Saltern Road, Lymington, S041 3QD
Tel: 01590 677071
Email: lymington@yachthavens.com www.yachthavens.com

VHF Ch 80
ACCESS H24

Lymington Yacht Haven has the enviable position of being the first marina that comes into sight on your port hand side as you make your way up the well-marked Lymington river channel. Nestled between the 500 acre Lymington to Keyhaven nature reserve and the famous Georgian market town of Lymington, there is something for everyone.

Lymington Yacht Haven is manned 24/7 for fuel and berthing and boasts the most modern luxury shore side facilities you will find in the UK. Bike and electric bike hire are available through the marina office to explore the beautiful New Forest.

FACILITIES AT A GLANCE

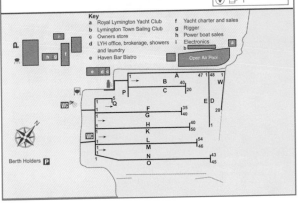

Key
a Royal Lymington Yacht Club
b Lymington Town Sailing Club
c Owners store
d LYH office, brokerage, showers and laundry
e Haven Bar Bistro
f Yacht charter and sales
g Rigger
h Power boat sales
i Electronics

OVER THE TOP

The First Lone Yachtsman to Sail Vertically Around the World

ADRIAN FLANAGAN

"One of the best-written and most gripping tales of recent years."
– Yachting World

Visit www.adlardcoles.com to buy at discount

BERTHON LYMINGTON MARINA

Berthon Lymington Marina Ltd
The Shipyard, Lymington, Hampshire, SO41 3YL
Tel: 01590 647405 Fax: 01590 647446
www.berthon.co.uk Email: marina@berthon.co.uk

VHF Ch 80
ACCESS H24

Situated approximately half a mile up river of Lymington Yacht Haven, on the port hand side, is Lymington Marina. Easily accessible at all states of the tide, it offers between 60 to 70 visitors' berths, with probably the best washrooms in the Solent. Its close proximity to the town centre and first rate services mean that booking is essential on busy weekends. Lymington Marina's parent, Berthon Boat Co, has state of the art facilities and a highly skilled work force of 100+ to deal with any repair, maintenance or refit.

Lymington benefits from having the New Forest on its doorstep and the Solent Way footpath provides an invigorating walk to and from Hurst Castle.

FACILITIES AT A GLANCE

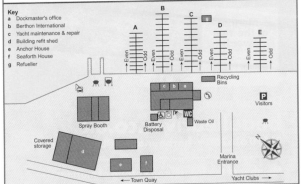

Key
a Dockmaster's office
b Berthon International
c Yacht maintenance & repair
d Building refit shed
e Anchor House
f Seaforth House
g Refueller

LYMINGTON TOWN QUAY

Lymington Harbour Commissioners
Bath Road, Lymington, S041 3SE
Tel: 01590 672014
Email: info@lymingtonharbour.co.uk

VHF Ch 66
ACCESS H24

New for 2020 (completion scheduled Jan), Town Quay Pontoon is being extended to accommodate 46 visiting boats up to 2m draft including 26 finger berths. It retains alongside berthing on the outermost pontoon for larger yachts. The turning area will reduce the fore and aft mid-stream moorings – 42 remain. The new berths will have power, water and wi-fi as well as new toilet and shower facilities in a block on the quay. The quay provides easy access to the historic cobbles, with its bars, restaurants and shops. The facilities of the town are close by with the Saturday market in the High Street. The New Forest is easily accessible by bus train and bicycle.

FACILITIES AT A GLANCE

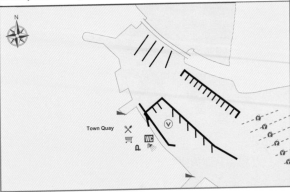

Town Quay

LYMINGTON HARBOUR

Lymington Harbour Commissioners
Bath Road, Lymington, SO41 3SE
Tel: 01590 672014
Email: info@lymingtonharbour.co.uk

VHF	Ch 66
ACCESS	H24

Lymington Harbour Commission provides dedicated walk ashore visitor berths at the Lymington Town Quay and at the Dan Bran pontoon which comes ashore adjacent to the Royal Lymington YC and Lymington Town SC. Dan Bran is accessible at all states of the tide inside the wave screen. Power is available along its 650' length with use of the facilities at Lymington Town SC and walk ashore access to the town and nearby nature reserves on the salt marsh. Sited between the marinas a short walk from Town Quay, it is ideal for club rallies/events and can accommodate up to 50 boats together. The sea water swimming bath adjacent to the pontoon is a popular venue for children and families.

FACILITIES AT A GLANCE

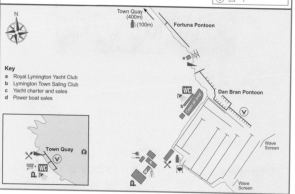

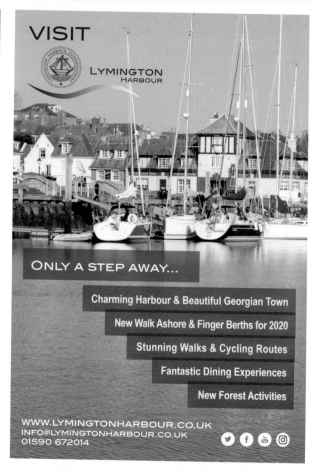
BUCKLERS HARD MARINA

Bucklers Hard
Beaulieu, New Forest, Hampshire, SO42 7XB
Tel: 01590 616200
www.beaulieuriver.co.uk   harbour.office@beaulieu.co.uk

VHF	Ch 68
ACCESS	H24

Situated on the Beaulieu River, Buckler's Hard Yacht Harbour is the ideal location from which to sail in the Solent or visit for a short stay to explore the surrounding New Forest. Recent investment in the TYHA 5 Gold Anchor marina offers improved facilities and technology to keep pace with modern demands, while preserving the unique character and charm of the unspoilt natural haven. Both permanent marina berths and river moorings are available. Visiting boats are welcome and advised to book in advance or radio Beaulieu River Radio on CH68 before entering the river

FACILITIES AT A GLANCE

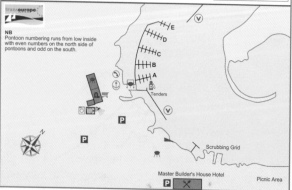

COWES YACHT HAVEN

Cowes Yacht Haven
Vectis Yard, Cowes, Isle of Wight, PO31 7BD
Tel: 01983 299975 Fax: 01983 200332
www.cowesyachthaven.com
Email: info@cowesyachthaven.com

VHF Ch 80
ACCESS H24

Situated virtually at the centre of the Solent, Cowes is best known as Britain's premier yachting centre and offers all types of facilities to yachtsmen. Cowes Yacht Haven, operating 24 hours a day, has very few permanent moorings and is dedicated to catering for visitors and events. At peak times it can become very crowded and for occasions such as Aberdeen Asset Management Cowes Week you need to book up in advance.

FACILITIES AT A GLANCE

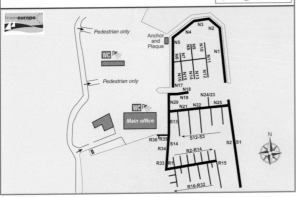

COWES HARBOUR SHEPARDS MARINA

Cowes Harbour Shepards Marina
Medina Road, Cowes, Isle of Wight, PO31 7HT
Tel: 01983 297821 Email: shepards.chc@cowes.co.uk
www.cowesharboursshepardsmarina.co.uk

VHF Ch 80
ACCESS H24

Shepards Marina is one of Cowes Harbour's main marina facilities offering a full range of services and amenities for yacht racing events, rallies, and catering also to the cruising sailor and powerboater. The marina has capacity for 130 visiting boats, 40 resident berth holders.

Visitor berths can be booked in advance, subject to availability. All berths benefit from water and electricity, free Wi-Fi, inclusive showers, and site-wide CCTV. Discounted rates are available for rallies of six or more boats, sailing schools, and winter berthing.

On site you will also find the Basque Kitchen restaurant, Girls for Sail, Island Divers, and Solent Sails. Fuel can be obtained from the fuel berth located 200m south of the chain ferry.

FACILITIES AT A GLANCE

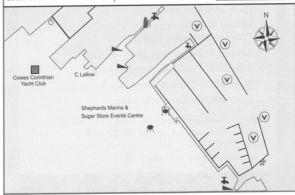

EAST COWES MARINA

East Cowes Marina
Britannia Way, East Cowes, Isle of Wight, PO32 6UB
Tel: 01983 293983
www.eastcowesmarina.co.uk
Email: berths@eastcowesmarina.co.uk

VHF Ch 80
ACCESS H24

Accommodating around 235 residential yachts and 150 visiting boats at all states of the tide, East Cowes Marina is situated on the quiet and protected east bank of the Medina River, about a quarter mile above the chain ferry. A small convenience store is just five minutes walk away. The new centrally heated shower and toilet facilities ensure the visitor a warm welcome at any time of the year, as does the on-site pub and restaurant.

Several water taxis provide a return service to Cowes, ensuring a quick and easy way of getting to West Cowes.

FACILITIES AT A GLANCE

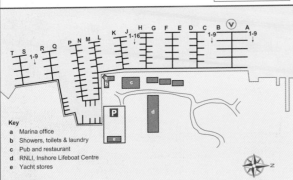

Key
a Marina office
b Showers, toilets & laundry
c Pub and restaurant
d RNLI, Inshore Lifeboat Centre
e Yacht stores

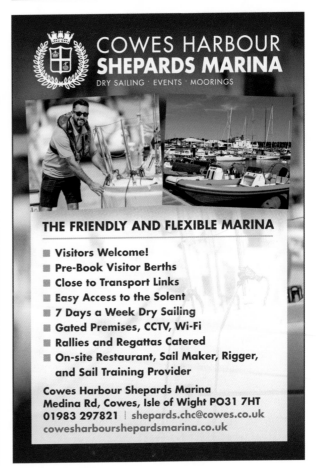

ISLAND HARBOUR MARINA

Island Harbour Marina
Mill Lane, Binfield, Newport, Isle of Wight, PO30 2LA
Tel: 01983 539994 Fax: 01983 523401
Email: info@island-harbour.co.uk

VHF Ch 80
ACCESS HW±4

Situated in beautiful rolling farmland about half a mile south of Folly Inn, Island Harbour Marina provides around 200 visitors' berths. Protected by a lock that is operated daily from 0800 – 2100 during the summer and from 0800 – 1730 during the winter, the marina is accessible for about three hours either side of HW for draughts of 1.5m.

Due to its secluded setting, the marina's on site chandlery also sells essential provisions and newspapers. A half hour walk along the river brings you to Newport, the capital and county town of the Isle of Wight.

FACILITIES AT A GLANCE

Key
a Control tower
b Bin store
c Chandlery
d Restaurant

HYTHE MARINA VILLAGE

Hythe Marina Village
Shamrock Way, Hythe, Southampton, SO45 6DY
Tel: 023 8020 7073
Email: hythe@mdlmarinas.co.uk
www.hythemarinavillage.co.uk

VHF Ch 80
ACCESS H24

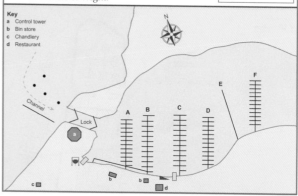

Situated on the western shores of Southampton Water, Hythe Marina Village is approached by a dredged channel leading to a lock basin. The lock gates are controlled H24 throughout the year with a waiting pontoon south of the approach basin.

Hythe Marina Village incorporates full marine services as well as on-site restaurants and a selection of shops can be found in the town centre, a 5 minute walk away. Forming an integral part of the New Forest Waterside, Hythe is the perfect base from which to explore Hampshire's pretty inland villages and towns, or alternatively you can catch the ferry to Southampton's Town Quay.

FACILITIES AT A GLANCE

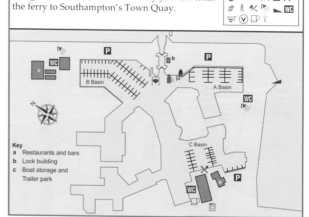

Key
a Restaurants and bars
b Lock building
c Boat storage and Trailer park

2

TOWN QUAY

Associated British Ports
Town Quay, Southampton, SO14 2AQ
Tel: 02380 234397 Mobile: 07764 293588
Email: info@townquay.com www.townquay.com

VHF Ch 80
ACCESS H24

In the heart of Southampton, Town Quay is walking distance from the City's cultural quarter, West Quay Shopping Centre and a variety of restaurants, bars and theatres making the marina a vibrant place to stay all year round.

The marina is accessible at all states of the tide and the reception is open 24 hours a day with free drinks and wi-fi. Free cycle hire and use of a gas BBQ on the 'chill out' deck is available.

Located on the eastern shores of Southampton Water, Town Quay offers unrivalled views of Southampton's busy maritime activity and direct access to the world famous cruising and racing waters of the Solent.

FACILITIES AT A GLANCE

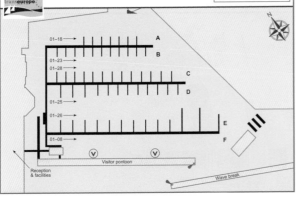

OCEAN VILLAGE MARINA

Ocean Village Marina
2 Channel Way, Southampton, SO14 3TG
Tel: 023 8022 9385
Email: oceanvillage@mdlmarinas.co.uk
www.oceanvillagemarina.co.uk

VHF Ch 80
ACCESS H24

The entrance to Ocean Village Marina lies on the port side of the River Itchen, just before the Itchen Bridge. With the capacity to accommodate large yachts and tall ships, the marina, accessible 24 hours a day, is a renowned home for international yacht races.

Situated at the heart of an exciting new waterside development incorporating shops, a cinema, restaurants and a £50m luxury spa hotel complex, Ocean Village offers a vibrant atmosphere for all visitors.

FACILITIES AT A GLANCE

Key
a Marina office, WC, showers, launderette
b Pitcher & Piano
c Banana Wharf
d Ocean Rooms Beauty
e Maritimo Lounge
f Dock office
g Harbour Hotel & Spa
h Harbour Lights Cinema

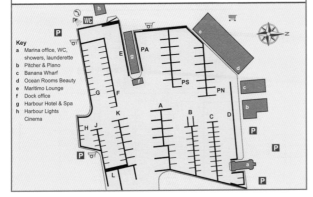

SHAMROCK QUAY

Shamrock Quay
William Street, Northam, Southampton, Hants, SO14 5QL
Tel: 023 8022 9461
Email: shamrockquay@mdlmarinas.co.uk
www.shamrockquay.co.uk

VHF Ch 80
ACCESS H24

Shamrock Quay, lying upstream of the Itchen Bridge on the port hand side, offers excellent facilities to yachtsmen. It also benefits from being accessible and manned 24 hours a day. On-site there is a 75-ton travel hoist and a 47-ton boat mover, and for dining out there is a choice of restaurants and bars.

The city centre is about two miles away, where among the numerous attractions are the Medieval Merchant's House in French Street, the Southampton City Art Gallery and the SeaCity Museum in the Civic Centre.

FACILITIES AT A GLANCE

Key
a Offices and shops
b Marina office
c Café

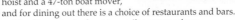
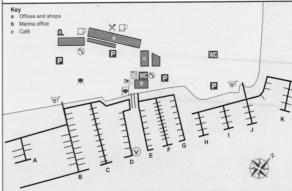

KEMPS QUAY

Kemp's Shipyard Ltd
Quayside Road, Southampton, SO18 1BZ
Tel: 023 8063 2323 Fax: 023 8022 6002
Email: enquiries@kempsquay.com

VHF
ACCESS HW±3.5

At the head of the River Itchen on the starboard side is Kemps Quay, a family-run marina with a friendly, old-fashioned feel. Accessible only 3½ hrs either side of HW, it has a limited number of deep water berths, the rest being half tide, drying out to soft mud. Its restricted access is, however, reflected in the lower prices.

Although situated on the outskirts of Southampton, a short bus or taxi ride will soon get you to the city centre. Besides a nearby BP Garage selling bread and milk, the closest supermarkets can be found in Bitterne Shopping Centre, which is five minutes away by bus.

FACILITIES AT A GLANCE

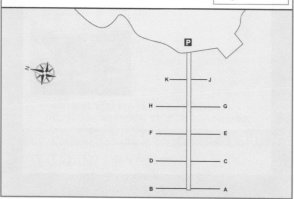

SAXON WHARF

Saxon Wharf
Lower York Street, Northam, Southampton, SO14 5QF
Tel: 023 8033 9490
Email: saxonwharf@mdlmarinas.co.uk
www.saxonwharfmarina.co.uk

VHF Ch 80
ACCESS H24

Placed on the River Itchen in Southampton, Saxon Wharf is a marine service centre specifically designed for the superyacht market. With a 200-ton boat hoist and heavy duty pontoons, Saxon Wharf is the ideal location for large vessels in need of secure, quick turnaround lift-outs, repair work or even full-scale refits.

With a Dry Stack facility boasting the largest capacity forklift truck in the UK, Saxon Wharf can now dry stack boats of up to 13m LOA. There is also ample storage ashore and 24-hour security. Shamrock Quay, where there are bars and restaurants, is within 300 metres of this location.

FACILITIES AT A GLANCE

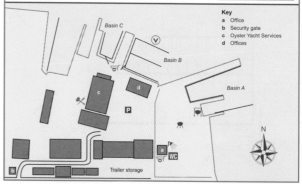

Key
a Office
b Security gate
c Oyster Yacht Services
d Offices

HAMBLE POINT MARINA

Hamble Point Marina
School Lane, Hamble, Southampton, SO31 4NB
Tel: 023 8045 2464
Email: hamblepoint@mdlmarinas.co.uk
www.hamblepointmarina.co.uk

VHF Ch 80
ACCESS H24

Situated virtually opposite Warsash, this is the first marina you will come to on the western bank of the Hamble. Accommodating yachts and power boats up to 30m in length, it offers easy access to the Solent.

The marina boasts extensive facilities including 137 dry stack berths for motorboats up to 10 metres and over 50 tenants who provide boat-owners with a wide range of marine services from boat repairs to electrical work. Hamble Point is within a 20-minute walk of Hamble Village, where there are a plethora of pubs and restaurants on offer.

FACILITIES AT A GLANCE

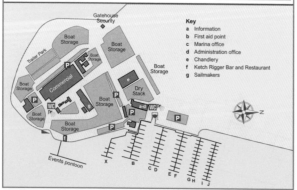

Key
a Information
b First aid point
c Marina office
d Administration office
e Chandlery
f Ketch Rigger Bar and Restaurant
g Sailmakers

PORT HAMBLE MARINA

Port Hamble Marina
Satchell Lane, Hamble, Southampton, SO31 4QD
Tel: 023 8045 2741
Email: porthamble@mdlmarinas.co.uk
www.porthamblemarina.co.uk

VHF Ch 80
ACCESS H24

Port Hamble Marina is situated on the River Hamble right in the heart of the South Coast's sailing scene. With thousands of visitors every year, this busy marina is popular with racing enthusiasts and cruising vessels looking for a vibrant atmosphere. The picturesque Hamble village, with its inviting pubs and restaurants, is only a few minutes walk away.

On site, Port Hamble also offers excellent amenities including luxurious all-new male and female facilities, alongside boutique style extension shower rooms. Banana Wharf bar and restaurant provides the perfect spot to meet, eat and drink by the water whilst petrol and diesel is available seven days a week. Locally there are several companies on hand who cater for every boating need.

FACILITIES AT A GLANCE

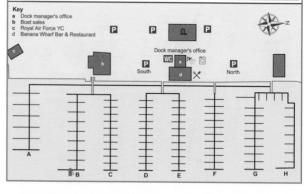

Key
a Dock manager's office
b Boat sales
c Royal Air Force YC
d Banana Wharf Bar & Restaurant

2

MERCURY YACHT HARBOUR

Mercury Yacht Harbour
Satchell Lane, Hamble, Southampton, SO31 4HQ
Tel: 023 8045 5994
Email: mercury@mdlmarinas.co.uk
www.mercuryyachtharbour.co.uk

VHF Ch 80
ACCESS H24

Mercury Yacht Harbour is the third marina from seaward on the western bank of the River Hamble, tucked away in a picturesque, wooded site adjacent to Badnam Creek. Enjoying deep water at all states of the tide, it accommodates yachts up to 24m LOA and boasts an extensive array of facilities.

The on-site chandlery stocks a plethora of essential items, and for a good meal look no further than the Gaff Rigger bar and restaurant whose balcony offers striking views over the water. Hamble Village is only a 20-minute walk away.

FACILITIES AT A GLANCE

Key
a Toilets and showers
b Launderette
c Chandlery
d Gaff Rigger
  Bar & Restaurant
e Dockmaster,
  marina manager's office
f Waste disposal
g Recycling area

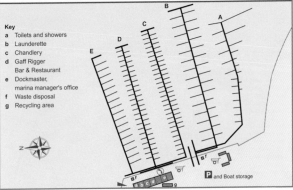

UNIVERSAL MARINA

Universal Marina
Crableck Lane, Sarisbury Green, Southampton, SO31 7ZN
Tel: 01489 574272 Fax: 01489 574273
Email: info@universalmarina.co.uk

VHF Ch 80
ACCESS H24

Universal Marina is one of the few remaining independent marinas offering south coast moorings. Universal Marina's unique location is unbeatable, tucked in between the oak trees on the East Bank of the Hamble where 68 acres of natural wildlife and marshlands surrounds the busy and friendly marina. Positioned only minutes off the M27, it is one of the most accessible marinas on the south coast. The 250 berth complex, features all the latest facilities required by the modern day boat owner, recently upgraded pontoons, power, water and wifi available to each berth. Visitors are welcome & although there are no dedicated visitor berths these are available by prior arrangement.

FACILITIES AT A GLANCE

trans-europe

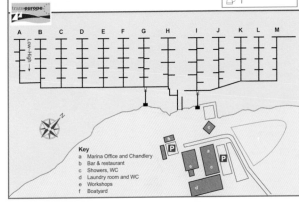

Key
a Marina Office and Chandlery
b Bar & restaurant
c Showers, WC
d Laundry room and WC
e Workshops
f Boatyard

SWANWICK MARINA

Swanwick Marina
Swanwick, Southampton, Hampshire, SO31 1ZL
Tel: 01489 884081 Fax: 01489 579073
Email: swanwick@premiermarinas.com
www.premiermarinas.com

VHF Ch 80
ACCESS H24

Situated on the east bank of the River Hamble next to Bursledon Bridge, Swanwick Marina is accessible at all states of the tide and can accommodate yachts up to 20m LOA.

The marina's fully-licensed bar and bistro, The Boat House, over-looking the river, is open for breakfast, lunch and dinner all year round. Alternatively, just a short row or walk away is the celebrated Jolly Sailor pub in Bursledon on the west bank, made famous for being the local watering hole in the British television series *Howard's Way*.

FACILITIES AT A GLANCE

Key
a Marina office
b Pub/restaurant
c Chandlery
d Boat sales offices

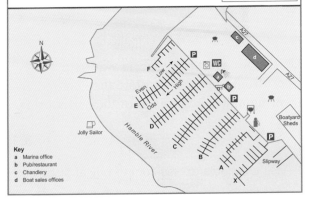

RYDE LEISURE HARBOUR

Ryde Harbour
The Esplanade, Ryde, Isle of Wight, PO33 1JA
Tel: 01983 613879 Fax: 01983 613903
www.rydeharbour.com Email: ryde.harbour@iow.gov.uk

VHF Ch 80
ACCESS HW±2

Known as the 'gateway to the Island', Ryde, with its elegant houses and abundant shops, is among the Isle of Wight's most popular resorts. Its well-protected harbour is conveniently close to the exceptional beaches as well as to the town's restaurants and amusements.

Drying to 2.5m and therefore only accessible to yachts that can take the ground, the harbour accommodates 90 resident boats as well as up to 75 visiting yachts. Fin keel yachts may dry out on the harbour wall.

Ideal for family cruising, Ryde offers a wealth of activities, ranging from ten pin bowling and ice skating to crazy golf and tennis.

FACILITIES AT A GLANCE

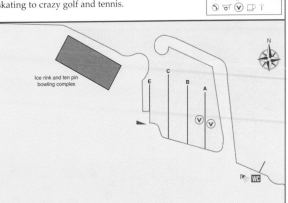

BEMBRIDGE HARBOUR

Bembridge Harbour
Harbour Office, The Duver, St Helens, Ryde
Isle of Wight, PO33 1YB
Tel: 01983 872828 Fax: 01983 872922
Email: thorpemalcolm@btconnect.com
www.bembridgeharbour.co.uk

VHF	Ch 80
ACCESS	HW±2.5

Bembridge is a compact, pretty harbour whose entrance, although restricted by the tides (recommended entry for a 1.5m draught is 2½hrs before HW), is well sheltered in all but north north easterly gales. Offering excellent sailing clubs, beautiful beaches and fine restaurants, this Isle of Wight port is a first class haven with plenty of charm. With approximately 120 new visitors' berths on the Duver Marina pontoons, which can now be booked online, the marina at St Helen's Quay at the western end of the harbour is now allocated to annual berth holders only.

FACILITIES AT A GLANCE

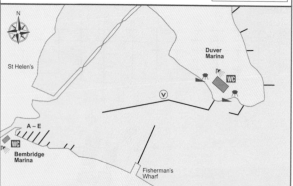

HASLAR MARINA

Haslar Marina
Haslar Road, Gosport, Hampshire, PO12 1NU
Tel: 023 9260 1201
www.haslarmarina.co.uk Email: sales@haslarmarina.co.uk

VHF	Ch 80
ACCESS	H24

This modern, purpose-built marina lies to port on the western side of Portsmouth Harbour entrance and is easily recognised by its prominent lightship incorporating a bar and restaurant. Accessible at all states of the tide, Haslar's extensive facilities do not however include fuel, the nearest being at the Gosport Marina only a few cables north.

Within close proximity is the Royal Navy Submarine Museum and the Museum of Naval Firepower 'Explosion' both worth a visit.

FACILITIES AT A GLANCE

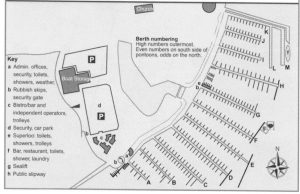

Key
a Admin. offices, security, toilets, showers, weather,
b Rubbish skips, security gate
c Bistro/bar and independent operators, trolleys
d Security, car park
e Superloo: toilets, showers, trolleys
f Bar, restaurant, toilets, shower, laundry
g Sealift
h Public slipway

Berth numbering
High numbers outermost.
Even numbers on south side of pontoons, odds on the north.

GOSPORT MARINA

Premier Gosport Marina
Mumby Road, Gosport, Hampshire, PO12 1AH
Tel: 023 9252 4811 Fax: 023 9258 9541
Email: gosport@premiermarinas.com
www.premiermarinas.com

VHF	Ch 80
ACCESS	H24

A few cables north of Haslar Marina, again on the port hand side, lies Gosport Marina. Boasting 519 fully-serviced, visitors' and 80 dry stack berths, its extensive range of facilities incorporates a fuel barge on its southern break-water as well as shower and laundry amenities. Numerous boatyard and engineering specialists are also located in and around the premises.

Within easy reach of the marina is Gosport town centre, offering a cosmopolitan selection of restaurants along with several supermarkets and shops.

FACILITIES AT A GLANCE

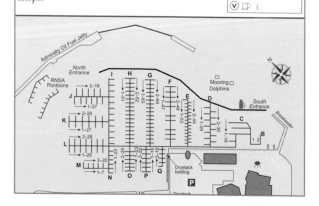

2

ROYAL CLARENCE MARINA

Royal Clarence Marina, Royal Clarence Yard
Weevil Lane, Gosport, Hampshire PO12 1AX
Tel: 02392 523523 Fax: 02392 523523
Email: info@royalclarencemarina.org
www.royalclarencemarina.org

VHF Ch 80
ACCESS H24

Royal Clarence Marina enjoys
a unique setting, with the
former Royal Navy victualling
yard as its backdrop. Only
five minutes from the entrance
of Portsmouth Harbour, this
Transeurope marina lies within
a deep-water basin giving 24/7
access for a draft of up to 4.5m.
This remarkably peaceful and calm marina has wide pontoon spacing,
little tidal flow, and exceptional protection from the swell produced in
Portsmouth Harbour. The new facilities, now just
opposite the marina, have been described as the best
on the South Coast and with two popular restaurants
onsite, makes a great location for visitors.

FACILITIES AT A GLANCE

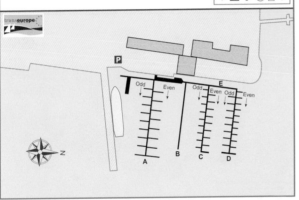

WICORMARINE YACHT HAVEN

WicorMarine Yacht Haven
Cranleigh Road, Portchester, Hampshire, PO16 9DR
Tel: 01329 237112 Fax: 01329 248595
Email: inbox@wicormarine.co.uk

VHF
ACCESS H24

WicorMarine Yacht Haven is
situated in the picturesque upper
reaches of Portsmouth Harbour
away from the hustle and bustle.
The walk-ashore pontoons and
traditional mid-river berths offer
an affordable alternative to busy
marinas and are only 30 mins from
the harbour entrance.

An excellent range of boatyard facilities including a 12T boat hoist,
undercover storage, H24 showers and toilets, diesel, fresh water, on
site repair services and a chandlery complete with
Calor Gas and Camping Gaz exchange.

The popular, licensed Salt Cafe is open to visitors
all year round where you can take in the stunning
views of the harbour from the waterfront deck.

FACILITIES AT A GLANCE

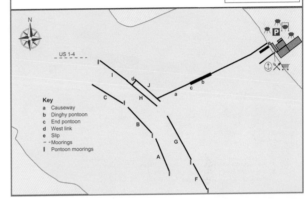

Key
a Causeway
b Dinghy pontoon
c End pontoon
d West link
e Slip
– Moorings
| Pontoon moorings

US 1-4

PORT SOLENT MARINA

Port Solent Marina
South Lockside, Portsmouth, PO6 4TJ
Tel: 023 9221 0765 Fax: 023 9232 4241
www.premiermarinas.com
Email: portsolent@premiermarinas.com

VHF Ch 80
ACCESS H24

Port Solent Marina is located
to the north east of Portsmouth
Harbour, not far from the historic
Portchester Castle. Accessible
via a 24-hour lock, this purpose
built marina offers a full range
of facilities. The Boardwalk
comprises an array of shops and
restaurants, while close by is a
David Lloyd Health Centre and a
large Odeon cinema.

No visit to Portsmouth Harbour is complete
without a trip to the Historic Dockyard, home to
Henry VIII's *Mary Rose*, Nelson's HMS *Victory*
and the first iron battleship, HMS *Warrior*, built
in 1860.

FACILITIES AT A GLANCE

Key
a Laundry, berth holders showers, toilets and baby change
b Portsmouth Harbour YC
c Chandlery, marine engineers
d Under cover boat shed
e Berth holders showers, toilets and public toilets, baby change
f David Lloyd Health and Fitness Club
g The Boardwalk - bars/restaurants
h Odeon cinema
i Marina control and Port Solent reception
j Residential building

Bridgeheads 1 2 3

SOUTHSEA MARINA

Southsea Marina
Fort Cumberland Road, PO4 9RJ
Tel: 02392 822719 Fax: 02392 822220
Email: southsea@premiermarinas.com
www.premiermarinas.com

VHF Ch 80
ACCESS HW±3

Southsea Marina is a small
and friendly marina located
on the western shore of
Langstone Harbour, an
expansive tidal bay situated
between Hayling Island and
Portsmouth. The channel
is clearly marked by seven
starboard and nine port hand
markers. A tidal gate allows
unrestricted movement in and out of the marina up
to 3 hours either side of HW operates the entrance.
The minimum depth in the marina entrance
during this period is 1.6m and a waiting pontoon
is available. There are excellent on site facilities
including a bar, restaurant and chandlery.

FACILITIES AT A GLANCE

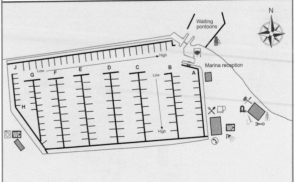

SPARKES MARINA

Sparkes Marina
38 Wittering Road, Hayling Island, Hampshire, PO11 9SR
Tel: 023 9246 3572
Email: sparkes@mdlmarinas.co.uk   www.sparkesmarina.co.uk

VHF Ch 80
ACCESS H24

Just inside the entrance to Chichester Harbour, on the eastern shores of Hayling Island, lies Sparkes Marina. Its facilities include 24-hour showers and toilets, a laundry room, an office/ reception, and Drift: Hayling Island bar and restaurant.

In addition to its berthing and marina services, Sparkes has many skilled professionals on site, including specialists in engineering, outboard engines, glass fibre repairs, rigging, sails and covers, marine carpentry, electrical, boat management and valeting. There is storage ashore for over 200 boats and a 40 ton mobile crane (lifting capacity 15 tons).

FACILITIES AT A GLANCE

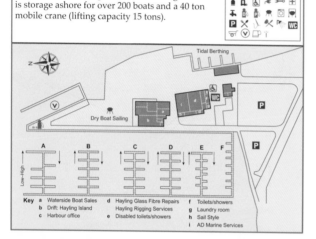

Key		
a	Waterside Boat Sales	d Hayling Glass Fibre Repairs	f Toilets/showers
b	Drift: Hayling Island	Hayling Rigging Services	g Laundry room
c	Harbour office	e Disabled toilets/showers	h Sail Style
			i AD Marine Services

NORTHNEY MARINA

Northney Marina
Northney Road, Hayling Island, Hampshire, PO11 0NH
Tel: 023 9246 6321
Email: northney@mdlmarinas.co.uk
www.northneymarina.co.uk

VHF Ch 80
ACCESS H24

Situated in Chichester Harbour, Northney Marina is set on the northern shore of Hayling Island in the well-marked Sweare Deep Channel, which branches off to port almost at the end of Emsworth Channel. This 228-berth marina offers excellent boatyard facilities, a provisions store and laundry area, diesel, a slipway, Salt Shack Café, wi-fi and 24/7 staff cover. There is also an events area for rallies.

FACILITIES AT A GLANCE

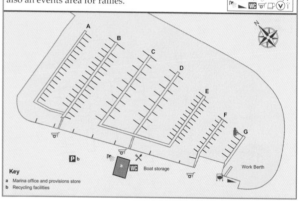

Key	
a	Marina office and provisions store
b	Recycling facilities

EMSWORTH YACHT HARBOUR

Emsworth Yacht Harbour Ltd
Thorney Road, Emsworth, Hants, PO10 8BP
Tel: 01243 377727 Fax: 01243 373432
Email: info@emsworth-marina.co.uk
www.emsworth-marina.co.uk

VHF
ACCESS HW±2

Accessible about one and a half to two hours either side of high water, Emsworth Yacht Harbour is a sheltered site, offering good facilities to yachtsmen.

Created in 1964 from a log pond, the marina is within easy walking distance of the pretty little town of Emsworth, which boasts at least 10 pubs, several high quality restaurants and two well-stocked convenience stores.

FACILITIES AT A GLANCE

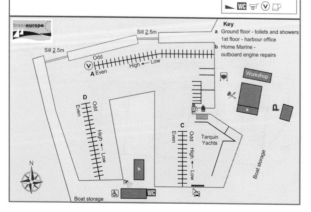

Key	
a	Ground floor - toilets and showers
	1st floor - harbour office
b	Home Marine -
	outboard engine repairs

CHICHESTER MARINA

Chichester Marina
Birdham, Chichester, West Sussex, PO20 7EJ
Tel: 01243 512731 Fax: 01243 513472
Email: chichester@premiermarinas.com
www.premiermarinas.com

VHF Ch 80
ACCESS HW±5

Chichester Marina, nestling in an enormous natural harbour, has more than 1,000 berths, making it one of the largest in the UK. Its approach channel can be easily identified by the CM SHM pile. The channel was dredged to 0.5m below CD in 2004, giving access of around five hours either side of HW at springs. Besides the wide ranging marine facilities, there are also a restaurant and small convenience store on site. Chichester, which is only about a five minute bus or taxi ride away, has several places of interest, the most notable being the cathedral.

FACILITIES AT A GLANCE

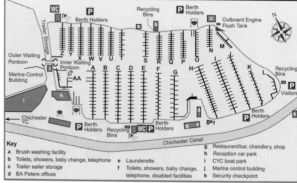

Key		
a	Brush washing facility	g Restaurant/bar, chandlery, shop
b	Toilets, showers, baby change, telephone	e Launderette	h Reception car park
c	Trailer sailer storage	f Toilets, showers, baby change,	i CYC boat park
d	BA Peters offices	telephone, disabled facilities	j Marina control building
			k Security checkpoint

2

BIRDHAM POOL MARINA

Birdham Pool Marina
Birdham Pool, Chichester, Sussex
Tel: 01243 512310 Fax: 01243 513163
Email: mikebraidley@castlemarinas.co.uk

| VHF | Ch 80 |
| ACCESS | HW±3·5 |

Birdham Pool is the UK's oldest marina, with a charm not found elsewhere. A recent programme of improvements sees 28 new berths, a new 30-ton crane to lift out boats up to 50ft long and 2m draft, brand new facilities block and new Marine Trades Centre showcasing traditional skilled craftsmen. Visitors will not be disappointed by the unique and picturesque setting, with views across the South Downs as well as Chichester Harbour. Access is HW±3·5, via a dredged channel marked by starboard hand piles.

FACILITIES AT A GLANCE

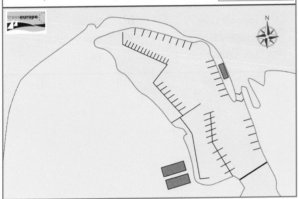

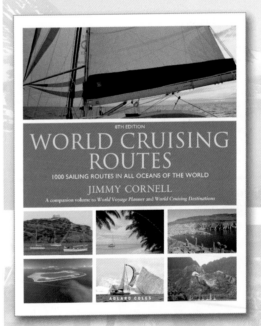
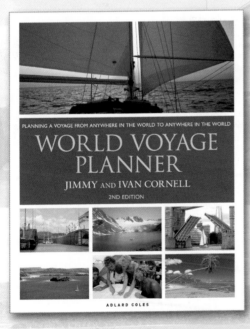

SOUTH EAST ENGLAND – Selsey Bill to North Foreland

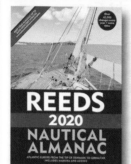
Key to Marina Plans symbols

🛢	Bottled gas	**P**	Parking
	Chandler	✕	Pub/Restaurant
♿	Disabled facilities		Pump out
	Electrical supply		Rigging service
	Electrical repairs		Sail repairs
	Engine repairs		Shipwright
✚	First Aid		Shop/Supermarket
	Fresh Water		Showers
D	Fuel - Diesel		Slipway
P	Fuel - Petrol	**WC**	Toilets
	Hardstanding/boatyard	☎	Telephone
@	Internet Café		Trolleys
	Laundry facilities	V	Visitors berths
	Lift-out facilities		Wi-Fi

Area 3 - South East England

MARINAS
Telephone Numbers
VHF Channel
Access Times

N. Foreland
Margate
Ramsgate

Ramsgate Royal Harbour Marina
01843 572100
Ch 14, 80 H24

S. Foreland

Dover

Folkestone

Dover Marina
01304 241663
Ch 80 H24

Lady Bee Marina
01273 593801
Ch 14 H24

Brighton Marina
01273 819919
Ch M, 80 H24

Rye

Shoreham

Littlehampton

Brighton

Harbour of Rye
01797 225225
Ch 14 HW±2

Littlehampton Marina
01903 713553
Ch 80
HW-3 to +2.5
Hillyards
01903 713327
HW-3 to +2.5

Newhaven
Newhaven Marina
01273 513881
Ch 80 H24

Eastbourne

Sovereign Harbour Marina
01323 470099
Ch 17 H24

N

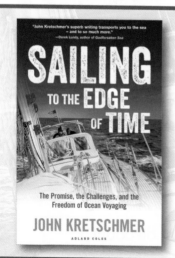

LITTLEHAMPTON MARINA

Littlehampton Marina
Ferry Road, Littlehampton, W Sussex
Tel: 01903 713553 Fax: 01903 732264
Email: sales@littlehamptonmarina.co.uk

VHF	Ch 80
ACCESS	HW-3 to +2.5

A typical English seaside town with funfair, promenade and fine sandy beaches, Littlehampton lies roughly midway between Brighton and Chichester at the mouth of the River Arun. It affords a convenient stopover for yachts either east or west bound, providing you have the right tidal conditions to cross the entrance bar with its charted depth of 0.7m. The marina lies about three cables above Town Quay and Fisherman's Quay, both of which are on the starboard side of the River Arun, and is accessed via a retractable footbridge that opens on request to the HM (note that you should contact him by 1630 the day before you require entry).

FACILITIES AT A GLANCE

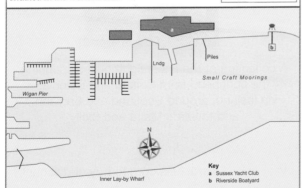

Key
a Marina offices
b Cafe

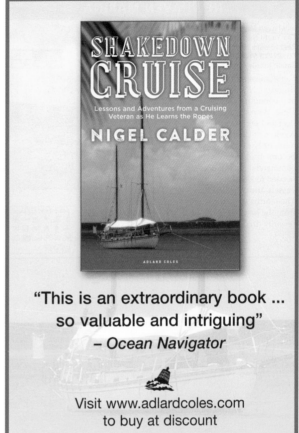

LADY BEE MARINA

Lady Bee Marina
138-140 Albion Street, Southwick
West Sussex, BN42 4EG
Tel: 01273 593801 Fax: 01273 870349

VHF	Ch 14
ACCESS	H24

Shoreham, only five miles west of Brighton, is one of the South Coast's major commercial ports handling, among other products, steel, grain, tarmac and timber. On first impressions it may seem that Shoreham has little to offer the visiting yachtsman, but once through the lock and into the eastern arm of the River Adur, the quiet Lady Bee Marina, with its Spanish waterside restaurant, can make this harbour an interesting alternative to the lively atmosphere of Brighton Marina. Run by the Harbour Office, the marina meets all the usual requirements, although fuel is available in cans from Southwick garage or from Corral's diesel pump situated in the western arm.

FACILITIES AT A GLANCE

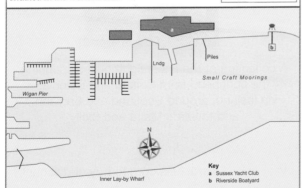

Key
a Sussex Yacht Club
b Riverside Boatyard

BRIGHTON MARINA

Brighton Marina
West Jetty, Brighton, East Sussex, BN2 5UP
Tel: 01273 819919 Fax: 01273 675082
Email: brighton@premiermarinas.com
www.premiermarinas.com

VHF	Ch M, 80
ACCESS	H24

Brighton Marina is the largest marina in the country and with its extensive range of shops, restaurants and facilities, is a popular and convenient stop-over for east and west-going passagemakers. Note, however, that it is not advisable to attempt entry in strong S to SE winds.

Only half a mile from the marina is the historic city of Brighton itself, renowned for being a cultural centre with a cosmopolitan atmosphere. Among its numerous attractions are the exotic Royal Pavilion, built for King George IV in the 1800s, and the Lanes, with its multitude of antiques shops.

FACILITIES AT A GLANCE

Key
a David Lloyd Heath & Fitness Club
b Bowling alley
c Casino/night club
d Multiplex cinema
e Yacht club
f Petrol station
g Mariners Quay
h Marina reception

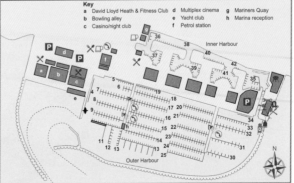

NEWHAVEN MARINA

Newhaven Marina
The Yacht Harbour, Fort Road, Newhaven
East Sussex, BN9 9BY
Tel: 01273 513881
Email: john.stirling@newhavenmarina.co.uk

VHF	Ch 80
ACCESS	H24

Some seven miles from Brighton, Newhaven lies at the mouth of the River Ouse. With its large fishing fleet and regular ferry services to Dieppe, the harbour has over the years become progressively commercial, therefore care is needed to keep clear of large vessels under manoeuvre.

The marina lies approximately quarter of a mile from the harbour entrance on the west bank and was recently dredged to allow full tidal access except on LWS.

FACILITIES AT A GLANCE

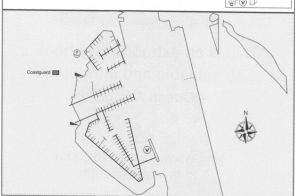

SOVEREIGN HARBOUR MARINA

Sovereign Harbour Marina
Pacific Drive, Eastbourne, East Sussex, BN23 5BJ
Tel: 01323 470099
Email: eastbourne@premiermarinas.com
www.premiermarinas.com

VHF	Ch 17
ACCESS	H24

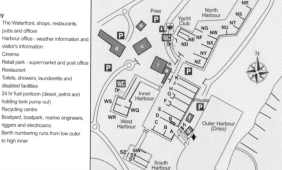

Opened in 1993 and taken over by Premier Marinas in 2007, Sovereign Harbour is accessible at all states of the tide and weather except for in strong NE to SE'ly winds. Entered via a lock H24, the Five Gold Anchor Award marina is part of one of the largest waterfront complexes in the UK, enjoying close proximity to shops, restaurants and a multiplex cinema. The Sovereign Harbour YC is on site and welcomes visitors to its bar and galley.

A short bus or taxi ride takes you to Eastbourne, where you will find shops and eating places to suit all tastes and budgets.

FACILITIES AT A GLANCE

Key
a The Waterfront, shops, restaurants, pubs and offices
b Harbour office - weather information and visitor's information
c Cinema
d Retail park - supermarket and post office
e Restaurant
f Toilets, showers, launderette and disabled facilities
g 24 hr fuel pontoon (diesel, petrol and holding tank pump out)
h Recycling centre
i Boatyard, boatpark, marine engineers, riggers and electricians
NB Berth numbering runs from low outer to high inner

HARBOUR OF RYE

Harbour of Rye
New Lydd Road, Camber, E Sussex, TN31 7QS
Tel: 01797 225225
Email: rye.harbour@environment-agency.gov.uk
www.environment-agency.gov.uk/harbourofrye

VHF	Ch 14
ACCESS	HW±2

The Strand Quay moorings are located in the centre of the historic town of Rye with all of its amenities a short walk away. The town caters for a wide variety of interests with the nearby Rye Harbour Nature Reserve, a museum, numerous antique shops and plentiful pubs, bars and restaurants. Vessels, up to a length of 15 metres, wishing to berth in the soft mud in or near the town of Rye should time their arrival at the entrance for not later than one hour after high water. Larger vessels should make prior arrangements with the Harbour Master. Fresh water, electricity, shower and toilet facilities are available.

FACILITIES AT A GLANCE

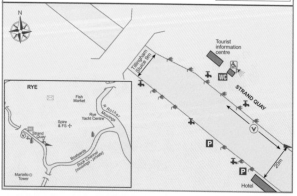

DOVER MARINA

Dover Harbour Board
Harbour House, Dover, Kent, CT17 9TF
Tel: 01304 241663 Fax: 01304 242549
Email: marina@doverport.co.uk www.doverport.co.uk/marina

VHF Ch 80
ACCESS H24

Nestling under the famous White Cliffs, Dover sits between South Foreland to the NE and Folkestone to the SW. Boasting a maritime history stretching back as far as the Bronze Age, Dover is today one of Britain's busiest commercial ports, with a continuous stream of ferries and cruise liners plying to and from their European destinations. However, over the past years the harbour has made itself more attractive to the cruising yachtsman, with the marina, set well away from the busy ferry terminal, offering three sheltered berthing options in the Tidal Harbour, Granville Dock and Wellington Dock.

FACILITIES AT A GLANCE

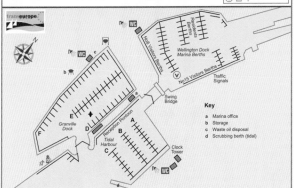

Key
a Marina office
b Storage
c Waste oil disposal
d Scrubbing berth (tidal)

ROYAL HARBOUR MARINA

Royal Harbour Marina, Ramsgate
Harbour Office, Military Road, Ramsgate, Kent, CT11 9LQ
Tel: 01843 572100
Email: portoframsgate@thanet.gov.uk
www.portoframsgate.co.uk

VHF Ch 14, 80
ACCESS H24

Steeped in maritime history, Ramsgate was awarded 'Royal' status in 1821 by George IV in recognition of the warm welcome he received when sailing from Ramsgate. Offering good shelter and modern facilities, including both red and white diesel, the Royal Harbour comprises an outer marina accessible H24 and an inner marina, entered approximately HW±2. Permission to enter or leave the Royal Harbour must be obtained from Port Control on channel 14 and berthing instructions can be obtained from the Dockmaster on channel 80. Full information may be found on the website.

FACILITIES AT A GLANCE

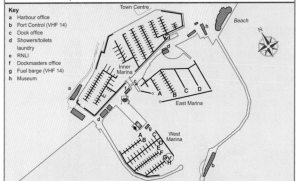

Key
a Harbour office
b Port Control (VHF 14)
c Dock office
d Showers/toilets
   laundry
e RNLI
f Dockmasters office
g Fuel barge (VHF 14)
h Museum

3

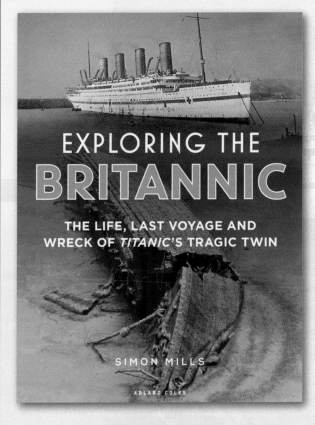

Exploring the Britannic

The complete story of RMS Titanic's tragic twin told through never before seen photographs of the wreck

Visit www.adlardcoles.com
to buy at discount

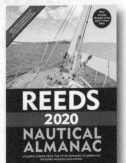
Key to Marina Plans symbols

Bottled gas		P Parking	
Chandler		Pub/Restaurant	
Disabled facilities		Pump out	
Electrical supply		Rigging service	
Electrical repairs		Sail repairs	
Engine repairs		Shipwright	
First Aid		Shop/Supermarket	
Fresh Water		Showers	
Fuel - Diesel		Slipway	
Fuel - Petrol		WC Toilets	
Hardstanding/boatyard		Telephone	
@ Internet Café		Trolleys	
Laundry facilities		V Visitors berths	
Lift-out facilities		Wi-Fi	

4

Area 4 - East England

MARINAS
Telephone Numbers, VHF Channel, Access Times

Gallions Pt Marina 020 7476 7054 Ch M, 80 HW±5
South Dock Marina 020 7252 2244 Ch M HW-2½ to +1½
Poplar Dock Marina 020 7308 9930 Ch 13 HW±1
St Katharine Haven 020 7264 5312 Ch 80 HW-2 to +1½
Chelsea Harbour 020 7225 9157 Ch 80 HW±1½
Brentford Dock Marina 020 8232 8941 HW±2½
Penton Hook Marina 01932 568681 Ch 80 H24
Windsor Marina 01753 853911 Ch 80 H24
Bray Marina 01628 623654 Ch 80 H24

Gt Yarmouth

Lowestoft — Royal Norfolk & Suffolk YC 01520 566726 Ch 14, 80 H24
Lowestoft Haven Marina 01520 580300 Ch M, 80 H24
Southwold — Lowestoft Cruising Club 07913 391950, H24

Suffolk Yacht Hbr 01473 659240 Ch 80 H24
Royal Harwich YC Marina 01473 780319 Ch 77 H24
Woolverstone Marina 01473 780206 Ch 80 H24
Fox's Marina 01473 689111 Ch 80 H24
Neptune Marina 01473 215204 Ch M, 80 H24
Ipswich Haven Marina 01473 236644 Ch M, 80 H24

Orford — Shotley Marina 01473 788982 Ch 80 H24

Ipswich

Harwich

Titchmarsh Marina 01255 672185 Ch 80 HW±5
Walton Yacht Basin 01255 675873 Ch 80 HW-¾ to +¼

Burnham Yacht Harbour 01621 782150 Ch 80 H24
Essex Marina 01702 258531 Ch 80 H24
Bridgemarsh Marina 01621 740414 Ch 80 HW±4
Fambridge Yacht Haven 01621 740370 Ch 80 H24
Fambridge Yacht Station 01621 742911 Ch 80 H24

Limehouse Marina 020 7308 9930 Ch 80 HW±3

Bradwell Marina 01621 776235 Ch M, 80 HW±4½
Blackwater Marina 01621 740264 Ch M HW±2
Tollesbury Marina 01621 869202 Ch 80 HW±2
Heybridge Basin 01621 853506 Ch 80 HW±1

R Thames

N. Foreland

Port Werburgh 01634 225107 Ch 80 HW±3

Chatham Maritime Marina 01634 899200

Gillingham Marina 01634 280022 Ch 80 HW±4½

Ramsgate

N

GILLINGHAM MARINA

Gillingham Marina
173 Pier Road, Gillingham, Kent, ME7 1UB
Tel: 01634 280022 Fax: 01634 280164
Email: berthing@gillingham-marina.co.uk
www.gillingham-marina.co.uk

VHF | Ch 80
ACCESS | HW±4.5

Gillingham Marina comprises a locked basin, accessible four and a half hours either side of high water, and a tidal basin upstream which can be entered approximately two hours either side of high water. Deep water moorings in the river cater for yachts arriving at other times.

Visiting yachts are usually accommodated in the locked basin, although it is best to contact the marina ahead of time. Lying on the south bank of the River Medway, the marina is approximately eight miles from Sheerness, at the mouth of the river, and five miles downstream of Rochester Bridge. Facilities include a well-stocked chandlery, brokerage and an extensive workshop.

FACILITIES AT A GLANCE

Key
a Workshop
b Showers & toilets
c Shop
d Laundry
e Play area
f Reception & club
g Tender storage
h Lead in pontoon
i Petrol & diesel
j Leisure centre

PORT WERBURGH

Port Werburgh
Vicarage Lane, Hoo, Rochester, Kent, ME3 9TW
Tel: 01634 252107 Fax: 01634 253477
Email: jillswann@wanttoliveafloat.com

VHF | Ch 80
ACCESS | HW±3

Hoo Marina has been purchased by Residential Marine Ltd and is now incorporated into Port Werburgh. The port, some eight miles upriver from Sheerness, can be approached either straight across the mud flats at HW or via the creek, which has access HW±3 for shallow draught boats. The path of the creek is marked by withies, which must be kept to port.

The port accommodates residential and leisure boats from 20–200ft and has a lifting service available for craft up to 17 tons; a dry dock is available for larger boats. There are no workshop facilities but boat owners are encouraged to work on their own boats. Security is provided by H24 CCTV coverage.

All berths are supplied with water and electricity and the onsite amenity block has showers, toilets and a laundry room. There is a grocery store adjacent and shops in Hoo village approximately half a mile distant. There is a frequent bus service to nearby Rochester.

FACILITIES AT A GLANCE

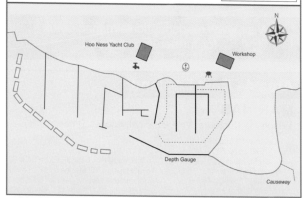

Limehouse Basin Marina

London

An oasis of calm in the heart of London

Fully serviced pontoons
Visitors welcome

020 7308 9930   bwml.co.uk   phil.cotman@bwml.co.uk

CHATHAM MARITIME MARINA

Chatham Maritime Marina, The Lock Building,
Leviathan Way, Chatham Maritime, Chatham, Medway, ME4 4LP
Tel: 01634 899200
Email: chatham@mdlmarinas.co.uk
www.chathammaritimemarina.co.uk

VHF Ch 80
ACCESS H24

Chatham Maritime Marina is situated on the banks of the River Medway in Kent, providing an ideal location from which to explore the surrounding area. There are plenty of secluded anchorages in the lower reaches of the Medway Estuary, while the river is navigable for some 13 miles from its mouth at Sheerness right up to Rochester, and even beyond for those yachts drawing less than 2m. Only 45 minutes from London by road, the marina is part of a multi-million pound leisure and retail development, accommodating 412 boats following a recent expansion.

FACILITIES AT A GLANCE

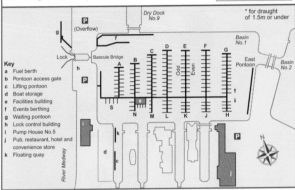

Key
a   Fuel berth
b   Pontoon access gate
c   Lifting pontoon
d   Boat storage
e   Facilities building
f   Events berthing
g   Waiting pontoon
h   Lock control building
i   Pump House No.5
j   Pub, restaurant, hotel and convenience store
k   Floating quay

LIMEHOUSE MARINA

BWML Limehouse Marina
46 Goodhart Place, London, E14 8EG
Tel: 020 7308 9930   Fax: 020 7363 0428
Email: limehouse.marina@bwml.co.uk   www.bwml.co.uk

VHF Ch 80
ACCESS HW±3

Limehouse Marina, situated where the canal system meets the Thames, is now considered the 'Jewel in the Crown' of the British inland waterways network. With complete access to 2,000 miles of inland waterway systems and with access to the Thames at most stages of the tide except around low water, the marina provides a superb location for river, canal and sea-going pleasure craft alike. Boasting a wide range of facilities and up to 90 berths, Limehouse Marina is housed in the old Regent's Canal Dock.

FACILITIES AT A GLANCE

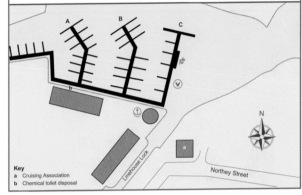

Key
a   Cruising Association
b   Chemical toilet disposal

GALLIONS POINT MARINA

Gallions Point Marina, Gate 14, Royal Albert Basin
Woolwich Manor Way, North Woolwich
London, E16 2QY.   Tel: 020 7476 7054   Fax: 020 7474 7056
Email: info@gallionspointmarina.co.uk
www.gallionspointmarina.co.uk

VHF Ch M, 80
ACCESS HW±5

Gallions Point Marina lies about 500 metres down-stream of the Woolwich Ferry on the north side of Gallions Reach. Accessed via a lock at the entrance to the Royal Albert Basin, the marina offers deep water pontoon berths as well as hard standing. Future plans to improve facilities include the development of a bar/restaurant, a chandlery and an RYA tuition school.

FACILITIES AT A GLANCE

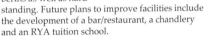

SOUTH DOCK MARINA

South Dock Marina
Rope Street, Off Plough Way
London, SE16 7SZ
Tel: 020 7252 2244 Fax: 020 7237 3806
Email: christopher.magro@southwark.gov.uk

VHF	Ch M
ACCESS	HW-2.5 to +1.5

South Dock Marina is housed in part of the old Surrey Dock complex on the south bank of the River Thames. Its locked entrance is immediately downstream of Greenland Pier, just a few miles down river of Tower Bridge. For yachts with a 2m draught, the lock can be entered HW-2½ to HW+1½ London Bridge, although if you arrive early there is a holding pontoon on the pier. The marina can be easily identified by the conspicuous arched rooftops of Baltic Quay, a luxury waterside apartment block. Once inside this secure, 200-berth marina, you can take full advantage of all its facilities as well as enjoy a range of restaurants and bars close by or visit historic maritime Greenwich.

FACILITIES AT A GLANCE

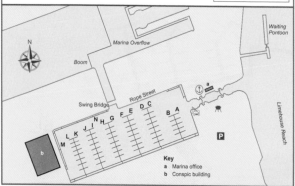

Key
a Marina office
b Conspic building

CHELSEA HARBOUR MARINA

Chelsea Harbour Marina
Estate Managements Office
C2-3 The Chambers, London, SW10 0XF
Tel: 07770 542783 Fax: 020 7352 7868
Email: harbourmaster@chelsea-harbour.co.uk

VHF	
ACCESS	HW±1.5

Chelsea Harbour is widely thought of as one of London's most significant maritime sites. It is located in the heart of SW London, therefore enjoying easy access to the amenities of Chelsea and the West End. On site is the Chelsea Harbour Design Centre, where 80 showrooms exhibit the best in British and International interior design, offering superb waterside views along with excellent cuisine in the Wyndham Grand.

The harbour lies approximately 48 miles up river from Sea Reach No 1 buoy in the Thames Estuary and is accessed via the Thames Flood Barrier in Woolwich Reach. With its basin gate operating one and a half hours either side of HW (+ 20 minutes at London Bridge), the marina welcomes visiting yachtsmen.

FACILITIES AT A GLANCE

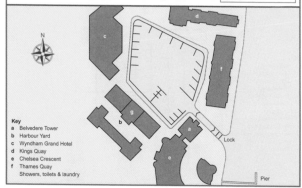

Key
a Belvedere Tower
b Harbour Yard
c Wyndham Grand Hotel
d Kings Quay
e Chelsea Crescent
f Thames Quay
    Showers, toilets & laundry

ST KATHARINE DOCKS

St Katharine's Marina Ltd
50 St Katharine's Way, London, E1W 1LA
Tel: 020 7264 5312
Email: ptetlow@skdocks.co.uk
www.skdocks.co.uk/marina

VHF	Ch 80
ACCESS	HW -2 to +1.5

St Katharine Docks Marina has been recently refurbished and offers 185 berths equipped for boats up to 40m in three separate, secure and calm basins. The historic docks are located next to Tower Bridge.

This is a unique marina benefiting from waterside dining, boutique shops and excellent transport links to the West End. Visitors are welcomed all year round and the marina provides its own calendar of events details of which can be found on the website and social media pages.

The marina is ideally situated for visiting the Tower of London, Tower Bridge, *HMS Belfast* and the City of London all of which can be reached on foot. A short river bus service away is Greenwich and the Cutty Sark and to the west the Shard and London Eye.

FACILITIES AT A GLANCE

Key
a Ivory House
b Dickens Inn
c Marina reception
d Tower Hotel

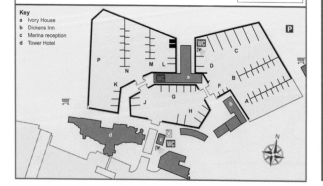

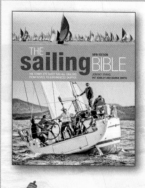

BRENTFORD DOCK MARINA

Brentford Dock Marina
2 Justin Close, Brentford, Middlesex, TW8 8QE
Tel: 020 8232 8941 Mob: 07970 143 987
E-mail: brentforddockmarina@gmail.com

VHF
ACCESS HW±2.5

Brentford Dock Marina is situated on the River Thames at the junction with the Grand Union Canal. Its hydraulic lock is accessible for up to two and a half hours either side of high water, although boats over 9.5m LOA enter on high water by prior arrangement. There is a grocery store on site. The main attractions within the area are the Royal Botanic Gardens at Kew and the Kew Bridge Steam Museum at Brentford.

FACILITIES AT A GLANCE

Key
a Shop
b Rubbish disposal
c Recycling bins
d Marina office and first aid
e Toilets, showers and slop out facilities

PENTON HOOK MARINA

Penton Hook Marina
Staines Road, Chertsey, Surrey, KT16 8PY
Tel: 01932 568681
Email: pentonhook@mdlmarinas.co.uk
www.pentonhookmarina.co.uk

VHF
ACCESS H24

Penton Hook, the largest inland marina in Europe, is situated on what is considered to be one of the most attractive reaches of the River Thames; close to the vibrant town of Staines-on-Thames and about a mile downstream from Runnymede.

Providing unrestricted access to the River Thames through a deep water channel below Penton Hook Lock, the marina can accommodate ocean-going craft of up to 30m LOA and is ideally placed for a visit to Thorpe Park, reputedly one of the country's most popular family leisure attractions.

FACILITIES AT A GLANCE

Key
a Information point
b Dock manager's office
c Yacht club
d Repairs and under cover storage

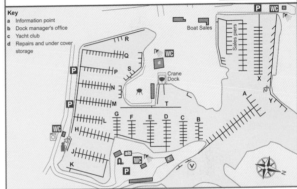

4

WINDSOR MARINA

Windsor Marina
Maidenhead Road, Windsor
Berkshire, SL4 5TZ
Tel: 01753 853911
Email: windsor@mdlmarinas.co.uk www.windsormarina.co.uk

VHF
ACCESS H24

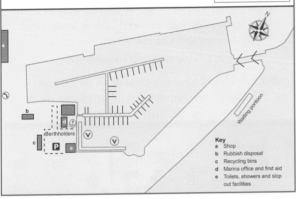

Situated on the outskirts of Windsor town on the south bank of the River Thames, Windsor Marina enjoys a peaceful garden setting. On site is the Windsor Yacht Club and fuel (diesel and petrol), enabling you to fill up as and when you need.

A trip to the town of Windsor, comprising beautiful Georgian and Victorian buildings, would not be complete without a visit to Windsor Castle. With its construction inaugurated over 900 years ago by William the Conqueror, it is the oldest inhabited castle in the world and accommodates a priceless art and furniture collection.

FACILITIES AT A GLANCE

Key
a Boat sales & engineers
b Recycling bins
c Dock office
d Trimmers
e Yacht club

BRAY MARINA

Bray Marina
Monkey Island Lane, Bray
Berkshire, SL6 2EB
Tel: 01628 623654
Email: bray@mdlmarinas.co.uk www.braymarina.co.uk

VHF
ACCESS H24

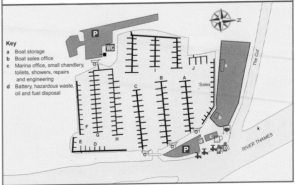

Bray Marina is situated in a country park setting among shady trees, providing berth holders with a tranquil mooring. From the marina there is direct access to the Thames and there are extensive well-maintained facilities available for all boat owners. The 400-berth marina boasts an active club, which holds social functions as well as boat training lessons and handling competitions, a small chandlery and engineering services.

Upstream is the National Trust property, Cliveden House, with its extensive gardens and woodlands. Cookham is home of the Queen's Swan Keeper, who can sometimes be seen in his traditional costume. Further on still is Hambledon Mill; from here the river is navigable as far as Lechlade.

FACILITIES AT A GLANCE

Key
a Boat storage
b Boat sales office
c Marina office, small chandlery, toilets, showers, repairs and engineering
d Battery, hazardous waste, oil and fuel disposal

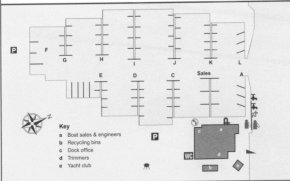

BURNHAM YACHT HARBOUR MARINA

Burnham Yacht Harbour Marina Ltd
Burnham-on-Crouch, Essex, CM0 8BL
Tel: 01621 782150 HM: 01621 786832
Email: admin@burnhamyachtharbour.co.uk

VHF	Ch 80
ACCESS	H24

Burnham Yacht Harbour is situated in the pretty town of Burnham-on-Crouch with its quaint shops, elegant quayside and riverside walks. The train station, with direct train links to London Liverpool Street Station, is within walking. There is provision of all facilities you would expect

to find from a modern secure marina with H24 tidal access, 350 fully serviced berths, the popular Swallowtail Restaurant and Bar, friendly staff, engineers, shipwrights, workshop, friendly staff, chandlery and yacht brokerage. The entrance is easily identified by a yellow pillar buoy with an 'X' topmark.

FACILITIES AT A GLANCE

Key
a Workshop
b Yacht sales
c Marina office
d Shower block
e The Swallowtail
f RNLI shore station
g Country park

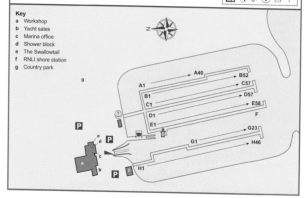

ESSEX MARINA

Essex Marina
Wallasea Island, Essex, SS4 2HF
Tel: 01702 258531 Fax: 01702 258227
Email: info@essexmarina.co.uk
www.essexmarina.co.uk

VHF	Ch 80
ACCESS	H24

Surrounded by beautiful countryside, Essex Marina is situated in Wallasea Bay, about half a mile up river of Burnham on Crouch. Boasting 500 deep water berths, including 50 swinging moorings, the marina can be accessed at all states of the tide. On site are a 70 ton boat hoist, a chandlery and brokerage

service as well as the Essex Marina Yacht Club.

Essex Marina is the home of Boats.co.uk. There is a ferry service which runs from Easter until the end of September, taking passengers across the river 6 days a week to Burnham, where you will find numerous shops and restaurants.

FACILITIES AT A GLANCE

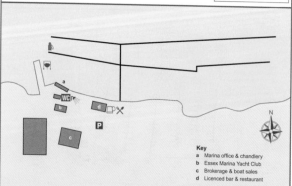

Key
a Marina office & chandlery
b Essex Marina Yacht Club
c Brokerage & boat sales
d Licenced bar & restaurant

BRIDGEMARSH MARINA

Bridgemarsh Marine
Fairholme, Bridge Marsh Lane, Althorne, Essex
Tel: 01621 740414 Mobile: 07968 696815 Fax: 01621 742216

VHF	Ch 80
ACCESS	HW±4

On the north side of Bridgemarsh Island, just beyond Essex Marina on the River Crouch, lies Althorne Creek. Here Bridgemarsh Marine accommodates over 100 boats berthed alongside pontoons supplied with water and electricity. A red beacon marks the entrance to the

creek, with red can buoys identifying the approach channel into the marina. Accessible four hours either side of high water, the marina has an on site yard with two docks, a slipway and crane. The village of Althorne is just a short walk away, from where there are direct train services (taking approximately one hour) to London.

FACILITIES AT A GLANCE

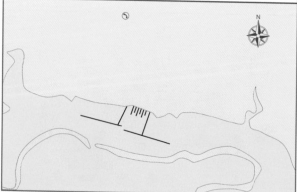

HEYBRIDGE BASIN

Heybridge Basin
Lock Hill, Heybridge Basin, Maldon, Essex, CM9 4RY
Tel: 07712 079764
Email: grant.everiss@waterways.org.uk
www.essexwaterways.com

| VHF | Ch 80 |
| ACCESS | HW±1 |

Towards the head of the River Blackwater and not far from Maldon, lies Heybridge Basin sea lock. It is situated at the lower end of the 14M Chelmer and Blackwater Navigation Canal and can be entered approximately 1-1.5hrs before HW for vessels drawing up to 2m. There is good holding ground in the river just outside the lock. There are in excess of 300 permanent moorings along the navigation and room for up to 20 rafting visiting vessels in the Basin, which has a range of facilities, including shower and laundry. Please book at least 24hrs in advance especially during the summer months. The manned lock is operational for tides between 0600 and 2000 during summer months (0800–1700 Apr–Oct).

FACILITIES AT A GLANCE

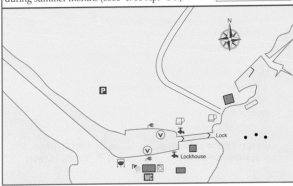

FAMBRIDGE YACHT HAVEN

Fambridge Yacht Haven
Church Road, North Fambridge, Essex, CM3 6LU
Tel: 01621 740370 www.yachthavens.com
Email: fambridge@yachthavens.com

| VHF | Ch 80 |
| ACCESS | H24 |

The Haven is split over two sites in the village of North Fambridge. The marina is located just under a mile upstream of its 'Yacht Station' facility with access via Stow Creek, which branches N off the R Crouch. The channel is straight and clearly marked to the ent of the Yacht Haven. Home to the West Wick Yacht Club, the marina has 220 berths to accommodate vessels up to 20m LOA. North Fambridge features the 500 year-old Ferry Boat Inn, a favourite haunt with the sailing fraternity. Burnham-on-Crouch is six miles down river, while the Essex and Kent coasts are within easy sailing distance. Excellent repair facilities can be found ashore together with undercover storage for vessels up to 19m LOA with a maximum weight of 40 tons.

FACILITIES AT A GLANCE

Key
a Marina reception
b Waste
c West Wick YC
d Boat Shed Essex
e Marina maintenance,
   workshop & stores
f Under cover storage
g Chandler

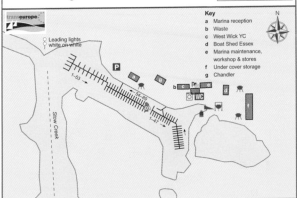

BRADWELL MARINA

Bradwell Marina, Port Flair Ltd, Waterside
Bradwell-on-Sea, Essex, CM0 7RB
Tel: 01621 776235 Fax: 01621 776393
Email: info@bradwellmarina.com
www.bradwellmarina.com

| VHF | Ch M, 80 |
| ACCESS | HW±4.5 |

Opened in 1984, Bradwell is a privately-owned marina situated in the mouth of the River Blackwater, serving as a convenient base from which to explore the Essex coastline or as a departure point for cruising further afield to Holland and Belgium.

The yacht basin can be accessed four and a half hours either side of HW and offers plenty of protection from all wind directions. With a total of 300 fully serviced berths, generous space has been allocated for manoeuvring between pontoons. Overlooking the marina is Bradwell Club House, incorporating a bar, restaurant, launderette and ablution facilities.

FACILITIES AT A GLANCE

Key
a Clubhouse
b Tower office

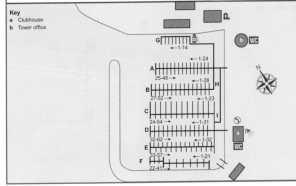

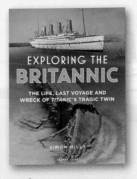

FAMBRIDGE YACHT STATION

Fambridge Yacht Station
Church Road, North Fambridge, Essex, CM3 6LU
Tel: 01621 742911 www.yachthavens.com
Email: fambridge@yachthavens.com

VHF Ch 80
ACCESS H24

The Yacht Station is located just under a mile downstream of Fambridge Yacht Haven and is set within the sheltered River Crouch directly between the rural villages of North and South Fambridge. Home to the North Fambridge Yacht Club, the Yacht Station has a 120m visitor pontoon providing deep water berthing alongside and foot access to mud berths and the North Fambridge. There are also 120 deep water swinging moorings in 4 straight E/W trots just off the visitor pontoon. A launch service operates 7 days a week during the summer, call in advance for times. As with the marina, excellent repair facilities can be found ashore for vessels with a maximum weight of 25t.

FACILITIES AT A GLANCE

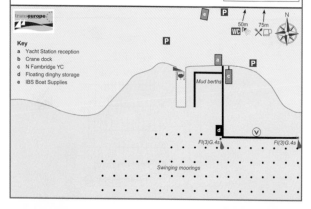

Key
a Yacht Station reception
b Crane dock
c N Fambridge YC
d Floating dinghy storage
e IBS Boat Supplies

Mud berths

Fl(3)G.4s   Fl(3)G.4s

Swinging moorings

Visitors welcome

Fambridge Yacht Haven
Full tidal access

– 220 sheltered & fully serviced pontoon berths
– 120 deepwater swinging moorings
– 120m visitor pontoon with full tidal access
– A TransEurope Marina
– FREE Wi-Fi for berth holders & visitors
– Walking distance from the famous Ferry Boat Inn
– Hassle-free Park & Ride Service
– Modern 40t & 25t slipway hoists & 30t mobile crane

Call 01621 740370 or VHF Ch 80
or visit yachthavens.com

Fambridge
Yacht Haven

BLACKWATER MARINA

Blackwater Marina
Marine Parade, Maylandsea, Essex
Tel: 01621 740264
Email: info@blackwater-marina.co.uk

VHF Ch M
ACCESS HW±2

Blackwater Marina is a place where families in day boats mix with Smack owners and yacht crews; here seals, avocets and porpoises roam beneath the big, sheltering East Coast skies and here the area's rich heritage of working Thames Barges and Smacks remains part of daily life today.
But it isn't just classic sailing boats that thrive on the Blackwater. An eclectic mix of motor cruisers, open boats and modern yachts enjoy the advantages of a marina sheltered by its natural habitat, where the absence of harbour walls allows uninterrupted views of some of Britain's rarest wildlife and where the 21st century shoreside facilities are looked after by experienced professionals, who are often found sailing on their days off.

FACILITIES AT A GLANCE

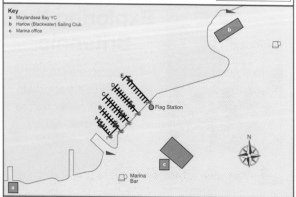

Key
a Maylandsea Bay YC
b Harlow (Blackwater) Sailing Club
c Marina office

Flag Station

Marina
Bar

TOLLESBURY MARINA

Tollesbury Marina
The Yacht Harbour, Tollesbury, Essex, CM9 8SE
Tel: 01621 869202 Fax: 01621 868489
email: harbourmaster@tollesburymarina.com

VHF Ch 80
ACCESS HW±2

Tollesbury Marina lies at the mouth of the River Blackwater in the heart of the Essex countryside. Within easy access from London and the Home Counties, it has been designed as a leisure centre for the whole family, with on-site activities comprising tennis courts and a covered heated swimming pool as well as a convivial bar and restaurant. Accommodating over 240 boats, the marina can be accessed two hours either side of HW and is ideally situated for those wishing to explore the River Crouch to the south and the Rivers Colne, Orwell and Deben to the north.

FACILITIES AT A GLANCE

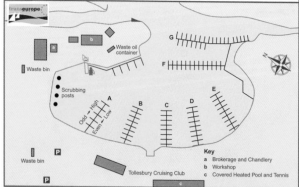

Waste oil
container

Waste bin

Scrubbing
posts

Waste bin

Tollesbury Cruising Club

Key
a Brokerage and Chandlery
b Workshop
c Covered Heated Pool and Tennis

TITCHMARSH MARINA

Titchmarsh Marina Ltd
Coles Lane, Walton on the Naze, Essex, CO14 8SL
Tel: 01255 672185 Fax: 01255 851901
Email: info@titchmarshmarina.co.uk
www.titchmarshmarina.co.uk

VHF	Ch 80
ACCESS	HW±5

Titchmarsh Marina sits on the south side of The Twizzle in the heart of the Walton Backwaters. As the area is designated a 'wetland of international importance', the marina has been designed and developed to function as a natural harbour. The 420 berths are well-sheltered by the high-grassed clay banks, offering good protection in all conditions. The marina entrance has a depth of 1.3m at LWS but once inside the basin this increases to around 2m; there is a tide gauge at the fuel berth. Among the excellent facilities onsite are the well-stocked chandlery and the Harbour Lights restaurant and bar serving food daily.

FACILITIES AT A GLANCE

Key
a Harbour master, chandlery (+ cycle hire) marine engineers, marine electronics
b Hardstanding
c Harbour Lights - restaurant and bar

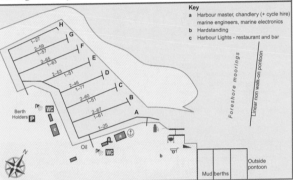

4

WALTON YACHT BASIN

Walton and Frinton Yacht Trust
Mill Lane, Walton on the Naze, CO14 8PF
Managed by Bedwell & Co Tel: 01255 675873
Mobile: 07957 848031

VHF	Ch 80
ACCESS	HW-0.75,HW+0.25

Walton Yacht Basin lies at the head of Walton Creek, an area made famous in Arthur Ransome's *Swallows & Amazons* and *Secret Waters*. The creek can only be navigated HW±2, although yachts heading for the Yacht Basin should arrive on a rising tide as the entrance gate is kept shut once the tide turns in order to retain the water inside. Before entering the gate, moor up against the Club Quay to enquire about berthing availability.

A short walk away is the popular seaside town of Walton, full of shops, pubs and restaurants. Its focal point is the pier which, overlooking superb sandy beaches, offers various attractions. Slightly further out of town, the Naze affords pleasant coastal walks with striking panoramic views.

FACILITIES AT A GLANCE

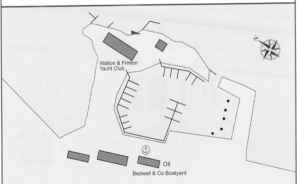

SUFFOLK YACHT HARBOUR

Suffolk Yacht Harbour Ltd
Levington, Ipswich, Suffolk, IP10 0LN
Tel: 01473 659240 Fax: 01473 659632
Email: info@syharbour.co.uk
www.syharbour.co.uk

VHF	Ch 80
ACCESS	H24

A friendly, independently-run marina on the East Coast of England, Suffolk Yacht Harbour enjoys a beautiful rural setting on the River Orwell, yet is within easy access of Ipswich, Woodbridge and Felixstowe. With approximately 550 berths, the marina offers extensive facilities while the Haven Ports Yacht Club provides a bar and restaurant.

FACILITIES AT A GLANCE

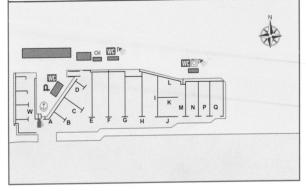

SHOTLEY MARINA

Shotley Marina Ltd
Shotley Gate, Ipswich, Suffolk, IP9 1QJ
Tel: 01473 788982 Fax: 01473 788868
Email: sales@shotleymarina.co.uk
www.shotleymarina.co.uk

VHF	Ch 80
ACCESS	H24

Based in the well protected Harwich Harbour where the River Stour joins the River Orwell, Shotley Marina is only eight miles from the county town of Ipswich. Entered via a lock at all states of the tide, its first class facilities include extensive boat repair and maintenance services as well as a well-stocked chandlery and on site bar and restaurant. The marina is strategically placed for sailing up the Stour to Manningtree, up the Orwell to Pin Mill or exploring the Rivers Deben, Crouch and Blackwater as well as the Walton Backwaters.

FACILITIES AT A GLANCE

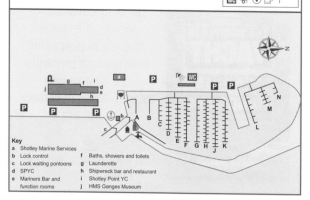

Key
a Shotley Marine Services
b Lock control
c Lock waiting pontoons
d SPYC
e Mariners Bar and function rooms
f Baths, showers and toilets
g Launderette
h Shipwreck bar and restaurant
i Shotley Point YC
j HMS Ganges Museum

ROYAL HARWICH YACHT CLUB MARINA

Royal Harwich Yacht Club Marina
Marina Road, Woolverstone, Suffolk, IP9 1AT
Tel: 01473 780319 Fax: 01473 780919 Berths: 07742 145994
www.royalharwichyachtclub.co.uk
Email: office.manager@royalharwich.co.uk

VHF	Ch 77
ACCESS	H24

This 54 berth marina is ideally situated at a mid point on the Orwell between Levington and Ipswich. The facility is owned and run by the Royal Harwich Yacht Club and enjoys a full catering and bar service in the Clubhouse. The marina benefits from full tidal access, and can accommodate yachts up to 14.5m on the hammerhead. Within the immediate surrounds, there are boat repair services, and a well stocked chandlery. The marina is situated a mile's walk from the world famous Pin Mill and is a favoured destination with visitors from Holland, Belgium and Germany. The marina welcomes racing yachts and cruisers, and is able to accommodate multiple bookings.

FACILITIES AT A GLANCE

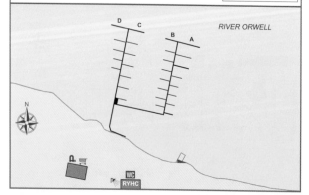

RIVER ORWELL

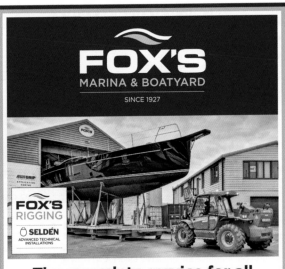

FOX'S MARINA

Fox's Marina & Boatyard
The Strand, Ipswich, Suffolk, IP2 8SA
Tel: 01473 689111
Email: foxs@foxsmarina.com www.foxsmarina.com

VHF Ch 80
ACCESS H24

Located on the picturesque River Orwell, Fox's provides good shelter in all conditions and access at all states of tide with 100 pontoon berths and ashore storage for 200 vessels. A 70T hoist is able to handle boats up to 80ft in length.

Fox's Marina & Boatyard offers a full range of in-house services and, with 10,000 sq ft of heated workshop space, are specialists in repairs and refits of sailing/motor yachts and commercial craft. Specific services include coppercoat and osmosis treatment, specialist GRP and gelcoat repairs, spray painting and varnishing, and custom stainless fabrication. Also on-site, Fox's Chandlery and Marine Store, is the largest stockist of marine chandlery and equipment, sailing, leisure and country clothing in East Anglia.

FACILITIES AT A GLANCE

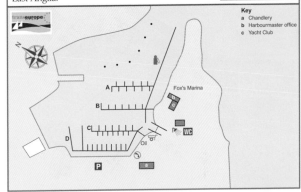

Key
a Chandlery
b Harbourmaster office
c Yacht Club

WOOLVERSTONE MARINA

Woolverstone Marina
Woolverstone, Ipswich, Suffolk, IP9 1AS
Tel: 01473 780206
Email: woolverstone@mdlmarinas.co.uk
www.woolverstonemarina.co.uk

VHF Ch 80
ACCESS H24

Woolverstone Marina is set in 22 acres of glorious parkland on the picturesque River Orwell. Within easy reach of the sea and a multitude of scenic destinations, this is a great base to start cruising. Walton Backwaters and the River Deben are only a short distance away. If you prefer longer distance cruising then Belgium and Holland are directly across the North Sea.

Besides boat repair services, an on-site chandlery and ablution facilities, the marina also incorporates a luxurious lodge park, yacht brokerage and an on-site restaurant and bar, which overlooks the river.

FACILITIES AT A GLANCE

Key
a Marina office, toilets, showers, and launderette
b Restaurant and Bar

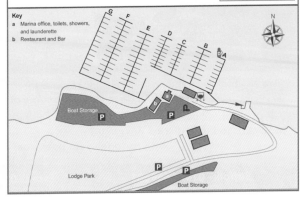

NEPTUNE MARINA

Neptune Marina Ltd
Neptune Quay, Ipswich, IP4 1QJ
Tel: 01473 215204
Email: enquiries@neptune-marina.com

VHF	Ch M, 80
ACCESS	H±2.5

Neptune Marina is situated at Neptune Quay on the historic waterfront, and ever-increasing shoreside developments. This 26-acre dock is accessible through a H24 lock gate, with a waiting pontoon outside. Onsite facilities include boatyard and lift-out facilities plus superfast wifi for boat owners.

The Neptune Marina building occupies an imposing position in the NE corner of the dock with quality coffee shop and associated retail units. There are a number of excellent restaurants along the quayside and adjacent to the marina.

The modern town centre catering for all needs is just a 10-minute walk away.

FACILITIES AT A GLANCE

Key
a Old Custom House
b Conference centre
c Floating French restaurant
d Bistro
e Bellway apartments
f Neptune Marina office & facilities
g Marina storage yard

IPSWICH HAVEN MARINA

Ipswich Haven Marina
Associated British Ports
New Cut East, Ipswich, Suffolk, IP3 0EA
Tel: 01473 236644 Fax: 01473 236645
Email: ipswichhaven@abports.co.uk

VHF	Ch M, 80
ACCESS	H24

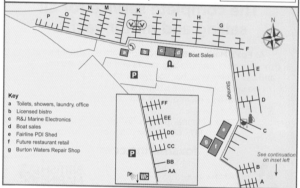

Lying at the heart of Ipswich, the Haven Marina enjoys close proximity to all the bustling shopping centres, restaurants, cinemas and museums that this County Town of Suffolk has to offer. The main railway station is only a 10-minute walk away, where there are regular connections to London, Cambridge and Norwich, all taking just over an hour to get to.

Within easy reach of Holland, Belgium and Germany, East Anglia is proving an increasingly popular cruising ground. The River Orwell, displaying breathtaking scenery, was voted one of the most beautiful rivers in Britain by the RYA.

FACILITIES AT A GLANCE

Key
a Toilets, showers, laundry, office
b Licensed bistro
c R&J Marine Electronics
d Boat sales
e Fairline PDI Shed
f Future restaurant retail
g Burton Waters Repair Shop

See continuation on inset left

LOWESTOFT HAVEN MARINA

Lowestoft Haven Marina
School Road, Lowestoft, Suffolk, NR33 9NB
Tel: 01502 580300
Email: lowestofthaven@abports.co.uk
www.lowestofthavenmarina.co.uk

VHF Ch M, 80
ACCESS H24

Lowestoft Haven Marina is based on Lake Lothing with easy access to both the open sea and the Norfolk Broads. The town centres of both Lowestoft and Oulton Broad are within a short distance of the marina.

The marina's 140 berths can accommodate vessels from 7–20m. Offering a full range of modern facilities the marina welcomes all visitors.

FACILITIES AT A GLANCE

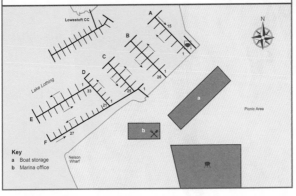

Key
a Boat storage
b Marina office

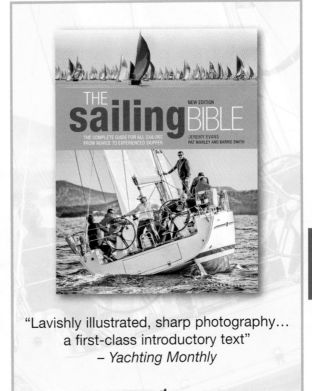
4

ROYAL NORFOLK & SUFFOLK YACHT CLUB

Royal Norfolk and Suffolk Yacht Club
Royal Plain, Lowestoft, Suffolk, NR33 0AQ
Tel: 01502 566726
Email: admin@rnsyc.org.uk   www.rnsyc.net

VHF Ch 14, 80
ACCESS H24

With its entrance at the inner end of the South Pier, opposite the Trawl Basin on the north bank, the Royal Norfolk and Suffolk Yacht Club marina occupies a sheltered position in Lowestoft Harbour. Lowestoft has always been an appealing destination to yachtsmen due to the fact that it can be accessed at any state of the tide, 24 hours a day. Note, however, that conditions just outside the entrance can get pretty lively when the wind is against tide. The clubhouse is enclosed in an impressive Grade 2 listed building overlooking the marina and its facilities include a bar and restaurant as well as a formal dining room.

FACILITIES AT A GLANCE

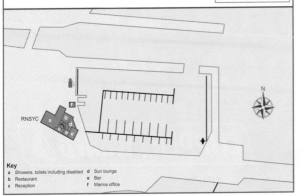

RNSYC

Key
a Showers, toilets including disabled   d Sun lounge
b Restaurant   e Bar
c Reception   f Marina office

LOWESTOFT CRUISING CLUB

Lowestoft Cruising Club
Off Harbour Road, Oulton Broad, Lowestoft, Suffolk, NR32 3LY
Tel: 07810 522515
www.lowestoftcruisingclub.co.uk

VHF
ACCESS H24

Lowestoft Cruising Club welcomes visitors and can offer a friendly atmosphere, some of the finest moorings and at very competitive rates. Whatever the weather, these moorings provide a calm, safe haven for visiting yachts and with the Mutford lock only 250 metres away, easy access onto the Norfolk and Suffolk Broads. Facilities include electricity and water, plus excellent showers, toilets and secure car parking. These moorings are the nearest ones to the railway stations (to Norwich and Ipswich), bus routes, shops, banks, pubs and restaurants in Oulton Broad.

FACILITIES AT A GLANCE

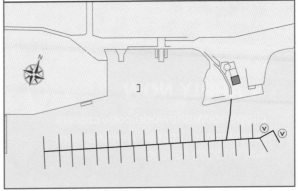

WORLD CLASS SKIPPERS WANTED

NO PRESSURE

Sir Robin Knox-Johnston
Founder of the Clipper Round the World Yacht Race

Join the elite and take on the world's longest yacht race, crewed exclusively by novice crew embarking on the race of their lives.

Clipper Race Skippers are exceptional. They have the fortitude to take on the toughest of mental challenges, and the physical endurance to successfully lead a team through Mother Nature's extreme environments on a 40,000 mile lap around the globe.

Now we're recruiting for the next edition of the Clipper Race. To qualify you must hold a Yachtmaster Ocean certificate [commercial endorsed] or International Yacht Training Master of Yachts.

↘ APPLY NOW

clipperroundtheworld.com/careers
raceskipper@clipper-ventures.com
+44 (0) 2392 526000

NORTH EAST ENGLAND - Great Yarmouth to Berwick-upon-Tweed

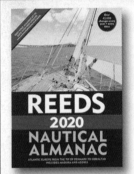

Reeds PDF ebooks

In response to popular demand, all the Reeds Almanacs are now available as searchable, highlightable PDF ebooks. (All ebooks incorporate the Marina Guide.)

Visit www.reedsnauticalalmanac.co.uk for further information

Key to Marina Plans symbols

Bottled gas		P	Parking
Chandler			Pub/Restaurant
Disabled facilities			Pump out
Electrical supply			Rigging service
Electrical repairs			Sail repairs
Engine repairs			Shipwright
First Aid			Shop/Supermarket
Fresh Water			Showers
Fuel - Diesel			Slipway
Fuel - Petrol		WC	Toilets
Hardstanding/boatyard			Telephone
Internet Café			Trolleys
Laundry facilities		V	Visitors berths
Lift-out facilities			Wi-Fi

Area 5 - North East England

5

MARINAS
Telephone Numbers
VHF Channel
Access Times

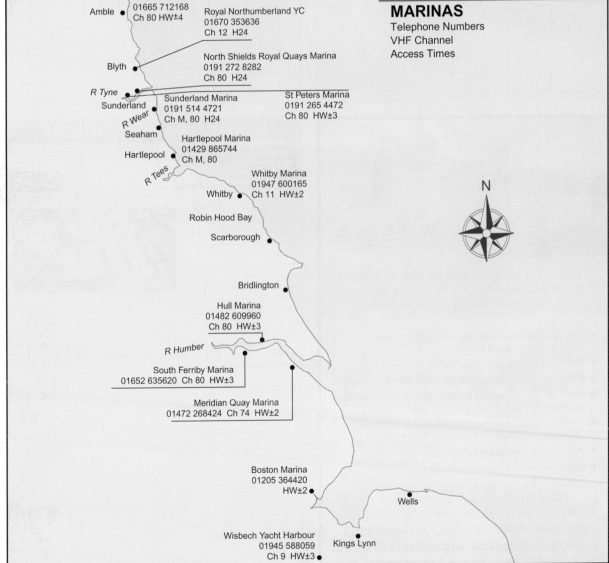

Amble — Amble Marina 01665 712168 Ch 80 HW±4

Royal Northumberland YC 01670 353636 Ch 12 H24

Blyth

North Shields Royal Quays Marina 0191 272 8282 Ch 80 H24

R Tyne

Sunderland — Sunderland Marina 0191 514 4721 Ch M, 80 H24

St Peters Marina 0191 265 4472 Ch 80 HW±3

R Wear

Seaham

Hartlepool — Hartlepool Marina 01429 865744 Ch M, 80

R Tees

Whitby Marina 01947 600165 Ch 11 HW±2

Whitby

Robin Hood Bay

Scarborough

Bridlington

Hull Marina 01482 609960 Ch 80 HW±3

R Humber

South Ferriby Marina 01652 635620 Ch 80 HW±3

Meridian Quay Marina 01472 268424 Ch 74 HW±2

Boston Marina 01205 364420 HW±2

Wells

Wisbech Yacht Harbour 01945 588059 Ch 9 HW±3

Kings Lynn

N

WISBECH YACHT HARBOUR

Wisbech Yacht Harbour
Harbour Master, Harbour Office, The Boathouse,
Harbour Square, Wisbech, Cambridgeshire PE13 3BH
Tel: 01945 588059 Fax: 01945 580589
Email: afoster@fenland.gov.uk www.fenland.gov.uk

VHF Ch 9
ACCESS HW±3

Regarded as the capital of the English Fens, Wisbech is situated about 25 miles north east of Peterborough and is a market town of considerable character and historical significance. Rows of elegant houses line the banks of the River Nene, with the North and South Brink still deemed two of the finest Georgian streets in England.

Wisbech Yacht Harbour, linking Cambridgeshire with the sea, is proving increasingly popular as a haven for small craft, despite the busy commercial shipping. In recent years the facilities have been developed and improved upon and the HM is always on hand to help with passage planning both up or downstream.

FACILITIES AT A GLANCE

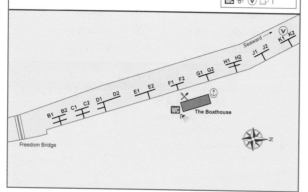

BOSTON GATEWAY MARINA

Boston Gateway Marina
Witham Bank East, Boston, Lincs, PE21 9JU
Tel: 07480 525230
Email: enquiries@bostongatewaymarina.co.uk

VHF
ACCESS H±2

Located near Boston Grand Sluice Lock on the sunny side of the River Witham, the marina is ideally situated for easy access to The Wash and is suitable for both sea-going and river boats. It is a short walk to the centre of the historic town of Boston, Lincolnshire, but retains a tranquil feel. The marina offers visitor, short-term and longer-term moorings to suit each individual customer. Power and water are available for all boats.

The town centre offers the normal variety of facilities within easy walking distance. Local tourist attractions include the 14th century St Botolph's Church – 'The Stump' – the 1390s Boston Guildhall Musuem and a 450-year old market to name but a few.

FACILITIES AT A GLANCE

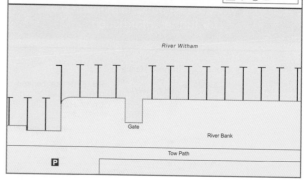

WISBECH
YACHT HARBOUR

HUMBER CRUISING ASSOCIATION

Humber Cruising Association
Fish Docks, Grimsby, DN31 3SD
Tel: 01472 268424
www.hcagrimsby.co.uk
Email: berthmaster@hcagrimsby.co.uk

VHF Ch 74
ACCESS HW±2

Situated in the locked fish dock of Grimsby, at the mouth of the River Humber, Meridian Quay Marina is run by the Humber Cruising Association and comprises approximately 200 alongside berths plus 30 more for visitors. Accessed two hours either side of high water via lock gates, the lock should be contacted on VHF Ch 74 (call sign 'Fish Dock Island') as you make your final approach. The pontoon berths are equipped with water and electricity; there is a fully licensed clubhouse. Also available are internet access and laundry facilities.

FACILITIES AT A GLANCE

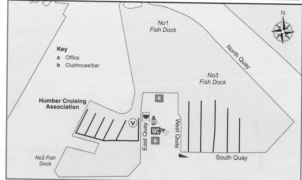

HULL MARINA

Hull Marina
W 13, Kingston Street, Hull, HU1 2DQ
Tel: 01482 609960 Fax: 01482 224148
Email: david.parkinson@bwml.co.uk
www.bwml.co.uk

| VHF | Ch 80 |
| ACCESS | HW±3 |

Situated on the River Humber, Hull Marina is literally a stone's throw from the bustling city centre with its array of arts and entertainments. Besides the numerous historic bars and cafés surrounding the marina, there are plenty of traditional taverns to be sampled in the Old Town, while also found here is the Street Life Museum, vividly depicting the history of the city.

Yachtsmen enter the marina via a tidal lock, operating HW±3, and should try to give 15 minutes' notice of arrival via VHF Ch 80. Hull is perfectly positioned for exploring the Trent, Ouse and the Yorkshire coast as well as across the North Sea to Holland or Belgium.

FACILITIES AT A GLANCE

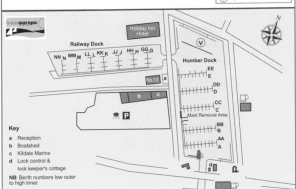

Key
a Reception
b Boatshed
c Kildale Marine
d Lock control &
   lock keeper's cottage
NB Berth numbers low outer
   to high inner.

5

SOUTH FERRIBY MARINA

South Ferriby Marina
Red Lane, South Ferriby, Barton on Humber, Lincs, DN18 6JH
Tel: 01652 635620 (Lock 635219) Mobile: 07828 312071
Email: enquiries@southferribymarina.com

VHF	Ch 74
ACCESS	HW±3

Situated at the entrance to the non-tidal River Ancholme the existing marina has been established since 1966 and is well placed to provide easy access to the River Humber and North Sea. This is a family run business providing a range of services including a boatyard and chandlery. Access is by way of lock at HW±3.

The marina has excellent road and rail services within easy reach, while South Ferriby village has two pubs and a Post Office/Spar Shop just a short walk away.

The picturesque River Ancholme is navigable for about 17 miles; the maximum headroom under bridges is 4.42 metres (14ft 6ins).

FACILITIES AT A GLANCE

Key
a Chandlery
b Shipwrights workshop

WHITBY MARINA

Whitby Marina
Whitby Harbour Office, Endeavour Wharf
Whitby, North Yorkshire YO21 1DN
Harbour Office: 01947 602354 Marina: 01947 600165
Email: port.services@scarborough.gov.uk

VHF	Ch 11
ACCESS	HW±2

The only natural harbour between the Tees and the Humber, Whitby lies some 20 miles north of Scarborough on the River Esk. The historic town is said to date back as far as the Roman times, although it is better known for its abbey, which was founded over 1,300 years ago by King Oswy of Northumberland. Another place of interest is the Captain Cook Memorial Museum, a tribute to Whitby's greatest seaman.

A swing bridge divides the harbour into upper and lower sections, with the marina being in the Upper Harbour. The bridge opens on request (VHF Ch 11) each half hour for two hours either side of high water.

FACILITIES AT A GLANCE

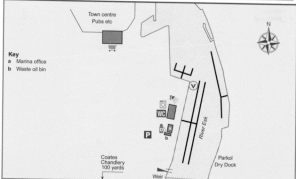

Key
a Marina office
b Waste oil bin

HARTLEPOOL MARINA

Hartlepool Marina
Lock Office, Slake Terrace, Hartlepool, TS24 0RU
Tel: 01429 865744 www.hartlepool-marina.com
Email: enquiries@hartlepool-marina.com

VHF	Ch M, 80
ACCESS	

Hartlepool Marina is a modern boating facility on the NE coast now boasting an extensively refurbished North amenity block. Nestling on the Tees Valley the multi award winning marina promotes up to 500 pontoon berths alongside a variety of reputable services all surrounded by an exciting array

of on water activities, a cosmopolitan mix of bistros, bars, restaurants, shopping, hotels and entertainment options.

Beautiful cruising waters and golden sands to the North and South of the marina approach which is channel dredged to CD and accessible via a lock: vessels wishing to enter should contact the Marina Lock Office on VHF Ch M/80 before arrival.

FACILITIES AT A GLANCE

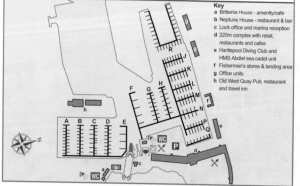

Key
a Brittania House - amenity/cafe
b Neptune House - restaurant & bar
c Lock office and marina reception
d 220m complex with retail, restaurants and cafes
e Hartlepool Diving Club and HMS Abdiel sea cadet unit
f Fisherman's stores & landing area
g Office units
h Old West Quay Pub, restaurant and travel inn

SUNDERLAND MARINA

The Marine Activities Centre
Sunderland Marina, Sunderland, SR6 0PW
Tel: 0191 514 4721 Fax: 0191 514 1847
Email: info@sunmac.org.uk

VHF	Ch M
ACCESS	H24

Sunderland Marina sits on the the River Wear and is easily accessible through the outer breakwater at all states of tide. A short walk away from the city centre and beautiful beaches, facilities on site include the Snowgoose café and the Marina Vista Italian restaurant. Other pubs, restaurants, hotels and cafes are located nearby on the waterfront.

Sunderland Yacht Club is also located nearby and welcomes visiting yachtsman to its clubhouse.

FACILITIES AT A GLANCE

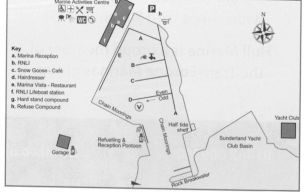

Key
a. Marina Reception
b. RNLI
c. Snow Goose - Café
d. Hairdresser
e. Marina Vista - Restaurant
f. RNLI Lifeboat station
g. Hard stand compound
h. Refuse Compound

NORTH SHIELDS ROYAL QUAYS MARINA

North Shields Royal Quays Marina
Coble Dene Road, North Shields, NE29 6DU
Tel: 0191 272 8282 Fax: 0191 272 8288
www.quaymarinas.com
Email: royalquaysmarina@quaymarinas.com

VHF Ch 80
ACCESS H24

North Shields Royal Quays Marina enjoys close proximity to the entrance to the River Tyne, allowing easy access to and from the open sea as well as being ideally placed for cruising further up the Tyne. Just over an hour's motoring upstream brings you to the heart of the city of Newcastle, where you can tie up on a security controlled visitors' pontoon right outside the Pitcher and Piano Bar.

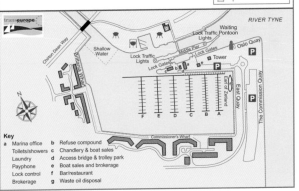

With a reputation for a high standard of service, the marina accommodates 300 pontoon berths, all of which are fully serviced. It is accessed via double sector lock gates which operate at all states of the tide and 24 hours a day.

FACILITIES AT A GLANCE

Key
a Marina office
   Toilets/showers
   Laundry
   Payphone
   Lock control
   Brokerage
b Refuse compound
c Chandlery & boat sales
d Access bridge & trolley park
e Boat sales and brokerage
f Bar/restaurant
g Waste oil disposal

ST PETERS MARINA

St Peters Marina, St Peters Basin
Newcastle upon Tyne, NE6 1HX
Tel: 0191 2654472 Fax: 0191 2762618
Email: info@stpetersmarina.co.uk
www.stpetersmarina.co.uk

VHF Ch 80
ACCESS HW±3

Nestling on the north bank of the River Tyne, some eight miles upstream of the river entrance, St Peters Marina is a fully serviced, 150-berth marina with the capacity to accommodate large vessels of up to 37m LOA. Situated on site is the Bascule Bar and Bistro, while a few minutes away is the centre of Newcastle. This city, along with its surrounding area, offers an array of interesting sites, among which are Hadrian's Wall, the award winning Gateshead Millennium Bridge and the Baltic Art Centre.

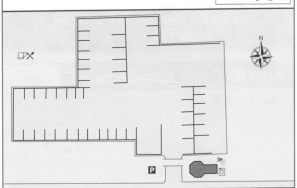

FACILITIES AT A GLANCE

ROYAL NORTHUMBERLAND YACHT CLUB

Royal Northumberland Yacht Club
South Harbour, Blyth, Northumberland, NE24 3PB
Tel: 01670 353636

VHF Ch 12
ACCESS H24

The Royal Northumberland Yacht Club is based at Blyth, a well-sheltered port that is accessible at all states of the tide and in all weathers except for when there is a combination of low water and strong south-easterly winds. The yacht club is a private club with some 75 pontoon berths and a further 20 fore and aft moorings.

Visitors usually berth on the north side of the most northerly pontoon and are welcome to use the clubship, HY *Tyne* – a wooden lightship built in 1880 which incorporates a bar, showers and toilet facilities. The club also controls its own boatyard, providing under cover and outside storage space plus a 20 ton boat hoist.

FACILITIES AT A GLANCE

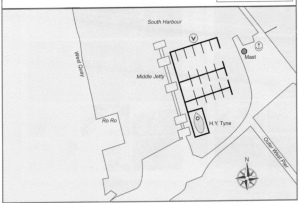

AMBLE MARINA

Amble Marina Ltd
Amble, Northumberland, NE65 0YP
Tel: 01665 712168
Email: marina@amble.co.uk www.amble.co.uk

VHF Ch 80
ACCESS HW±4

Amble Marina is a small family run business offering peace, security and a countryside setting at the heart of the small town of Amble. It is located on the banks of the beautiful River Coquet and at the start of the Northumberland coast's area of outstanding natural beauty. Amble Marina has 250 fully serviced berths for residential and visiting yachts. Cafés, bars, restaurants and shops are all within a short walk.

From your berth watch the sun rise at the harbour entrance and set behind Warkworth Castle or walk on wide, empty beaches. There is so much to do or if you prefer simply enjoy the peace, tranquillity and friendliness at Amble Marina.

FACILITIES AT A GLANCE

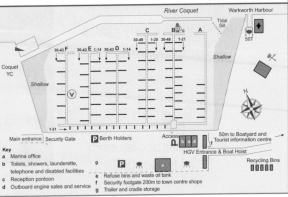

Key
a Marina office
b Toilets, showers, launderette, telephone and disabled facilities
c Reception pontoon
d Outboard engine sales and service
e Refuse bins and waste oil tank
f Security footgate 200m to town centre shops
g Trailer and cradle storage

SOUTH EAST SCOTLAND – Eyemouth to Rattray Head

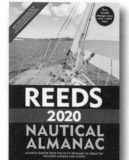
Key to Marina Plans symbols

Bottled gas		Parking
Chandler		Pub/Restaurant
Disabled facilities		Pump out
Electrical supply		Rigging service
Electrical repairs		Sail repairs
Engine repairs		Shipwright
First Aid		Shop/Supermarket
Fresh Water		Showers
Fuel - Diesel		Slipway
Fuel - Petrol		Toilets
Hardstanding/boatyard		Telephone
Internet Café		Trolleys
Laundry facilities		Visitors berths
Lift-out facilities		Wi-Fi

Area 6 - South East Scotland

MARINAS
Telephone Numbers
VHF Channel
Access Times

Aberdeen

Stonehaven

Montrose

Arbroath Harbour
01241 872166
Ch 11, 16   HW±3

Arbroath

Tayport

Port Edgar Marina
0131 3313330
Ch 80   H24

Port Edgar

Granton   Dunbar

Berwick-upon-Tweed

N

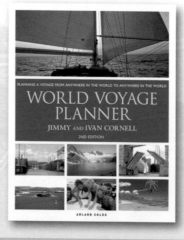
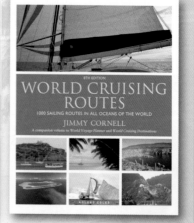

PORT EDGAR MARINA

Port Edgar Marina
Shore Road, South Queensferry
West Lothian, EH30 9SQ
Tel: 0131 331 3330 Fax: 0131 331 4878
Email: info@portedgar.co.uk

VHF Ch 80
ACCESS H24

Nestled between the iconic Forth Bridges, Edinburgh's 300 berth marina is the ideal base for exploring the Capital and the Forth coastline.

A short walk away is the historic High Street of Queensferry with a great selection of bars and restaurants. Situated 15 minutes away from Edinburgh Airport with easy road access, the secure site provides full boatyard facilities including a 25T slipway hoist, chandlery and café.

FACILITIES AT A GLANCE

Key
a Changing rooms and toilets
b Landing and trolleys
c Port Edgar Yacht Club
d Cafe
e Marina office
f Blue V
g Bosuns Locker

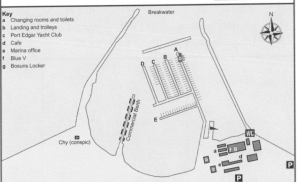

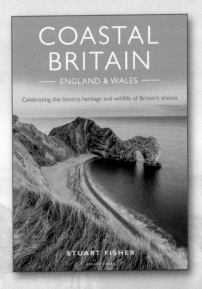
ARBROATH HARBOUR

Arbroath Harbour
Harbour Office, Arbroath, DD11 1PD
Tel: 01241 872166 Fax: 01241 878472
Email: harbourmaster@angus.gov.uk

VHF Ch 11
ACCESS HW±3

Arbroath harbour has 59 floating pontoon berths with security entrance which are serviced with electricity and fresh water to accommodate all types of leisure craft. Half height dock gates with walkway are located between the inner and outer harbours, which open and close at half tide, maintaining a minimum of 2.5m of water in the inner harbour.

The town of Arbroath offers a variety of social and sporting amenities to visiting crews and a number of quality pubs, restaurants, the famous twelfth century Abbey and Signal Tower Museum are located close to the harbour. Railway and bus stations are only 1km from the harbour with direct north and south connections.

FACILITIES AT A GLANCE

Key
a Signal Tower Museum
b Tourist Information
c RNLI
d Harbourmaster
e Harbour gates & walkway

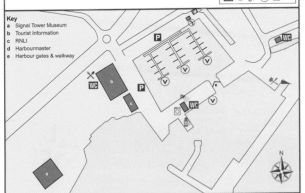

"Arbroath Harbour has 59 floating pontoon berths with security entrance which are serviced with electricity and fresh water to accommodate all types of leisure craft. Half height dock gates with a walkway are located between the inner and outer harbours, which open and close at half tide, maintaining a minimum of 2.5m of water in the inner harbour.

Other facilities in the harbour include free parking, toilets and showers, a crew room, fueling facilities, on site laundry facilities and boat builders' yard.

The town of Arbroath also offers a variety of social and sporting amenities to visiting crews and a number of quality pubs, restaurants, the famous twelfth century Abbey and Signal Tower Museum are located close to the harbour. The railway and bus stations are only 1km from the harbour with direct north and south connections."

Arbroath Harbour
Harbour Office Arbroath DD11 1PD

Harbour Master: Bruce Fleming
Tel: 01241 872166
Email: harbourmaster@angus.gov.uk

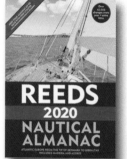
Key to Marina Plans symbols

	Bottled gas	P	Parking
	Chandler		Pub/Restaurant
	Disabled facilities		Pump out
	Electrical supply		Rigging service
	Electrical repairs		Sail repairs
	Engine repairs		Shipwright
	First Aid		Shop/Supermarket
	Fresh Water		Showers
	Fuel - Diesel		Slipway
	Fuel - Petrol	WC	Toilets
	Hardstanding/boatyard		Telephone
@	Internet Café		Trolleys
	Laundry facilities	V	Visitors berths
	Lift-out facilities		Wi-Fi

Area 7 - North East Scotland

MARINAS
Telephone Numbers
VHF Channel
Access Times

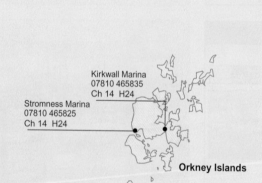

Shetland Islands

Kirkwall Marina
07810 465835
Ch 14 H24

Stromness Marina
07810 465825
Ch 14 H24

Orkney Islands

Scrabster

Wick
Wick Marina
01955 602030
Ch 14 H24

Helmsdale

Ullapool

Whitehills Marina
01261 861291
Ch 14 H4

Banff Harbour Marina
01261 815544
Ch 12 HW±4

Inverness Marina
07526 446348
Ch 12

Inverness

Buckie   Banff   Macduff

Caley Marina
01463 236539
Ch 74 H24

Findhorn

Peterhead

Peterhead Bay Marina
01779 477868
Ch 14 H24

Burghead

Lossiemouth 01343 813066
Ch 12 HW±4

Seaport Marina
01463 725500
Ch 74 HW±4

Nairn Marina
01667 456008
Ch 10 HW±2

Hopeman

Mallaig

Aberdeen

N

PETERHEAD BAY MARINA

Peterhead Port Authority
Harbour Office, West Pier, Peterhead, AB42 1DW
Tel: 01779 477868/483600
Email: marina@peterheadport.co.uk
www.peterheadport.co.uk

VHF	Ch 14
ACCESS	H24

Based in the south west corner of Peterhead Bay Harbour, the marina provides one of the finest marine leisure facilities in the east of Scotland. In addition to the services on site, there are plenty of nautical businesses in the vicinity, ranging from ship chandlers and electrical servicing to boat repairs and surveying.

Due to its easterly location, Peterhead affords an ideal stopover for those yachts heading to or from Scandinavia as well as for vessels making for the Caledonian Canal.

FACILITIES AT A GLANCE

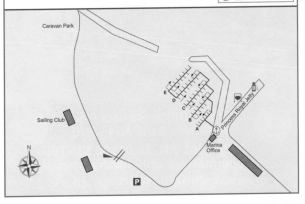

SET SAIL FOR
PETERHEAD BAY MARINA
North East Scotland's Finest Marina

- Fully serviced pontoons
- Shower, toilet & laundry facilities
- Wifi
- Access at all states of the tide
- Visiting yachtsmen welcome
- Annual charge: £114/m length
- Visitor rate from £13/night & £65/week
- Annual berths £114/m

Harbour Office, West Pier, Peterhead, Aberdeenshire AB42 1DW
Tel: 01779 483600   Fax: 01779 475715   Web: www.peterheadport.co.uk

7

BANFF HARBOUR MARINA

Banff Harbour Marina
Harbour Office, Quayside, Banff, Aberdeenshire, AB45 1HQ
Tel: 01261 815544 Fax: 01261 815544
Email: james.henderson@aberdeenshire.gov.uk

VHF	Ch 12
ACCESS	HW±4

A former fishing and cargo port now used as a recreational harbour. Banff offers excellent facilities to both regular and visiting users. The marina now provides 92 berths, of which 76 are serviced pontoon berths and 16 unserviced, traditional moorings, in one of the safest harbours on the NE coast of Scotland.

The outer basin offers adequate berthing for visitors and a tidal area for regulars.

The harbour is tidal with a sandy bottom. Movement during low water neaps is no problem for the shallow drafted boat.

FACILITIES AT A GLANCE

Key
a   Harbourmasters Office

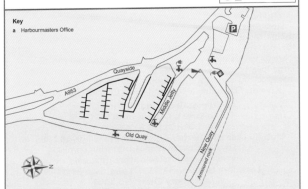

NAIRN MARINA

Nairn Marina
Nairn Harbour, Nairnshire, Scotland
Tel: 01667 456008 Fax: 01667 452877
Email: nairn.harbourmaster@virgin.net

VHF	Ch 10
ACCESS	HW±2

Nairn is a small town on the coast of the Moray Firth. Formerly renowned both as a fishing port and as a holiday resort dating back to Victorian times, it boasts miles of award-winning, sandy beaches, famous castles such as Cawdor, Brodie and Castle Stuart, and two championship golf courses. Other recreational activities include horse riding or walking through spectacular countryside.

The marina lies at the mouth of the River Nairn, entry to which should be avoided in strong N to NE winds. The approach is made from the NW at or around high water as the entrance is badly silted and dries out.

FACILITIES AT A GLANCE

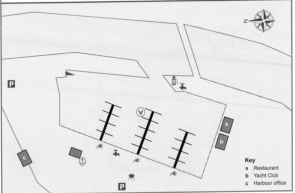

Key
a   Restaurant
b   Yacht Club
c   Harbour office

WHITEHILLS MARINA

Whitehills Harbour Commissioners
Whitehills, Banffshire AB45 2NQ
Tel: 01261 861427
www.whitehillsharbour.co.uk
Email: harbourmaster@whitehillsharbour.co.uk

VHF	Ch 14
ACCESS	H24

Built in 1900, Whitehills is a Trust Harbour fully maintained and run by nine commissioners elected from the village. It was a thriving fishing port up until 1999, but due to changes in the fishing industry, was converted into a marina during 2000.

Photo by Colin Heggie

Three miles west of Banff Harbour the marina benefits from good tidal access – although there is just 1.5m at springs – comprising 38 serviced berths, with electricity, as well as eight non-serviced berths.

Whitehills village has a wide range of facilities including a convenience store, a cafe/fish & chip shop, two pubs, a fresh fish shop as well as two good restaurants. It is also a great base for families, with an excellent playpark at Blackpots, just a short walk from the harbour.

FACILITIES AT A GLANCE

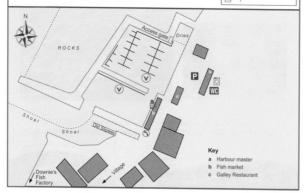

Key
a   Harbour master
b   Fish market
c   Galley Restaurant

LOSSIEMOUTH MARINA

Marina Office
Lossiemouth, Moray, IV31 6PB
Tel: 01343 813066 Mob: 07969 213521
Email: info@lossiemouthmarina.com

VHF	Ch 12
ACCESS	HW±4

Approximately halfway between Inverness and Peterhead, the marina provides over 115 berths. The East Basin and visitor berth area were upgraded in 2018 and the dedicated visitor finger pontoons lie just inside the East Basin, providing free water and electricity. Visitor packs can be collected from the marina office (Mon–Fri 9am-4pm) or from the Steamboat Inn. Modern toilet and shower blocks with laundry facilities are located in both basins. Diesel, local shops, restaurants and ATM are all within short walking distance. The marina has excellent undercover workshop facilities, dredging equipment, a 25 tonne sublift, and crane for masting/demasting.

FACILITIES AT A GLANCE

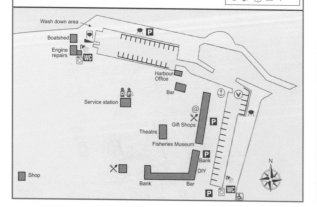

INVERNESS MARINA

Inverness Marina
Longman Drive, Inverness, IV1 1SU
Tel: 01463 220501
Email: info@invernessmarina.com
www.invernessmarina.com

VHF   Ch 12
ACCESS   H24

The marina is situated in the Inverness firth just one mile from the city centre and half a mile from the entrance to the Caledonian Canal. It has a minimum depth of 3m, 24hr access and 150 fully serviced berths. On site are a chandlery and services including rigging, engineering, electronics and boat repair.

Inverness has excellent transport networks to the rest of the UK and Europe and, as the gateway to the Highlands is a great location as a base for a touring golf courses, historic sites and the Whisky Trail. The marina is a perfect base for cruising Orkney, Shetland and Scandinavia.

FACILITIES AT A GLANCE

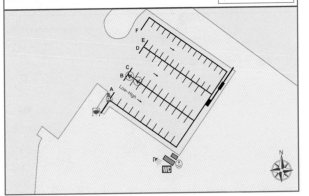

SEAPORT MARINA

Seaport Marina
Muirtown Wharf, Inverness, IV3 5LE
Tel: 01463 725500
Email: caledonian@scottishcanals.co.uk
www.scottishcanals.co.uk

VHF   Ch 74
ACCESS   HW±4

Seaport Marina is based at Muirtown Basin at the eastern entrance of the Caledonian Canal; a 60 mile coast-to-coast channel slicing through the majestic Great Glen. Only a 15 minute walk from the centre of Inverness, the Marina is an ideal base for visiting the Highlands.

Photo courtesy of D Edes

There are shops and amenities nearby, as well as chandlers, boat repair services and a slipway. The marina also offers a variety of winter mooring packages and details of transit and short term licences, including the use of the Caledonian Canal can be found on the above website.

FACILITIES AT A GLANCE

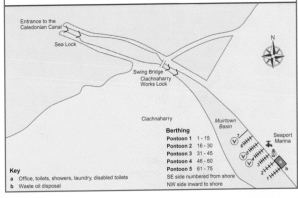

Entrance to the
Caledonian Canal

Sea Lock

Swing Bridge
Clachnaharry
Works Lock

Clachnaharry   Muirtown Basin

Berthing
Pontoon 1   1 - 15
Pontoon 2   16 - 30
Pontoon 3   31 - 45
Pontoon 4   46 - 60
Pontoon 5   61 - 75
SE side numbered from shore
NW side inward to shore

Seaport Marina

Key
a   Office, toilets, showers, laundry, disabled toilets
b   Waste oil disposal

CALEY MARINA

Caley Marina
Canal Road, Inverness, IV3 8NF
Tel: 01463 236539   Fax: 01463 238323
Email: info@caleymarina.com
www.caleymarina.com

VHF   Ch 74
ACCESS   H24

Caley Marina is a family run business based near Inverness. With the four flight Muirtown locks and the Kessock Bridge providing a dramatic backdrop, the marina runs alongside the Caledonian Canal which, opened in 1822, is regarded as one of the most spectacular waterways in Europe. Built as a short cut between the North Sea and the Atlantic Ocean, thus avoiding the potentially dangerous Pentland Firth on the north coast of Scotland, the canal is around 60 miles long and takes about three days to cruise from east to west. With the prevailing winds behind you, it takes slightly less time to cruise in the other direction.

FACILITIES AT A GLANCE

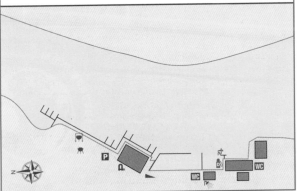

WICK MARINA

Wick Marina
Harbour Office, Wick, Caithness, KW1 5HA
Tel: 01955 602030   Fax: 01955 605936
Email: malcolm.bremner@wickharbour.co.uk

VHF   Ch 14, 16
ACCESS   H24

This is the most northerly marina on the British mainland and the last stop before the Orkney and Shetland Islands. Situated an easy five minutes walk from the town centre Wick Marina accommodates 70 fully serviced berths with all the support facilities expected in a modern marina including a boat lift.

This part of Scotland with its rugged coastline and rich history is easily accessible by air and a great starting point for cruising in the northern isles, Moray Firth, Caledonian Canal and Scandinavia, a comfortable 280-mile sail.

FACILITIES AT A GLANCE

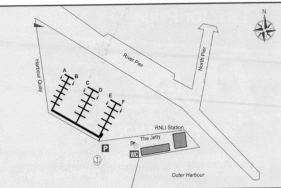

River Pier
North Pier
Harbour Quay
RNLI Station
The Jetty
Outer Harbour

7

KIRKWALL MARINA

Kirkwall Marina
Harbour Street, Kirkwall, Orkney, KW15
Tel: 07810 465835 Fax: 01856 871313
Email: info@orkneymarinas.co.uk www.orkneymarinas.co.uk

VHF	Ch 14
ACCESS	H24

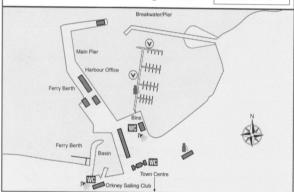

The Orkney Isles, comprising 70 islands in total, provides some of the finest cruising grounds in Northern Europe. The Main Island, incorporating the ancient port of Kirkwall, is the largest, although 16 others have lively communities and are rich in archaeological sites as well as spectacular scenery and wildlife.

Kirkwall Marina, an all year facility, is located within the harbour and just yards from the visitor attractions of this ancient port. Local shops, hotels and restaurants are all within walking distance.

FACILITIES AT A GLANCE

STROMNESS MARINA

Stromness Marina
Stromness, Orkney, KW16
Tel: 07810 465825 Fax: 01856 871313
Email: info@orkneymarinas.co.uk
www.orkneymarinas.co.uk

VHF	Ch 14
ACCESS	H24

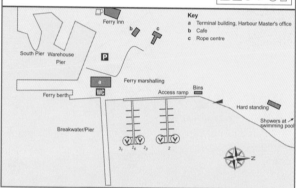

Stromness lies on the south-western tip of the Orkney Isles' Mainland. Sitting beneath the rocky ridge known as Brinkie's Brae, it is considered one of Orkney's major seaports, with sailors first attracted to the fine anchorage provided by the bay of Hamnavoe.

Stromness offers comprehensive facilities including a chandlery and repair services. Also on hand are an internet café and a fitness suite and swimming pool as well as car and bike hire.

FACILITIES AT A GLANCE

Key
a Terminal building, Harbour Master's office
b Cafe
c Rope centre

NORTH WEST SCOTLAND – Cape Wrath to Crinan Canal

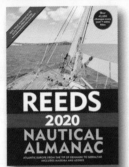
Key to Marina Plans symbols

	Bottled gas	P	Parking
	Chandler	✗	Pub/Restaurant
	Disabled facilities		Pump out
	Electrical supply		Rigging service
	Electrical repairs		Sail repairs
	Engine repairs		Shipwright
	First Aid		Shop/Supermarket
	Fresh Water		Showers
	Fuel - Diesel		Slipway
	Fuel - Petrol	WC	Toilets
	Hardstanding/boatyard		Telephone
@	Internet Café		Trolleys
	Laundry facilities	V	Visitors berths
	Lift-out facilities		Wi-Fi

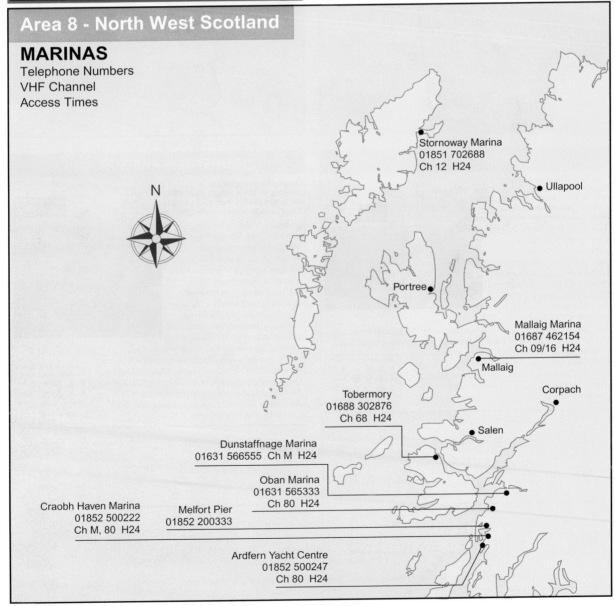

Area 8 - North West Scotland

MARINAS
Telephone Numbers
VHF Channel
Access Times

N

Stornoway Marina
01851 702688
Ch 12 H24

Ullapool

Portree

Mallaig Marina
01687 462154
Ch 09/16 H24

Mallaig

Corpach

Tobermory
01688 302876
Ch 68 H24

Salen

Dunstaffnage Marina
01631 566555 Ch M H24

Oban Marina
01631 565333
Ch 80 H24

Craobh Haven Marina
01852 500222
Ch M, 80 H24

Melfort Pier
01852 200333

Ardfern Yacht Centre
01852 500247
Ch 80 H24

8

STORNOWAY MARINA

Stornoway Port Authority
Amity House, Esplanade Quay,
Stornoway, Isle of Lewis, HS1 2XS
Tel: 01851 702688 Fax: 01851 705714
Email: sypa@stornowayport.com

VHF	Ch 12
ACCESS	HW24

Stornoway Marina is sheltered and has easy access at all states of the tide and weather conditions. Vessels up to 24 metres in length and 3 metres draft can be accommodated.

The 80-berth marina provides a safe haven for island hoppers and days sailors. The marina is particularly popular as it is located right in the heart of the bustling town centre. Fresh water, electricity, wi-fi, toilet, shower and laundry facilities are available quayside for all visitors.

FACILITIES AT A GLANCE

MALLAIG MARINA

Mallaig Marina
East Bay, Mallaig, Inverness-shire, PH41 4QS
Tel: 07824 331031 Fax: 01687 462172
Email: info@mallaigharbourauthority.com

VHF	Ch 09, 16
ACCESS	H24

Mallaig Marina is truly the gateway to the Western Isles. Now in its eighth year of operation the 50-berth Marina – part funded by EC Sail West project – provides the ideal location for experiencing and exploring the magnificent sailing opportunities available on the West Coast of Scotland. Shower/toilet/laundrette facilities are housed in the Mallaig Marina Centre.

The village centre, only 300m from the Marina, offers plenty of options for the discerning diner, shopper or tourist. Fishing boats still operate from the busy harbour, ferries, large and small, sail to Skye/Small Isles/Inverie and there is the daily arrival of The Jacobite Steam Train.

FACILITIES AT A GLANCE

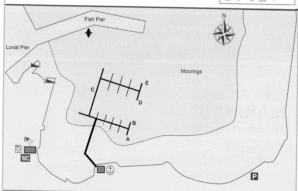

TOBERMORY

Tobermory Harbour Authority
Taigh Solais, Tobermory, Isle of Mull, PA75 6NR
Mob: 07917 832497 Tel: 01688 302876
www.tobermoryharbour.co.uk
Email: admin@tobermoryharbour.co.uk

VHF	Ch 68
ACCESS	0800–2000

Tobermory is the iconic Scottish west coast destination, a natural historic harbour and protected anchorage. The harbour pontoons are located on the west shore of Tobermory Bay with direct access to the town. To supplement 50 pontoon berths there are also 30 swinging moorings for hire – look for the blue moorings with white top.

Within easy walking distance, Tobermory offers an exceptional array of shops, bars and restaurants with local produce. Mull Aquarium in the Harbour Building is Europe's first catch and release aquarium. Situated adjacent to the main car par, the pontoon has easy access to public transport to and from mainland ferry links.

FACILITIES AT A GLANCE

Key a Tobermory Harbour
         Association office
      b Recycling
      c Cruise ship tenders
         and charter boats
      d Large vessels
      e Shallow draft vessels

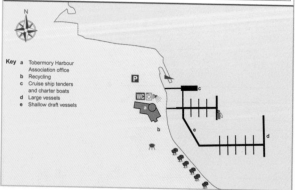

DUNSTAFFNAGE MARINA

Dunstaffnage Marina Ltd
Dunbeg, by Oban, Argyll, PA37 1PX
Tel: 01631 566555 Fax: 01631 571044
Email: info@dunstaffnagemarina.com

VHF	Ch M
ACCESS	H24

Located just two to three miles north of Oban, Dunstaffnage Marina has been renovated to include an additional 36 fully serviced berths, a new breakwater providing shelter from NE'ly to E'ly winds and an increased amount of hard standing. Also on site is the Wide Mouthed Frog, offering a convivial bar, restaurant and accommodation with stunning views of the 13th century Dunstaffnage Castle.

The marina is perfectly placed to explore Scotland's west coast and Hebridean Islands. Only 10M NE up Loch Linnhe is Port Appin, while sailing 15M S, down the Firth of Lorne, brings you to Puldohran where you can walk to an ancient hostelry situated next to the C18 Bridge Over the Atlantic.

FACILITIES AT A GLANCE

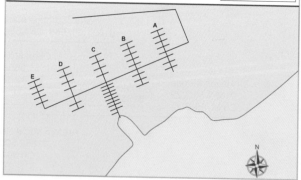

OBAN MARINA

Oban Marina & Yacht Services Ltd
Isle of Kerrera, Oban, Argyll, PA34 4SX
Tel: 01631 565333
Email: info@obanmarina.com www.obanmarina.com

VHF Ch 80
ACCESS H24

Oban Marina is perfectly situated at the gateway to the Western Isles on the picturesque Isle of Kerrera. In sight of the town of Oban, it is a well serviced and popular marina offering access at all tides.

With 100 pontoons berths and 30 moorings, easily accessible diesel fuel berth, free wifi, shower block and laundry, this friendly, small marina offers visitors a warm welcome. A complementary ferry service runs to and from Oban – must be pre-booked, see website for details – where all the major facilities including restaurants, chandlery, banks and transport links are available.

FACILITIES AT A GLANCE

Key
a Reception
b Showers/toilets
c Bar & grill
d Shed

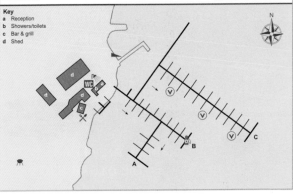

MELFORT PIER AND HARBOUR

Melfort Pier and Harbour
Kilmelford, by Oban, Argyll
Tel: 01852 200333
Email: melharbour@aol.com www.mellowmelfort.com

VHF
ACCESS

Melfort Pier & Harbour is situated on the shores of Loch Melfort, one of the most peaceful lochs on the south west coast of Scotland. Overlooked by the Pass of Melfort and the Braes of Lorn, it lies approximately 18 miles north of Lochgilphead and 16 miles south of Oban. Its onsite facilities include showers, laundry, free Wi-Fi access and parking – pets welcome. Fuel, power and water are available at nearby Kilmelford Yacht Haven.

For those who want a few nights on dry land, Melfort Pier & Harbour offers lochside houses, each one equipped with a sauna, spa bath and balcony offering stunning views over the loch - available per night.

FACILITIES AT A GLANCE

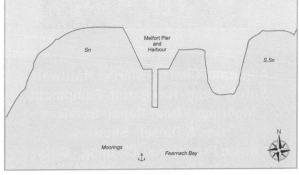

CRAOBH MARINA

Craobh Marina
By Lochgilphead, Argyll, Scotland, PA31 8UA
Tel: 01852 500222 Fax: 01852 500252
Out of hours: 07702 517038
Email: info@craobhmarina.co.uk www.craobhmarina.co.uk

VHF Ch 80
ACCESS H24

Craobh Marina is idyllically situated in the heart of Scotland's most sought after cruising grounds. Not only does Craobh offer ready access to a wonderful choice of scenic cruising throughout the western isles, the marina is conveniently close to Glasgow and its international transport hub.

Craobh Marina has been developed from a near perfect natural harbour, offering secure and sheltered berthing for up to 250 vessels to 40m LOA and with a draft of 4m. With an unusually deep and wide entrance Craobh Marina provides shelter and a warm welcome for all types of craft.

FACILITIES AT A GLANCE

Key
a Office, chandlery, facilities
b Boat shed
c Waste, recycle
d Bar, restaurant, shop
e Holiday cottages

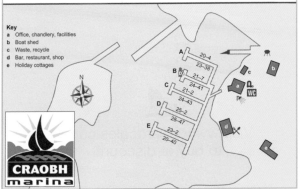

CRAOBH marina

ARDFERN YACHT CENTRE

Ardfern Yacht Centre
Ardfern, by Lochgilphead, Argyll, PA31 8QN
Tel: 01852 500247 Fax: 01852 500624
www.ardfernyacht.co.uk Email: office@ardfernyacht.co.uk

VHF Ch 80
ACCESS H24

Developed around an old pier once frequented by steamers, Ardfern Yacht Centre lies at the head of Loch Craignish, one of Scotland's most sheltered and picturesque sea lochs. With several islands and protected anchorages nearby, Ardfern is an ideal place from which to cruise the west coast of Scotland and the Outer Hebrides.

The Yacht Centre comprises pontoon berths and swinging moorings as well as a workshop, boat storage and well-stocked chandlery, while a grocery store and eating places can be found in the village. Among the onshore activities available locally are horse riding, cycling, and walking.

FACILITIES AT A GLANCE

Key
a Workshop
b Showers, toilets and launderette
c Chandlery and office

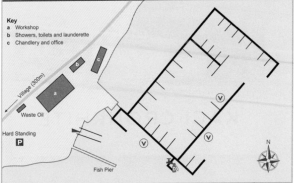

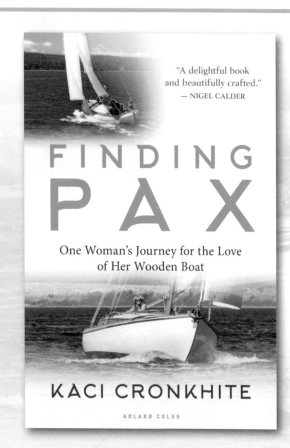

SOUTH WEST SCOTLAND – Crinan Canal to Mull of Galloway

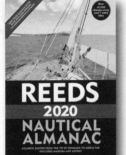
Key to Marina Plans symbols

🜒	Bottled gas	P	Parking
♤	Chandler	✕	Pub/Restaurant
♿	Disabled facilities	⚓	Pump out
🔌	Electrical supply		Rigging service
🔌	Electrical repairs		Sail repairs
🔧	Engine repairs	✕	Shipwright
✚	First Aid	🛒	Shop/Supermarket
⚓	Fresh Water		Showers
D	Fuel - Diesel		Slipway
P	Fuel - Petrol	WC	Toilets
🛠	Hardstanding/boatyard	☎	Telephone
@	Internet Café		Trolleys
⊡	Laundry facilities	Ⓥ	Visitors berths
	Lift-out facilities		Wi-Fi

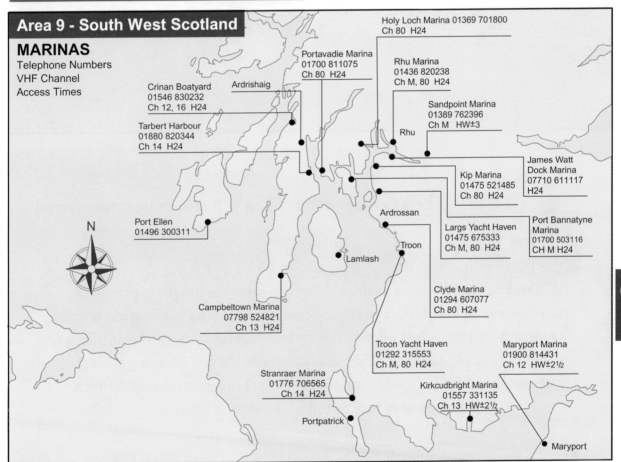

Area 9 - South West Scotland

MARINAS
Telephone Numbers
VHF Channel
Access Times

Holy Loch Marina 01369 701800
Ch 80 H24

Portavadie Marina
01700 811075
Ch 80 H24

Rhu Marina
01436 820238
Ch M, 80 H24

Ardrishaig

Crinan Boatyard
01546 830232
Ch 12, 16 H24

Sandpoint Marina
01389 762396
Ch M HW±3

Tarbert Harbour
01880 820344
Ch 14 H24

Rhu

James Watt
Dock Marina
07710 611117
H24

Kip Marina
01475 521485
Ch 80 H24

Ardrossan

Largs Yacht Haven
01475 675333
Ch M, 80 H24

Port Bannatyne
Marina
01700 503116
CH M H24

Port Ellen
01496 300311

Troon

Lamlash

Clyde Marina
01294 607077
Ch 80 H24

N

Campbeltown Marina
07798 524821
Ch 13 H24

Troon Yacht Haven
01292 315553
Ch M, 80 H24

Maryport Marina
01900 814431
Ch 12 HW±2½

Stranraer Marina
01776 706565
Ch 14 H24

Kirkcudbright Marina
01557 331135
Ch 13 HW±2½

Portpatrick

Maryport

9

PORT ELLEN MARINA

Port Ellen Marina
Port Ellen, Islay, Argyll, PA42 7DB
Tel: 07464 151200 www.portellenmarina.co.uk
Email: portellenmarina@outlook.com

VHF
ACCESS H24

A safe and relaxed marina
for visitors to the *Malt Whisky
Island*. There are seven classic
distilleries and yet another still
(private) to start production
soon. If you are planning a
cruise to the north then superb
sailing will take you onward via
Craighouse on Jura. Meeting
guests or short term storage is
trouble free with the excellent
air and ferry services connecting
to Glasgow. Once on Islay you
will be tempted to extend your stay so be warned,
check www.portellenmarina.com for the many
reasons to visit, from golf to music.

FACILITIES AT A GLANCE

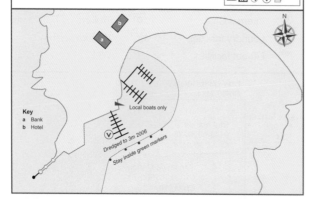

Key
a Bank
b Hotel

Local boats only

Dredged to 3m 2006
Stay inside green markers

CRINAN BOATYARD

Crinan Boatyard Ltd
Crinan, Lochgilphead, Argyll, PA31 8SW
Tel: 01546 830232 Fax: 01546 830281
Email: info@crinanboatyard.co.uk
www.crinanboatyard.co.uk

VHF Ch 12, 16
ACCESS H24

Situated at the westerly
entrance of the scenic Crinan
Canal, Crinan Boatyard offers
swinging moorings nightly
or longer term, a fuelling/
loading berth, a well stocked
Chandlery, heads, showers,
laundry and an experienced
work force for repair work
all on site. A hotel and coffee
shop, just a short walk away at
the Canal basin, great walking and the historic Kilmartin Glen close
by are some of the attractions on shore.

The nearby town of Lochgilphead 7 miles away
offers shopping and good travel links to Glasgow
(85 miles) and its International Airport.

FACILITIES AT A GLANCE

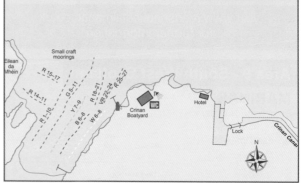

Small craft
moorings
Eilean
da
Mhéin
R 15-17
R 14-11
G 5-11
R 18-21
R 25-27
R 1-10
Y 7-9
B 6-8
W 6-8
V8 22-24
Crinan
Boatyard
WC
Hotel
Lock
Crinan Canal
N

Port Ellen
MARINA

The welcome in Port Ellen will always be remembered

**This non-profit marina enables visitors to enjoy the unique experiences
available around Port Ellen and Islay, including many sites of historical interest,
a footpath trail from Port Ellen to three world famous malt whisky distilleries,
top class eating establishments, abundant wild life and stunning scenery,
as well as providing a safe comfortable haven for yachts passing through
the sound of Jura or round the Mull of Kintyre.**

Pontoons will be open from 1st April until 31st October.

Visitor shower and toilet facilities are included in the berthing fee,
also slot machine laundry is available.

32 berths have inclusive water and power.

www.portellenmarina.co.uk   T: 07464 151200   E: portellenmarina@outlook.com

Coastal
Communities
Fund

Registered charity SC032157

TARBERT HARBOUR

Tarbert Harbour Authority
Harbour Office, Garval Road, Tarbert, Argyll, PA29 6TR
Tel: 01880 820344
Email: info@tarbertharbour.co.uk

VHF	Ch 14
ACCESS	H24

East Loch Tarbert is situated on the western shores of Loch Fyne. The naturally sheltered harbour is accessible through an easily navigated narrow entrance, and is a prefect stopping point for those heading north to the Crinan Canal.

The pontoons can accommodate up to 100 visiting vessels of various sizes, with fresh water, electricity and wi-fi available FOC. Toilet, shower and laundry facilities are accessible 24/7, and the unique recreation area and community marquee are available to use - perfect for families, gatherings and musters. The marina pontoons are situated at the heart of the heritage village of Tarbert, which boasts a busy festival calendar and offers a wide range of amenities.

FACILITIES AT A GLANCE

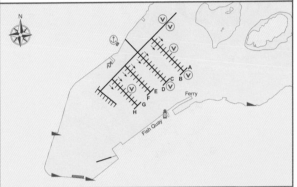

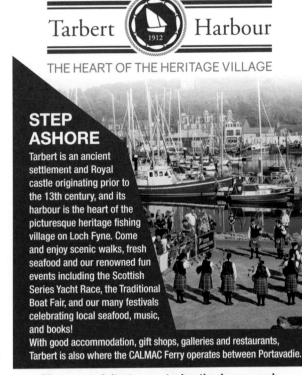

TARBERT Harbour
1912
THE HEART OF THE HERITAGE VILLAGE

STEP ASHORE

Tarbert is an ancient settlement and Royal castle originating prior to the 13th century, and its harbour is the heart of the picturesque heritage fishing village on Loch Fyne. Come and enjoy scenic walks, fresh seafood and our renowned fun events including the Scottish Series Yacht Race, the Traditional Boat Fair, and our many festivals celebrating local seafood, music, and books!

With good accommodation, gift shops, galleries and restaurants, Tarbert is also where the CALMAC Ferry operates between Portavadie.

Plan your visit at www.tarbertharbour.co.uk

Tel: 01880 820 344
Tarbert Harbour, Loch Fyne, Argyll, Scotland PA29 6TR

9

PORT BANNATYNE MARINA

Port Bannatyne Marina
Marine Road, Port Bannatyne, PA20 0LT
Tel: 01700 503116 Mobile: 07711 319992
Email: portbannatynemarina@btconnect.com

VHF	Ch M1
ACCESS	H24

Nestled in the bay at Port Bannatyne on the Isle of Bute, the marina is set in breathtakingly beautiful surroundings. The shore facilities include toilets and showers, lifting and winter storage and all boat repairs. Free wi-fi is available throughout the marina. Protected by a breakwater and accessible H24 the marina is dredged to –2.4m CD.

The village of Port Bannatyne offers a Post Office for essential groceries and three pubs. There are frequent bus services to both Rothesay and Ettrick Bay where a walk along a beautiful beach with amazing views can be completed with either a meal or tea and cake at the beach side restaurant.

FACILITIES AT A GLANCE

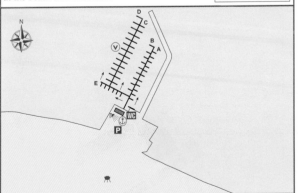

PORTAVADIE MARINA

Portavadie Marina
Portavadie, Loch Fyne, Argyll, PA21 2DA
Tel: 01700 811075 Fax: 01700 811074
Email: info@portavadiemarina.com

VHF	Ch 80
ACCESS	H24

Portavadie Marina offers deep and sheltered berthing to residential and visiting boats in an area renowned for its superb cruising waters. Situated on the east side of Loch Fyne in close proximity to several islands and the famous Kyles of Bute, Portavadie is within easy sailing distance of the Crinan Canal, giving access to the Inner and Outer Hebrides. The marina has 230 berths 60 of which are reserved for visitors, plus comprehensive on shore facilities, including a choice of restaurants, bars and self catering accommodation. There is also a shop and small chandlery overlooking the marina, a dedicated fuel berth for petrol and diesel and bike hire.

This unspoiled area of Argyll which is less than two hours by road from Glasgow offers an ideal base for boat owners looking for a safe and secure haven.

FACILITIES AT A GLANCE

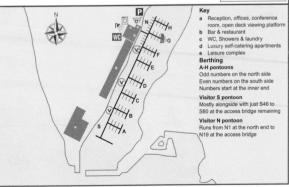

Key
a Reception, offices, conference room, open deck viewing platform
b Bar & restaurant
c WC, Showers & laundry
d Luxury self-catering apartments
e Leisure complex
Berthing
A-H pontoons
Odd numbers on the north side
Even numbers on the south side
Numbers start at the inner end
Visitor S pontoon
Mostly alongside with just S46 to S60 at the access bridge remaining
Visitor N pontoon
Runs from N1 at the north end to N19 at the access bridge

CAMPBELTOWN MARINA

Campbeltown Marina Ltd
Dubh Artach, Roading, Campbeltown, PA28 6LU
Tel: 07798 524821
Email: campbeltownmarina@btinternet.com

VHF	Ch 13
ACCESS	H24

Campbeltown Marina is a brand new facility opened in June 2015 and is situated in the town centre at the head of the deep, sheltered waters of Campbeltown Loch on the SE aspect of the Kintyre Peninsula. It is within easy reach of the Antrim Coast, Ayrshire and the Upper Clyde. Diesel is available at the Old Quay and gas is across the road. Petrol can be bought a 5-minute walk away and a well stocked chandlery is situated in the town centre.

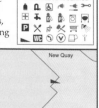

Campbeltown is the perfect getaway destination with plenty to offer the whole family. Golf, cycling and walking routes, modern swimming pool and horse riding are some of the activities on offer. Situated directly in the town centre there is a wide choice of shops, cafes, bars, restaurants and supermarkets within easy walking distance.

FACILITIES AT A GLANCE

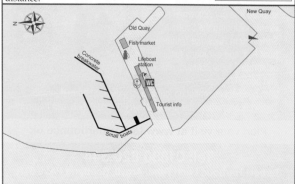

HOLY LOCH MARINA

Holy Loch Marina
Rankin's Brae, Sandbank, Dunoon, PA23 8FE
Tel: 01369 701800
Email: info@holylochmarina.co.uk www.holylochmarina.co.uk

VHF	Ch 80
ACCESS	H24

Holy Loch Marina, the marine gateway to Loch Lomond and the Trossachs National Park, lies on the south shore of the loch, roughly half a mile west of Lazaretto Point. Holy Loch is among the Clyde's most beautiful natural harbours and, besides being a peaceful location, offers an abundance of wildlife, places of local historical interest as well as excellent walking and cycling through the Argyll Forest Park. The marina can be entered in all weather conditions and is within easy sailing distance of Loch Long and Upper Firth.

FACILITIES AT A GLANCE

Key
a Office/Harbourmaster
b Boat storage
c Holy Loch Sailing Club
d Pier

Sandbank Village

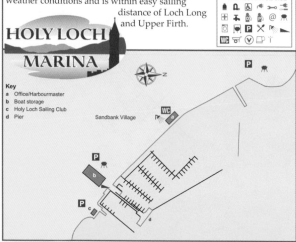

RHU MARINA

Rhu Marina
Rhu, Dunbartonshire, G84 8LH
Tel: 01436 820238
Email: rhumarina@quaymarinas.com

VHF	Ch M, 80
ACCESS	H24

Located on the north shore of the Clyde Estuary, Rhu Marina is accessible at all states of the tide and can accommodate yachts up to 24m in length. It also operates 40 swinging moorings in the bay adjacent to the marina, with a ferry service provided.

Within easy walking distance of the marina is Rhu village, a conservation village incorporating a few shops, a pub and the beautiful Glenarn Gardens as well as the Royal Northern & Clyde Yacht Club. A mile or two to the east lies the holiday town of Helensburgh, renowned for its attractive architecture and elegant parks and gardens, while Glasgow city is just 25 miles away and can be easily reached by train.

FACILITIES AT A GLANCE

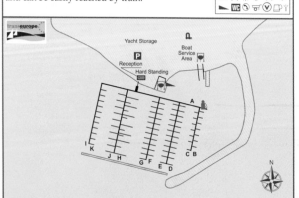

SANDPOINT MARINA

Sandpoint Marina Ltd
Sandpoint, Woodyard Road, Dumbarton, G82 4BG
Tel: 01389 762396 Fax: 01389 732605
Email: sales@sandpoint-marina.co.uk
www.sandpoint-marina.co.uk

VHF	
ACCESS	HW±3

Lying on the north bank of the Clyde estuary on the opposite side of the River Leven from Dumbarton Castle, Sandpoint Marina provides easy access to some of the most stunning cruising grounds in the United Kingdom. It is an independently run marina, offering a professional yet personal service to every boat owner. Among the facilities to hand are an on site chandlery, storage areas, a 40 ton travel hoist and 20 individual workshop units.

Within a 20-minute drive of Glasgow city centre, the marina is situated close to the shores of Loch Lomond, the largest fresh water loch in Britain.

FACILITIES AT A GLANCE

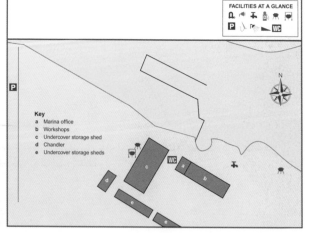

Key
a Marina office
b Workshops
c Undercover storage shed
d Chandler
e Undercover storage sheds

KIP MARINA

Kip Marina, The Yacht Harbour
Inverkip, Renfrewshire, Scotland, PA16 0AS
Tel: 01475 521485 Fax: 01475 568410
www.kipmarina.co.uk Email: info@kipmarina.co.uk

VHF Ch 80
ACCESS H24

Inverkip is a small village which lies on the south shores of the River Kip as it enters the Firth of Clyde. Once established for fishing, smuggling and, in the 17th century, witch-hunts, it became a seaside resort in the 1860s as a result of the installation of the railway. Today it is a yachting centre, boasting a state-of-the-art marina with over 600 berths and full boatyard facilities. With the capacity to accommodate yachts of up to 23m LOA, Kip Marina offers direct road and rail access to Glasgow and its international airport, therefore making it an ideal location for either a winter lay up or crew changeover.

FACILITIES AT A GLANCE

Key
a Boat sales, chandlery and reception
b Workshop and contractors
c Chartroom bar and restaurant

JAMES WATT DOCK MARINA

James Watt Dock Marina
East Hamilton Street
Greenock, Renfrewshire, PA15 2TD
Tel: 01475 729838
www.jwdmarina.co.uk Email: info@jwdmarina.co.uk

VHF 80
ACCESS H24

Based in the historic James Watt Dock alongside the stunning Victorian Sugar Shed, this new marina opened in May 2011 and is the first step in establishing an exciting new River Clyde waterfront development only 23 miles from Glasgow and 15 miles from the airport. James Watt Dock will have all the usual amenities expected of a modern marina.

Within easy reach of Greenock's cinema, pool, ice rink, restaurants and shops, and with nearby transport connections, the marina will be a great location for both visitors and regular berthers.

FACILITIES AT A GLANCE

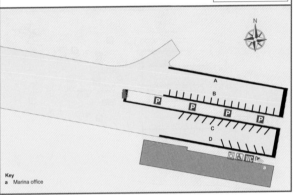

Key
a Marina office

9

LARGS YACHT HAVEN

Largs Yacht Haven Ltd
Irvine Road, Largs, Ayrshire, KA30 8EZ
Tel: 01475 675333
Email: largs@yachthavens.com www.yachthavens.com

VHF	Ch M, 80
ACCESS	H24

Largs Yacht Haven offers a superb location among lochs and islands, with numerous fishing villages and harbours nearby. Sheltered cruising can be enjoyed in the inner Clyde, while the west coast and Ireland are only a day's sail away. With a stunning backdrop of the Scottish mountains, Largs incorporates 700 fully serviced berths and provides a range of on site facilities including chandlers, sailmakers, divers, engineers, shops, restaurants and club.

A 20-minute coastal walk brings you to the town of Largs, which has all the usual amenities as well as good road and rail connections to Glasgow.

FACILITIES AT A GLANCE

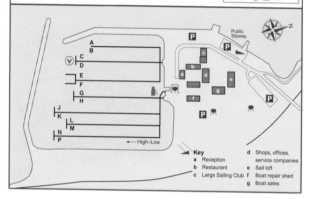

Key
a Reception
b Restaurant
c Largs Sailing Club
d Shops, offices, service companies
e Sail loft
f Boat repair shed
g Boat sales

CLYDE MARINA

Clyde Marina Ltd
The Harbour, Ardrossan, Ayrshire, KA22 8DB
Tel: 01294 607077 Fax: 01294 607076
www.clydemarina.com Email: info@clydemarina.com

VHF	Ch 80
ACCESS	H24

CLYDE MARINA

Situated on the Clyde Coast between Irvine and Largs, Clyde Marina is Scotland's third largest marina and boatyard. It is set in a landscaped environment boasting a 50T hoist and active boat sales. A deep draft marina berthing vessels up to 30m LOA, draft up to 5m. Peviously accommodated vessels include tall ships and Whitbread 60s plus a variety of sail and power craft. Fully serviced pontoons plus all the yard facilities you would expect from a leading marina including boatyard and boatshed for repairs or storage. Good road and rail connections and only 30 minutes from Glasgow and Prestwick airports.

FACILITIES AT A GLANCE

key
a Winter storage shed
b Secure winter hard standing area

Numbering starts from shoreside.
For pontoons B–E from shoreside:
Even nos - starboard side of pontoon
Odd nos - port side of pontoon

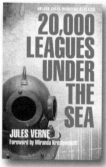

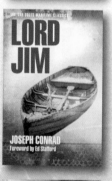

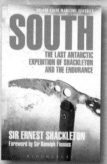
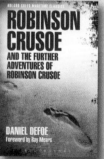

TROON YACHT HAVEN

Troon Yacht Haven Ltd
The Harbour, Troon, Ayrshire, KA10 6DJ
Tel: 01292 315553
Email: troon@yachthavens.com
www.yachthavens.com

VHF	Ch 80
ACCESS	H24

Troon Yacht Haven, situated on the Southern Clyde Estuary, benefits from deep water at all states of the tide. Tucked away in the harbour of Troon, it is well sheltered and within easy access of the town centre.

There are plenty of cruising opportunities to be had from here, whether it be hopping across to the Isle of Arran, with its peaceful anchorages and mountain walks, sailing round the Mull or through the Crinan Canal to the Western Isles, or heading for the sheltered waters of the Clyde.

FACILITIES AT A GLANCE

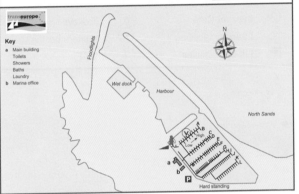

Key
a Main building
   Toilets
   Showers
   Baths
   Laundry
b Marina office

STRANRAER MARINA

Stranraer Marina
Militia House, English Street, Dumfries, DG1 2HR
Tel: 01776 706565 Mob: 07734 073421
Email: dgfirst-harbouradministration@dumgal.gov.uk

VHF	Ch 14
ACCESS	H24

Stranraer marina is at the southern end of beautiful Loch Ryan with H24 access and modern facilities.

The town centre with full facilities is only a short walk from the marina. A new 30T boat crane, boat transporter and hard standing proving very popular. The marina provides an excellent base for touring the picturesque Mull of Galloway.

It should be noted that the marina is exposed in strong N winds. Two ferry terminals are located on the E side of the loch approximately 6M N of the marina and extra care should be taken in this area.

FACILITIES AT A GLANCE

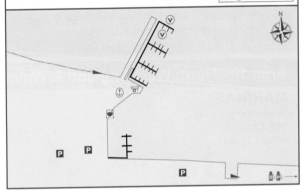

KIRKCUDBRIGHT MARINA

Kirkcudbright Marina
Militia House, English Street, Dumfries, DG1 2HR
Tel: 01557 331135 Mob: 07709 479663
Email: dgfirst-harbouradministration@dumgal.gov.uk

VHF	Ch 16, 73
ACCESS	HW±2.5

A very well sheltered picturesque marina accessed HW+/-2.5 hrs via a 3.5 mile long, narrow channel that is well marked and lit, contact should be made with Range Safety vessel 'Gallovidian' prior to approach. Limited visitors berths so vessels should contact the harbour master in advance.

The marina is only 250m from the centre of Kirkcudbright, an historic 'artist's' town where visitors may enjoy a wide range of facilities and tourist attractions including castle, museum, tollbooth, art galleries and traditional shops. There is a superb programme of summer festivities.

FACILITIES AT A GLANCE

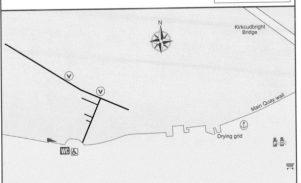

MARYPORT MARINA

Maryport Development Ltd
Marine Road, Maryport, Cumbria, CA15 8AY
Tel: 01900 814431
www.maryportmarina.com
Email: enquires@maryportmarina.com

VHF	Ch 12,16
ACCESS	HW±2.5

Maryport Marina is located in the historic Senhouse Dock, which was originally built for sailing clippers in the late 19th century. The old stone harbour walls provide good shelter to the 190 berths from the prevailing south westerlies.

Maryport town centre and its shops, pubs and other amenities is within easy walking distance from the marina. Maryport a perfect location from which to explore the west coast of Scotland as well as the Isle of Man and the Galloway Coast. For those who wish to venture inland, then the Lake District is only seven miles away.

FACILITIES AT A GLANCE

Key
a Marina Office
b Boat repair facility
c Coastguard building
d Fish handling building
e Wet fish shop
f Aquarium, cafe
g Play area
h Amenity block

9

NW ENGLAND, ISLE OF MAN & N WALES – Mull of Galloway to Bardsey Is

Reeds PDF ebooks

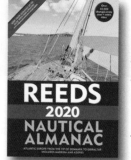

In response to popular demand, all the Reeds Almanacs are now available as searchable, highlightable PDF ebooks. (All ebooks incorporate the Marina Guide.)

Visit www.reedsnauticalalmanac.co.uk for further information

Key to Marina Plans symbols

Bottled gas		Parking	
Chandler		Pub/Restaurant	
Disabled facilities		Pump out	
Electrical supply		Rigging service	
Electrical repairs		Sail repairs	
Engine repairs		Shipwright	
First Aid		Shop/Supermarket	
Fresh Water		Showers	
Fuel - Diesel		Slipway	
Fuel - Petrol		Toilets	
Hardstanding/boatyard		Telephone	
Internet Café		Trolleys	
Laundry facilities		Visitors berths	
Lift-out facilities		Wi-Fi	

Area 10 - North West England & Wales

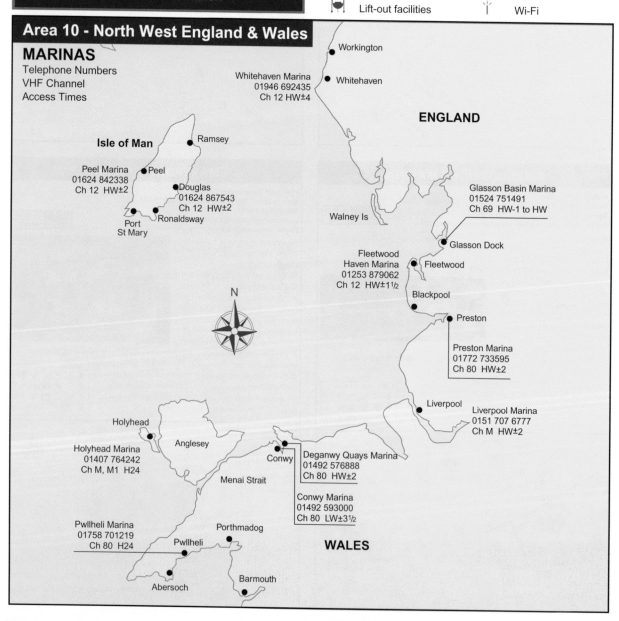

MARINAS
Telephone Numbers
VHF Channel
Access Times

Workington

Whitehaven Marina
01946 692435
Ch 12 HW±4

Whitehaven

ENGLAND

Isle of Man

Ramsey

Peel Marina
01624 842338
Ch 12 HW±2

Peel

Douglas
01624 867543
Ch 12 HW±2

Glasson Basin Marina
01524 751491
Ch 69 HW-1 to HW

Walney Is

Port
St Mary

Ronaldsway

Glasson Dock

Fleetwood
Haven Marina
01253 879062
Ch 12 HW±1½

Fleetwood

N

Blackpool

Preston

Preston Marina
01772 733595
Ch 80 HW±2

Liverpool

Liverpool Marina
0151 707 6777
Ch M HW±2

Holyhead

Holyhead Marina
01407 764242
Ch M, M1 H24

Anglesey

Conwy

Deganwy Quays Marina
01492 576888
Ch 80 HW±2

Menai Strait

Conwy Marina
01492 593000
Ch 80 LW±3½

Pwllheli Marina
01758 701219
Ch 80 H24

Pwllheli

Porthmadog

WALES

Abersoch

Barmouth

WHITEHAVEN MARINA

Whitehaven Marina Ltd
Harbour Office, Bulwark Quay, Whitehaven, Cumbria, CA28 7HS
Tel: 01946 692435
Email: enquiries@whitehavenmarina.co.uk
www.whitehavenmarina.co.uk

VHF	Ch 12
ACCESS	HW±4

Whitehaven Marina can be found at the south-western entrance to the Solway Firth, providing a strategic departure point for those yachts heading for the Isle of Man, Ireland or Southern Scotland. The harbour is one of the more accessible ports of refuge in NW England, affording a safe entry in most weathers. The approach channel across the outer harbour is dredged to about 1.0m above chart datum, allowing entry into the inner harbour via a sea lock at around HW±4. Over 100 new walk ashore berths were installed in 2013.

FACILITIES AT A GLANCE

Conveniently situated for visiting the Lake District, Whitehaven is an attractive Georgian town, renowned in the C18 for its rum and slave imports.

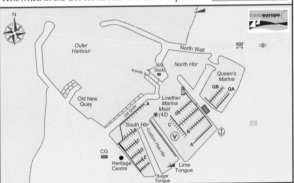

BWML GLASSON BASIN MARINA

BWML, Glasson Basin Marina
School Lane, Glasson Dock, Lancaster, LA2 0AW
Tel: 01524 751491 Fax: 01524 752626
Email: barnaby.hayward@bwml.co.uk
www.bwml.co.uk

VHF	Ch 69
ACCESS	HW-1 to HW

Glasson Basin Marina lies on the River Lune, west of Sunderland Point. Access is via the outer dock which opens 45 minutes before HW. Liverpool and thence via BWB lock into the inner basin. It is recommended to leave Lune No. 1 Buoy approx 1.5 hrs before HW. Contact the dock on Channel 69. The Marina can only be contacted by telephone. All the necessary requirements can be found either on site or within easy reach of Glasson Dock, including boat, rigging and sail repair services as well as a launderette, ablution facilities, shops and restaurants.

FACILITIES AT A GLANCE

Key
a   Marina office
b   Glasson Sailing Club
c   Harbour House

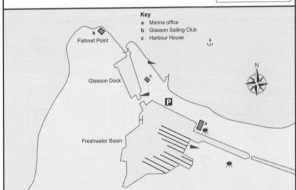

Glasson Basin Marina

Lancashire

Fully serviced pontoons

Visitors welcome

Comprehensive chandlery

Fully serviced boatyard and workshops with 50 tonne hoist

Professional workshop services including rigging and spray painting

We are a proud agent of Z Spars UK for yacht masts and rigging requirements

01524 751491   **bwml.co.uk**   **barnaby.hayward@bwml.co.uk**

DOUGLAS MARINA

Douglas Marina
Sea Terminal Building, Douglas, IM1 2RF
Tel: 01624 686627 Fax: 01624 686612
www.gov.im/harbours/
Email: enquiries.harboursdoi@gov.im

VHF	Ch 12, 16
ACCESS	HW±2

Douglas Marina is accessible HW±2 with 2.5m retained at LW. The depth of water inside the marina can vary so please advise draft. The maximum length accommodated on pontoons is 15m. Wall berths are also available. Douglas Marina Operations Centre requires clearance for entrance to the outer harbour due to commercial traffic. Please inform arrival on VHF Ch 12 10 minutes before port entry.

The marina has many facilities including electricity, fresh water, diesel, lift out, drying pad, gas, chandlery and showers/toilet facilities.

Douglas Marina is in the heart of the Isle of Man's capital so all local amenities and excellent transport links such as the Steam Railway are just a short walk away.

FACILITIES AT A GLANCE

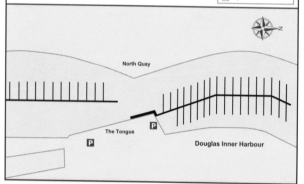

PEEL MARINA

Peel Marina
The Harbour Office, East Quay, Peel, IM5 1AR
Tel: 01624 842338 Fax: 01624 843610
www.gov.im/harbours/
Email: harbours@gov.im

VHF	Ch 12
ACCESS	HW±2

The Inner harbour has provision on pontoons for visiting vessels up 15m with rafting also available on the harbour walls. Access is available HW±2hrs with a maximum draft of 2.5m retained at low water but this does vary so please advise vessel dimensions on approach via VHF Ch 12.

Fresh water and electricity are available on all pontoon and some wall berths. Diesel fuel is available at the quayside with petrol sourced from a local forecourt in Peel.

Peel is a lovely active fishing port with many local amenities and a beautiful castle overlooking the harbour.

FACILITIES AT A GLANCE

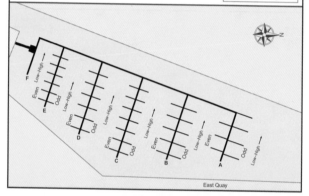

FLEETWOOD HAVEN MARINA

Fleetwood Haven Marina
c/o ABP, Port & Marina Office, Fleetwood, FY7 8BP
Tel: 01253 879062 Fax: 01253 879063
Email: fleetwoodhaven@abports.co.uk

VHF	Ch 12
ACCESS	HW±1.5

Fleetwood Haven Marina provides a good location from which to cruise Morecambe Bay and the Irish Sea. To the north west is the Isle of Man, the north is the Solway Firth and the Clyde Estuary, while to the south west is Conwy, the Menai Straits and Holyhead.

Tucked away in a protected dock which dates to 1835, the marina has 266 full service berths and offers extensive facilities including a 75-tonne boat hoist, laundry and a first class shower/bathroom block.

Call Fleetwood Dock Radio on VHF Channel 12 (Tel 01253 872351) for permission to enter the dock channel.

FACILITIES AT A GLANCE

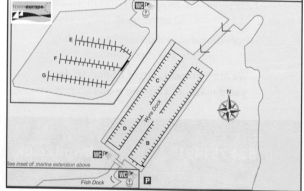

PRESTON MARINA

Preston Marine Services Ltd
The Boathouse, Navigation Way, Preston, PR2 2YP
Tel: 01772 733595 Fax: 01772 731881
Email: info@prestonmarina.co.uk www.prestonmarina.co.uk

| VHF | Ch 80 |
| ACCESS | HW±2 |

Preston Marina forms part of the comprehensive Riversway Docklands development, meeting all the demands of modern day boat owners. With the docks' history dating back over 100 years, today the marina comprises 40 acres of fully serviced pontoon berths sheltered behind the lock gates.

Lying 15 miles up the River Ribble, which itself is an interesting cruising ground with an abundance of wildlife, Preston is well placed for sailing to parts of Scotland, Ireland or Wales. The Docklands development includes a wide choice of restaurants, shops and cinemas as well as being in easy reach of all the cultural and leisure facilities provided by a large town.

FACILITIES AT A GLANCE

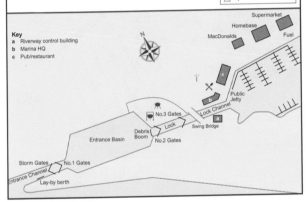

Key
a Riverway control building
b Marina HQ
c Pub/restaurant

LIVERPOOL MARINA

Liverpool Marina
Coburg Wharf, Sefton Street, Liverpool, L3 4BP
Tel: 0151 707 6777 Fax: 0151 707 6770
Email: mail@liverpoolmarina.co.uk

| VHF | Ch M |
| ACCESS | HW±2 |

Liverpool Marina is ideally situated for yachtsmen wishing to cruise the Irish Sea. Access is through a computerised lock that opens two and a half hours either side of high water between 0600 and 2200 daily. Once in the marina, you can enjoy the benefits of the facilities on offer, including a first class club bar and restaurant.

Liverpool is a thriving cosmopolitan city, with attractions ranging from numerous bars and restaurants to museums, art galleries and the Beatles Story.

FACILITIES AT A GLANCE

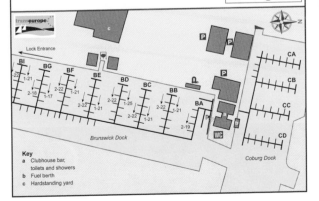

Key
a Clubhouse bar, toilets and showers
b Fuel berth
c Hardstanding yard

CONWY MARINA

Conwy Marina
Conwy, LL32 8EP
Tel: 01492 593000
Email: jroberts@quaymarinas.com
www.quaymarinas.com

| VHF | Ch 80 |
| ACCESS | LW±3.5 |

Situated in an area of outstanding natural beauty, with the Mountains of Snowdonia National Park providing a stunning backdrop, Conwy is the first purpose-built marina to be developed on the north coast of Wales. Enjoying a unique site next to the 13th century Conwy Castle, the third of Edward I's great castles, it provides a convenient base from which to explore the cruising grounds of the North Wales coast. The unspoilt coves of Anglesey and the beautiful Menai Straits prove a popular destination, while further afield are the Llyn Peninsula and the Islands of Bardsey and Tudwells. The marina incorporates about 500 fully serviced berths which are accessible through a barrier gate at half tide.

FACILITIES AT A GLANCE

Key
a Main services
   Marina office
   Network Yacht Brokers
   Seawake
b Toilets/showers
   Laundry store
   Yachtshop
   The Mulberry Stores
   Rowlands Marine Electronics

DEGANWY MARINA

Deganwy Marina
Deganwy, Conwy, LL31 9DJ
Tel: 01492 576888 Fax: 01492 580066
Email: enquiries@deganwymarina.co.uk
www.deganwymarina.co.uk

VHF	Ch 80
ACCESS	HW±3

Deganwy Marina is located in the centre of the north Wales coastline on the estuary of the Conwy River and sits between the river and the small town of Deganwy with the beautiful backdrop of the Vardre hills. The views from the marina across the Conwy

River are truly outstanding with the medieval walled town and Castle of Conwy outlined against the foothills of the Snowdonia National Park.

Deganwy Marina has 165 fully serviced berths, which are accessed via a tidal gate between half tide and high water.

FACILITIES AT A GLANCE

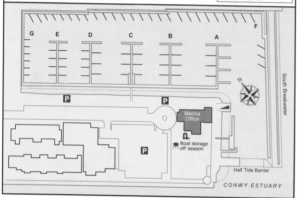

HOLYHEAD MARINA

Holyhead Marina Ltd
Newry Beach, Holyhead, Gwynedd, LL65 1YA
Tel: 01407 764242 Fax: 01407 769152
Email: info@holyheadmarina.co.uk

VHF	Ch M
ACCESS	H24

One of the few natural deep water harbours on the Welsh coast, Anglesey is conveniently placed as a first port of call if heading to North Wales from the North, South or West. Its marina at Holyhead, accessible at all states of the tide, is sheltered by Holyhead Mountain as well as an enormous harbour

breakwater and extensive floating breakwaters, therefore offering good protection from all directions.

Anglesey boasts numerous picturesque anchorages and beaches in addition to striking views over Snowdonia, while only a tide or two away are the Isle of Man and Eire.

FACILITIES AT A GLANCE

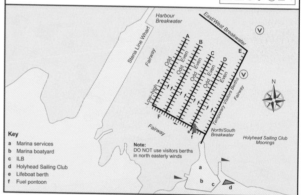

Key
a Marina services
b Marina boatyard
c ILB
d Holyhead Sailing Club
e Lifeboat berth
f Fuel pontoon

Note:
DO NOT use visitors berths in north easterly winds

PWLLHELI MARINA

Pwllheli Marina
Glan Don, Pwllheli, North Wales, LL53 5YT
Tel: 01758 701219 Fax: 01758 701443
Email: hafanpwllheli@gwynedd.llwy.cymru

VHF	Ch 80
ACCESS	

Pwllheli is an old Welsh market town providing the gateway to the Llyn Peninsula, which stretches out as far as Bardsey Island to form an 'Area of Outstanding Natural Beauty'. Enjoying the spectacular backdrop of the Snowdonia Mountains, Pwllheli's numerous attractions

include an open-air market every Wednesday, 'Neuadd Dwyfor', offering a mix of live theatre and latest films, and beautiful beaches.

Pwllheli Marina is situated on the south side of the Llyn Peninsula. One of Wales' finest marinas and sailing centres, it has over 400 pontoon berths and excellent onshore facilities.

FACILITIES AT A GLANCE

Key
a Marina offices
   Toilets
   Showers
   Baby change
   Launderette
b Domestic refuse point
c Short stay boat park
d Pwllheli sailing club
e Chandlery
f Events pontoons

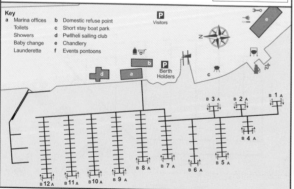

SOUTH WALES & BRISTOL CHANNEL – Bardsey Island to Land's End

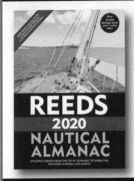

Reeds PDF ebooks

In response to popular demand, all the Reeds Almanacs are now available as searchable, highlightable PDF ebooks. (All ebooks incorporate the Marina Guide.)

Visit www.reedsnauticalalmanac.co.uk for further information

Key to Marina Plans symbols

Bottled gas		P	Parking
Chandler			Pub/Restaurant
Disabled facilities			Pump out
Electrical supply			Rigging service
Electrical repairs			Sail repairs
Engine repairs			Shipwright
First Aid			Shop/Supermarket
Fresh Water			Showers
Fuel - Diesel			Slipway
Fuel - Petrol		WC	Toilets
Hardstanding/boatyard			Telephone
@ Internet Café			Trolleys
Laundry facilities		V	Visitors berths
Lift-out facilities			Wi-Fi

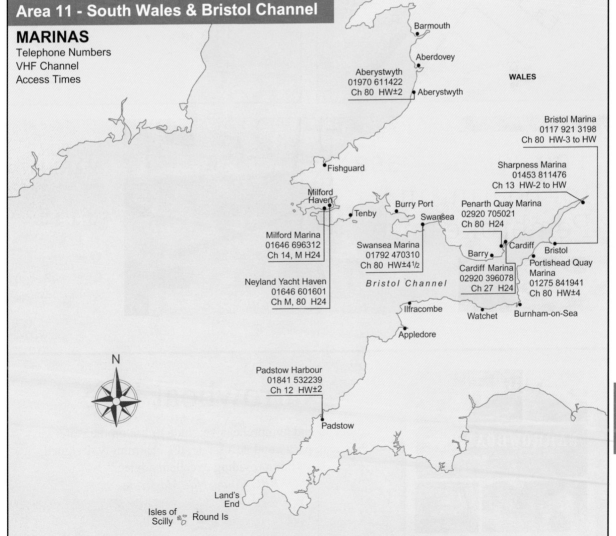

Area 11 - South Wales & Bristol Channel

MARINAS
Telephone Numbers
VHF Channel
Access Times

Barmouth

Aberdovey

Aberystwyth
01970 611422
Ch 80 HW±2
• Aberystwyth

WALES

Bristol Marina
0117 921 3198
Ch 80 HW-3 to HW

Sharpness Marina
01453 811476
Ch 13 HW-2 to HW

Fishguard

Milford Haven

Burry Port

Swansea

Penarth Quay Marina
02920 705021
Ch 80 H24

Tenby

Milford Marina
01646 696312
Ch 14, M H24

Swansea Marina
01792 470310
Ch 80 HW±4½

Cardiff

Barry

Bristol

Cardiff Marina
02920 396078
Ch 27 H24

Portishead Quay Marina
01275 841941
Ch 80 HW±4

Neyland Yacht Haven
01646 601601
Ch M, 80 H24

Bristol Channel

Ilfracombe

Watchet

Burnham-on-Sea

Appledore

Padstow Harbour
01841 532239
Ch 12 HW±2

N

Padstow

Land's End

Isles of Scilly Round Is

11

ABERYSTWYTH MARINA

Aberystwyth Marina
Trefechan, Aberystwyth, Ceredigion, SY23 1AS
Tel: 01970 611422 Fax: 01970 624122
Email: aber@themarinegroup.co.uk

VHF | Ch 80
ACCESS | HW±2

Aberystwyth Marina offers 165 first class berths providing safe, secure and sheltered moorings for motor boats and yachts.

The onsite chandlery has a selection of clothing, safety equipment, ropes, maintenance, navigation and electrical equipment. The brokerage has a range of motor boats and yachts for sale. In addition, the marina offers a range of boatyard and engine servicing. Other facilities include a slipway and 10t hoist.

Aberystwyth has a range of cafes, seaside fish and chip shops, restaurants, pubs and bars, many a short walk from the marina. The seafront, Promenade and pier is a great location for a walk and to look out over the Irish Sea.

FACILITIES AT A GLANCE

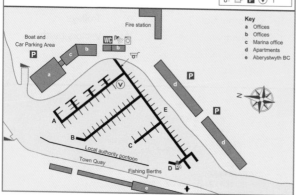

Key
a Offices
b Offices
c Marina office
d Apartments
e Aberystwyth BC

MILFORD MARINA

Milford Marina
Milford Docks, Milford Haven, Pembrokeshire, SA73 3AF
Tel: 01646 696312 Fax: 01646 696314
Email: enquiries@milfordmarina.com www.milfordmarina.com

VHF | Ch 14
ACCESS | H24

Set within one of the deepest natural harbours in the world, Milford Marina is situated in a non-tidal basin within the UK's only coastal National Park, the ideal base for discovering the fabulous coastline in Pembrokeshire, Wales and Ireland. Continued investment has meant that the marina provides safe, secure and sheltered boat berths with a full range of shoreside facilities in the heart of SW Wales.

Accessed via an entrance lock (with waiting pontoons both inside and outside the lock), the marina is perfect for exploring the picturesque upper reaches of the River Cleddau or cruising out beyond St Ann's Head to the unspoilt islands of Skomer, Skokholm and Grassholm.

FACILITIES AT A GLANCE

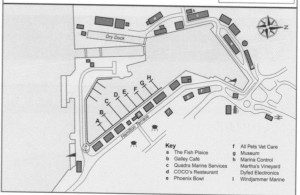

Key
a The Fish Plaice
b Galley Café
c Quadra Marine Services
d COCO's Restaurant
e Phoenix Bowl
f All Pets Vet Care
g Museum
h Marina Control
   Martha's Vineyard
   Dyfed Electronics
i Windjammer Marine

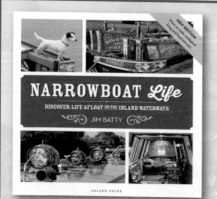

NEYLAND YACHT HAVEN

Neyland Yacht Haven Ltd
Brunel Quay, Neyland, Pembrokeshire, SA73 1PY
Tel: 01646 601601
Email: neyland@yachthavens.com www.yachthavens.com

VHF	Ch M, 80
ACCESS	H24

Approximately 10 miles from the entrance to Milford Haven lies Neyland Yacht Haven. Tucked away in a well protected inlet just before the Cleddau Bridge, this marina has 420 berths and can accommodate yachts up to 25m LOA with draughts of up to 2.5m. The marina is divided into two basins, with the lower one enjoying full tidal access, while entry to the upper one is restricted by a tidal sill. Visitor and annual berthing enquiries welcome.

Offering a comprehensive range of services, Neyland Yacht Haven is within a five minute walk of the town centre where the various shops and takeaways cater for most everyday needs; bicycle hire is also available. The Yacht Haven is a member of the TransEurope Group.

FACILITIES AT A GLANCE

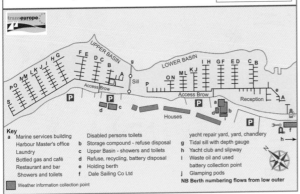

Key
a Marine services building
    Harbour Master's office
    Laundry
    Bottled gas and café
    Restaurant and bar
    Showers and toilets
b Storage compound - refuse disposal
c Upper Basin - showers and toilets
d Refuse, recycling, battery disposal
e Holding berth
f Dale Sailing Co Ltd
    Disabled persons toilets
g Tidal sill with depth gauge
h Yacht club and slipway
i Waste oil and used battery collection point
j Glamping pods
    yacht repair yard, yard, chandlery

NB Berth numbering flows from low outer

◻ Weather information collection point

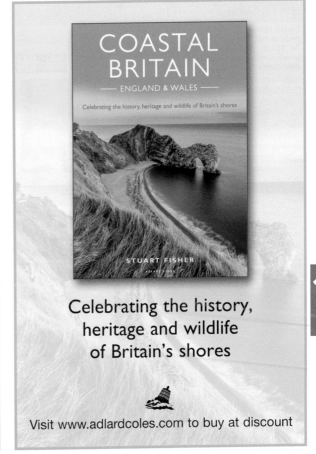
11

SWANSEA MARINA

Swansea Marina
Lockside, Maritime Quarter, Swansea, SA1 1WG
Tel: 01792 470310 Fax: 01792 463948
www.swansea.gov.uk/swanseamarina
Email: swanmar@swansea.gov.uk

VHF	Ch 80
ACCESS	HW±4.5

At the hub of the city's redeveloped and award winning Maritime Quarter, Swansea Marina can be accessed HW±4½ hrs via a lock. Surrounded by a plethora of shops, restaurants and marine businesses to cater for most yachtsmen's needs, the marina is in close proximity to the picturesque Gower coast, where there is no shortage of quiet sandy beaches off which to anchor. It also provides the perfect starting point for cruising to Ilfracombe, Lundy Island, the North Cornish coast or West Wales.

Within easy walking distance of the marina is the city centre, boasting a covered shopping centre and market. For those who prefer walking or cycling, take the long promenade to the Mumbles fishing village from where there are plenty of coastal walks.

FACILITIES AT A GLANCE

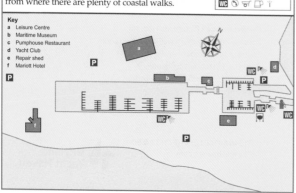

Key
a   Leisure Centre
b   Maritime Museum
c   Pumphouse Restaurant
d   Yacht Club
e   Repair shed
f   Marriott Hotel

PENARTH QUAYS MARINA

Penarth Quays Marina
Penarth, Vale of Glamorgan, CF64 1TQ
Tel: 02920 705021
Email: sjones@quaymarinas.com
www.quaymarinas.com

VHF	Ch 80
ACCESS	H24

Penarth Quays Marina has been established in the historic basins of Penarth Docks for over 20 years and is the premier boating facility in the region. The marina is Cardiff Bay's only 5 Gold Anchor marina and provides an ideal base for those using the Bay and the Bristol Channel. With 24hr access there is always water available for boating. Penarth and Cardiff boast an extensive range of leisure facilities, shops and restaurants making this marina an ideal base or destination. The marina has a blue flag and is a member of the TransEurope Group.

FACILITIES AT A GLANCE

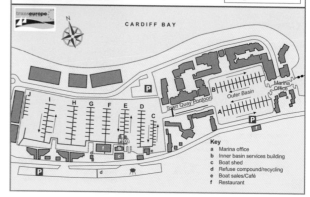

Key
a   Marina office
b   Inner basin services building
c   Boat shed
d   Refuse compound/recycling
e   Boat sales/Café
f   Restaurant

CARDIFF MARINA

Cardiff Marina
Watkiss Way, Cardiff, CF11 0SY
Tel: 02920 396078 Fax: 02920 345116
Email: info@themarinegroup.co.uk
www.themarinegroup.co.uk

VHF	Ch M
ACCESS	H24

A sheltered haven on the River Ely, Cardiff Marina offers 350 fully serviced berths within Cardiff Bay. Adjacent to Cardiff Marina, the waterside setting of Bayscape, a new mixed-use development of 115 apartments, is also home to the brand-new marina management suite, laundry and washrooms. The south facing terrace of the lounge bar, is a great location for berth holders to relax and unwind. Marina facilities also include a 50t Sealift, platform crane for mast work and brokerage. In addition, Cardiff Marine Village is home to Cardiff Marine Services, Wales' leading boatyard and refit and repair centre. The 3-acre site also has ample space for hard standing storage.

FACILITIES AT A GLANCE

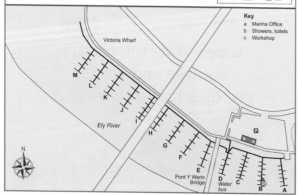

Key
a   Marina Office
b   Showers, toilets
c   Workshop

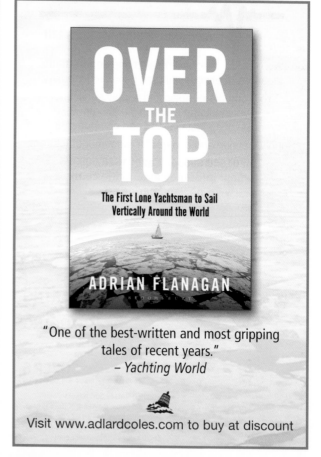

BRISTOL MARINA

Bristol Marina Ltd
Hanover Place, Bristol, BS1 6UH
Tel: 0117 921 3198 Fax: 0117 929 7672
Email: info@bristolmarina.co.uk

VHF	Ch 80
ACCESS	HW-3 to HW

Situated in the heart of the city, Bristol is a fully serviced marina providing over 100 pontoon berths for vessels up to 20m LOA. Among the facilities are a new fuelling berth and pump out station as well as an on site chandler and sailmaker. It is situated on the south side of the Floating Harbour, about eight miles from the mouth of the River Avon. Accessible from seaward via the Cumberland Basin, passing through both Entrance Lock and Junction Lock, it can be reached approximately three hours before HW.

Shops, restaurants, theatres and cinemas are all within easy reach of the marina, while local attractions include the SS *Great Britain*, designed by Isambard Kingdom Brunel, and the famous Clifton Suspension Bridge, which has an excellent visitors' centre depicting its fascinating story.

FACILITIES AT A GLANCE

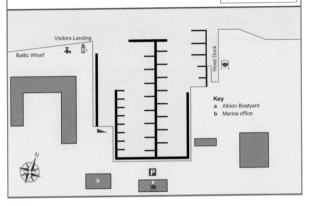

Key
a Albion Boatyard
b Marina office

PORTISHEAD QUAYS MARINA

Portishead Quays Marina
Newfoundland Way, Portishead, North Somerset, BS20 7DF
Tel: 01275 841941
Email: portisheadmarina@quaymarinas.com
www.quaymarinas.com

VHF	Ch 80
ACCESS	HW±3.5

Portishead Marina is a popular destination for cruising in the Bristol Channel. Providing an excellent link between the inland waterways at Bristol and Sharpness and offering access to the open water and marinas down channel. The entrance to the Marina is via a lock, with a minimum access of HW+/- 3.5hrs. Contact the Marina on VHF Ch 80 ahead of time for next available lock. The Marina provides 320 fully serviced berths and can accommodate vessels up to 40m LOA, draft up to 5.5m. The marina has a 35 tonnes boat hoist and the boatyard offers all the facilities you would expect from a Quay Marinas site.

FACILITIES AT A GLANCE

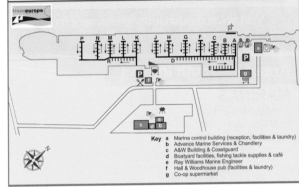

Key
a Marina control building (reception, facilities & laundry)
b Advance Marine Services & Chandlery
c A&W Building & Coastguard
d Boatyard facilities, fishing tackle supplies & café
e Ray Williams Marine Engineer
f Hall & Woodhouse pub (facilities & laundry)
g Co-op supermarket

PADSTOW HARBOUR

Padstow Harbour Commissioners
The Harbour Office, Padstow, Cornwall, PL28 8AQ
Tel: 01841 532239 Fax: 01841 533346
Email: padstowharbour@btconnect.com
www.padstow-harbour.co.uk

VHF	Ch 12, 16
ACCESS	HW±2

Padstow is a small commercial port with a rich history situated 1.5 miles from the sea within the estuary of the River Camel. The inner harbour is serviced by a tidal gate – part of the 1988–1990 flood defence scheme, which is open approximately two hours either side of high water. A minimum of 3m of water is maintained in the inner harbour at all times. Onshore facilities are excellent, please enquire at the Harbour Office.

This is a thriving fishing port, so perhaps it wasn't surprising that celebrity chefs like Rick Stein and Paul Ainsworth would set up shop in the town. This is a great resting point for everything Cornish from surf and coastal walks to fish and chips and cream teas.

FACILITIES AT A GLANCE

Key a Residents' pontoons
b Harbour office
* Electricity and water points
1-20 around harbour denote ladder numbers

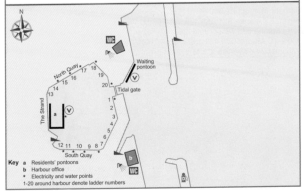
11

SOUTH IRELAND – Malahide, clockwise to Liscannor Bay

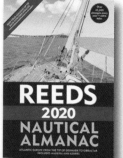
Key to Marina Plans symbols

	Bottled gas	P	Parking
	Chandler		Pub/Restaurant
	Disabled facilities		Pump out
	Electrical supply		Rigging service
	Electrical repairs		Sail repairs
	Engine repairs		Shipwright
	First Aid		Shop/Supermarket
	Fresh Water		Showers
	Fuel - Diesel		Slipway
	Fuel - Petrol	WC	Toilets
	Hardstanding/boatyard		Telephone
@	Internet Café		Trolleys
	Laundry facilities	V	Visitors berths
	Lift-out facilities		Wi-Fi

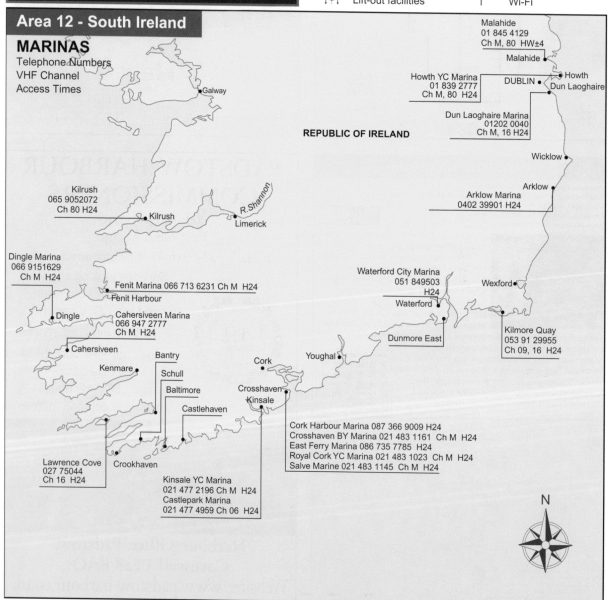

Area 12 - South Ireland

MARINAS
Telephone Numbers
VHF Channel
Access Times

REPUBLIC OF IRELAND

Malahide
01 845 4129
Ch M, 80 HW±4

Howth YC Marina
01 839 2777
Ch M, 80 H24

Dun Laoghaire Marina
01202 0040
Ch M, 16 H24

Galway

Kilrush
065 9052072
Ch 80 H24

R.Shannon

Limerick

Wicklow

Arklow
Arklow Marina
0402 39901 H24

Dingle Marina
066 9151629
Ch M H24

Fenit Marina 066 713 6231 Ch M H24
Fenit Harbour

Cahersiveen Marina
066 947 2777
Ch M H24

Dingle

Cahersiveen

Kenmare

Bantry

Schull

Baltimore

Castlehaven

Waterford City Marina
051 849503
H24
Waterford

Wexford

Kilmore Quay
053 91 29955
Ch 09, 16 H24

Dunmore East

Cork

Youghal

Crosshaven
Kinsale

Cork Harbour Marina 087 366 9009 H24
Crosshaven BY Marina 021 483 1161 Ch M H24
East Ferry Marina 086 735 7785 H24
Royal Cork YC Marina 021 483 1023 Ch M H24
Salve Marine 021 483 1145 Ch M H24

Lawrence Cove
027 75044
Ch 16 H24

Crookhaven

Kinsale YC Marina
021 477 2196 Ch M H24
Castlepark Marina
021 477 4959 Ch 06 H24

N

MALAHIDE MARINA

Malahide Marina
Malahide, Co. Dublin
Tel: +353 1 845 4129 Fax: +353 1 845 4255
Email: info@malahidemarina.net
www.malahidemarina.net

VHF	Ch M, 80
ACCESS	HW±4

Malahide Marina, situated just 10 minutes from Dublin Airport and 20 minutes north of Dublin's city centre, is a fully serviced marina accommodating up to 350 yachts. Capable of taking vessels of up to 75m in length, its first class facilities include a boatyard with hard standing for approximately 170 boats and a 30-ton mobile hoist. Its on site restaurant provides a large seating area in convivial surroundings. The village of Malahide has plenty to offer the visiting yachtsmen, with a wide variety of eating places, nearby golf courses and tennis courts as well as a historic castle and botanical gardens.

FACILITIES AT A GLANCE

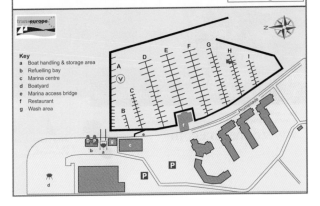

Key
a Boat handling & storage area
b Refuelling bay
c Marina centre
d Boatyard
e Marina access bridge
f Restaurant
g Wash area

HOWTH MARINA

Howth Marina
Howth Marina, Harbour Road, Howth, Co. Dublin
Tel: +353 1 8392777 Fax: +353 1 8392430
Email: marina@hyc.ie
www.hyc.ie

VHF	Ch M, 80
ACCESS	H24

Based on the north coast of the rugged peninsula that forms the northern side of Dublin Bay, Howth Marina is ideally situated for north or south-bound traffic in the Irish Sea. Well sheltered in all winds, it can be entered at any state of the tide. Overlooking the marina is Howth Yacht Club, which has in recent years been expanded and is now said to be the largest yacht club in Ireland. With good road and rail links, Howth is in easy reach of Dublin's airport and ferry terminal, making it an obvious choice for crew changeovers.

FACILITIES AT A GLANCE

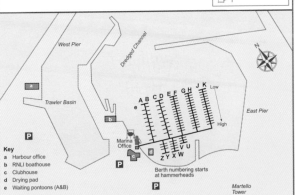

Key
a Harbour office
b RNLI boathouse
c Clubhouse
d Drying pad
e Waiting pontoons (A&B)

DUN LAOGHAIRE MARINA

Dun Laoghaire Marina
Harbour Road, Dun Laoghaire, Co Dublin, Eire
Tel: +353 1 202 0040 Fax: +353 1 202 0043
Email: info@dlmarina.com   www.dlmarina.com

VHF | Ch M, 16
ACCESS | H24

Dun Laoghaire Marina – Gateway to Dublin and the first marina in the Republic of Ireland to be awarded five Gold anchors by THYA and also achieved the ICOMIA 'Clean Marina' accreditation – is the largest marina in Ireland. 24 hour access in all weather conditions. The town centre is located within 400m. Serviced berthing for 820 boats from 6m to 23m with visitors mainly on the hammerheads.

Larger vessels up to 46m and 160 tonnes can be berthed alongside breakwater pontoons. Minimum draft is 3.8m LWS. Three phase power is available. With Dublin rail station 12km and airport 35km, this is an ideal base for Irish culture and entertainment, as well as crew changes etc. Easy access to Dublin Bay, home to the biennial Dun Laoghaire Regatta.

FACILITIES AT A GLANCE

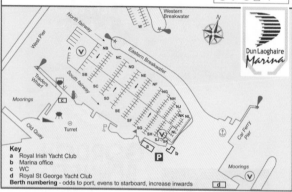

Key
a   Royal Irish Yacht Club
b   Marina office
c   WC
d   Royal St George Yacht Club
Berth numbering - odds to port, evens to starboard, increase inwards

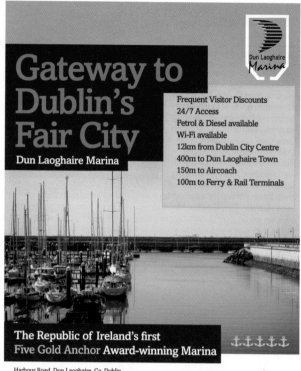

Gateway to Dublin's Fair City
Dun Laoghaire Marina

Frequent Visitor Discounts
24/7 Access
Petrol & Diesel available
Wi-Fi available
12km from Dublin City Centre
400m to Dun Laoghaire Town
150m to Aircoach
100m to Ferry & Rail Terminals

The Republic of Ireland's first
Five Gold Anchor **Award-winning Marina**

Harbour Road, Dun Laoghaire, Co. Dublin
T: 00353 1 2020040 F: 00353 1 2020043 E: info@dlmarina.com

www.dlmarina.com

ARKLOW MARINA

Arklow Marina
North Quay, Arklow, Co. Wicklow, Eire
Mobiles: 087 2375189 or 087 2588078
Email: personnel@asl.ie
www.arklowmarina.com

VHF |
ACCESS | H24

Arklow is a popular fishing port and seaside town situated at the mouth of the River Avoca, 16 miles south of Wicklow and 11 miles north east of Gorey. The town is ideally placed for visiting the many beauty spots of County Wicklow including Glenmalure, Glendalough and Clara Lara, Avoca (Ballykissangel).

Arklow Marina is on the north bank of the river (dredged 2014) just upstream of the commercial quays, with 42 berths in an inner harbour and 30 berths on pontoons outside the marina entrance. Vessels over 14m LOA should moor on the river pontoons.

FACILITIES AT A GLANCE

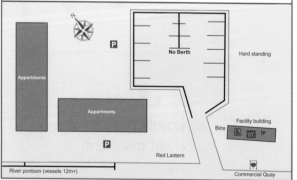

KILMORE QUAY

Kilmore Quay
Wexford, Ireland
Tel: +353 53 9129955 www.kilmorequaymarina.com
Email: assistant.marineofficer@wexfordcoco.ie

VHF | Ch 09, 16
ACCESS | H24

Located in the SE corner of Ireland, Kilmore Quay is a small rural fishing village situated approximately 14 miles from the town of Wexford and 12 miles from Rosslare ferry port.

Its 55-berthed marina, offering shelter from the elements as well as various on shore facilities, including diesel available 24/7, has become a regular port of call for many cruising yachtsmen. With several nearby areas of either historical or natural significance accessible using local bike hire, Kilmore is renowned for its 'green' approach to the environment.

FACILITIES AT A GLANCE

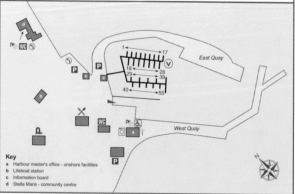

Key
a   Harbour master's office - onshore facilities
b   Lifeboat station
c   Information board
d   Stella Maris - community centre

WATERFORD CITY MARINA

Waterford City Marina
Waterford, Ireland
Tel: +353 87 238 4944
Email: jcodd@waterfordcouncil.ie

VHF
ACCESS H24

Famous for its connections with Waterford Crystal, manufactured in the city centre, Waterford is the capital of the SE region of Ireland. As a major city, it benefits from good rail links with Dublin, and Limerick, a regional airport with daily flights to Britain and an extensive bus service to surrounding towns and villages. The marina is found on the banks of the River Suir, in the heart of this historic Viking city dating back to the ninth century. Yachtsmen can make the most of Waterford's wide range of shops, restaurants and bars without having to walk too far from their boats. With 100 fully serviced berths and first rate security, Waterford City Marina now provides shower, toilet and laundry facilities in its new reception building.

FACILITIES AT A GLANCE

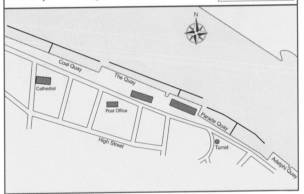

CROSSHAVEN BOATYARD MARINA

Crosshaven Boatyard Marina
Crosshaven, Co Cork, Ireland
Tel: +353 214 831161 Fax: +353 214 831603
Email: info@crosshavenboatyard.com

VHF Ch M
ACCESS H24

One of three marinas at Crosshaven, Crosshaven Boatyard was founded in 1950 and originally made its name from the construction of some of the most world-renowned yachts, including *Gypsy Moth* and Denis Doyle's *Moonduster*. Nowadays, however, the yard has diversified to provide a wide range of services to both the marine leisure and professional industries. Situated on a safe and sheltered river only 12 miles from Cork City Centre, the marina boasts 100 fully-serviced berths along with the capacity to accommodate yachts up to 35m LOA with a 4m draught. In addition, it is ideally situated for cruising the stunning south west coast of Ireland.

FACILITIES AT A GLANCE

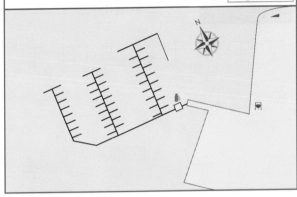

SALVE MARINE

Salve Marine
Crosshaven, Co Cork, Ireland
Tel: +353 21 483 1145 Fax: +353 21 483 1747
Email: salvemarine@eircom.net

VHF Ch M
ACCESS H24

Crosshaven is a picturesque seaside resort providing a gateway to Ireland's south and south west coasts. Offering a variety of activities to suit all types, its rocky coves and quiet sandy beaches stretch from Graball to Church Bay and from Fennell's Bay to nearby Myrtleville. Besides a selection of craft shops selling locally produced arts and crafts, there are plenty of pubs, restaurants and takeaways to suit even the most discerning of tastes. Lying within a few hundred metres of the village centre is Salve Marine, accommodating yachts up to 43m LOA with draughts of up to 4m. Its comprehensive services range from engineering and welding facilities to hull and rigging repairs.

FACILITIES AT A GLANCE

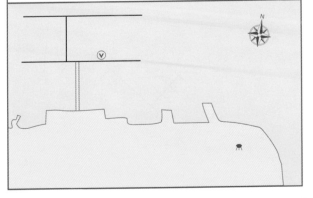

CORK HARBOUR MARINA

Cork Harbour Marina
Monkstown, Co Cork, Ireland
Tel: +353 87 366 9009
Email: info@corkharbourmarina.ie www.corkharbourmarina.ie

VHF
ACCESS H24

Located in the picturesque town of Monkstown, Cork Harbour Marina is in the heart of Cork Harbour. The marina can cater for all boat types with a draft of up to 7m and the marina is accessible at all phases of the tide.

Within strolling distance from the marina is the 'Bosun' restaurant and 'Napoli', an Italian delicatessen. There is also a sailing club, tennis club and golf club located nearby. Monkstown is just a short riverside walk from Passage West, with all the amenities one might require.

There is a frequent bus service from the marina gates to Cork City. Cork Harbour Marina is 15km from Cork International Airport.

FACILITIES AT A GLANCE

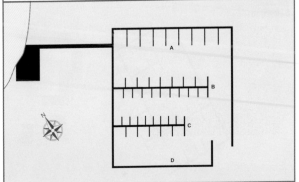

ROYAL CORK YACHT CLUB

Royal Cork Yacht Club Marina
Crosshaven, Co Cork, Ireland
Tel: +353 21 483 1023 Fax: +353 21 483 2657
Email: mark@royalcork.com   www.royalcork.com

VHF	Ch M
ACCESS	H24

Founded in 1720, the Royal Cork Yacht Club is the oldest and one of the most prominent yacht clubs in the world. Organising, among many other events, the prestigious biennial Volvo Cork Week, it boasts a number of World, European and national sailors among its membership.

The Yacht Club's marina is situated at Crosshaven, on the hillside at the mouth of the Owenabue River, just inside the entrance to Cork Harbour. The harbour is popular with yachtsmen as it is accessible and well sheltered in all weather conditions. It also benefits from the Gulf Stream producing a temperate climate practically all year round.

FACILITIES AT A GLANCE

Blue Flag
An Taisce

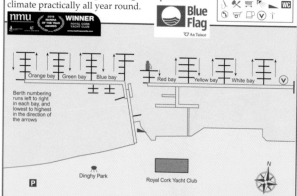

KINSALE YACHT CLUB MARINA

Kinsale Yacht Club Marina
Kinsale, Co Cork, Ireland
Tel: +353 21 4772196 Fax: +353 21 4774455
Email: kyc@iol.ie

VHF	Ch M
ACCESS	H24

Kinsale is a natural, virtually land-locked harbour on the estuary of the Bandon River, approximately 12 miles south west of Cork harbour entrance. Home to a thriving fishing fleet as well as frequented by commercial shipping, it boasts two fully serviced marinas, with the Kinsale Yacht Club & Marina being the closest to the town. Visitors to this marina automatically become temporary members of the club and are therefore entitled to make full use of the facilities, which include a fully licensed bar and restaurant serving evening meals on Wednesdays, Thursdays and Saturdays. Fuel, water and repair services are also available.

FACILITIES AT A GLANCE

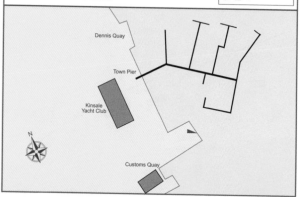

Dennis Quay

Town Pier

Kinsale Yacht Club

Customs Quay

CASTLEPARK MARINA

Castlepark Marina Centre
Kinsale, Co Cork, Ireland
Tel: +353 21 4774959
Email: info@castleparkmarina.com

VHF	Ch 16, 14
ACCESS	H24

Situated on the south side of Kinsale Harbour, Castlepark is a small marina with deep water pontoon berths that are accessible at all states of the tide. Surrounded by rolling hills, it boasts its own beach as well as being in close proximity to the parklands of James Fort and a traditional Irish pub. The attractive town of Kinsale, with its narrow streets and slate-clad houses, lies just 1.5 miles away by road or five minutes away by ferry. Known as Ireland's 'fine food centre', it incorporates a number of gourmet food shops and high quality restaurants as well as a wine museum.

FACILITIES AT A GLANCE

trans-europe

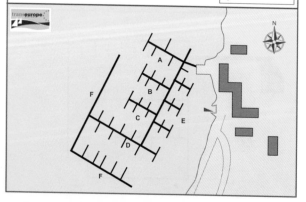

LAWRENCE COVE MARINA

Lawrence Cove Marina
Lawrence Cove, Bere Island, Co Cork, Ireland
Tel: +353 27 75044 mob: +353 879 125930
Email: rachelsherig@gmail.com
www.lawrencecovemarina.ie

VHF	Ch 16
ACCESS	H24

Lawrence Cove enjoys a peaceful location on an island at the entrance to Bantry Bay. Privately owned and run, it offers sheltered and secluded waters as well as excellent facilities and fully serviced pontoon berths. A few hundred yards from the marina you will find a shop, pub and restaurant, while the mainland, with its various attractions, can be easily reached by ferry. Lawrence Cove lies at the heart of the wonderful cruising grounds of Ireland's south west coast and, just two hours from Cork airport, is an ideal place to leave your boat for long or short periods.

FACILITIES AT A GLANCE

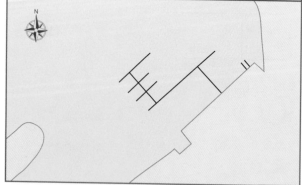

CAHERSIVEEN MARINA

Cahersiveen Marina
The Pier, Cahersiveen, Co. Kerry, Ireland
Tel: +353 66 9472777
Email: acardsiveen@gmail.com
www.cahersiveenmarina.ie

VHF **Ch 24**
ACCESS **H24**

Situated two miles up Valentia River from Valentia Harbour, Cahersiveen Marina is well protected in all wind directions and is convenient for sailing to Valentia Island and Dingle Bay as well as for visiting some of the spectacular uninhabited islands in the surrounding area. Boasting a host of sheltered sandy beaches, the region is renowned for salt and fresh water fishing as well as being good for scuba diving.

Within easy walking distance of the marina lies the historic town of Cahersiveen, incorporating an array of convivial pubs and restaurants.

FACILITIES AT A GLANCE

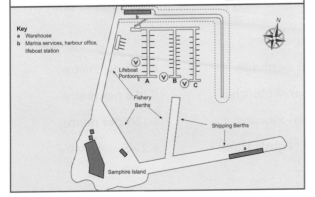

DINGLE MARINA

Dingle Marina
c/o Dingle Fishery Harbour Centre, Strand Street, Dingle, Co Kerry, Ireland
Tel: +353 (0)87 925 4115 Fax: +353 (0)69 5152546
Email:dingleharbour@agriculture.gov.ie
www.dinglemarina.ie

VHF **Ch 14**
ACCESS **H24**

Dingle is Ireland's most westerly marina, lying at the heart of the sheltered Dingle Harbour, and is easily reached both day and night via a well buoyed approach channel. The surrounding area is an interesting and unfrequented cruising ground, with several islands, bays and beaches for the yachtsman to explore.

The marina lies in the heart of the old market town, renowned for its hospitality and traditional Irish pub music. Besides enjoying the excellent seafood restaurants and 52 pubs, other recreational pastimes include horse riding, golf, climbing and diving.

FACILITIES AT A GLANCE

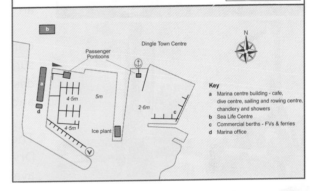

Key
a Marina centre building - cafe, dive centre, sailing and rowing centre, chandlery and showers
b Sea Life Centre
c Commercial berths - FVs & ferries
d Marina office

FENIT HARBOUR MARINA

Fenit Harbour & Marina
Fenit, Tralee, Co. Kerry, Republic of Ireland
Tel: +353 66 7136231 Fax: +353 66 7136473
Email: info@fenitharbour.com www.fenitharbour.com

VHF **Ch M**
ACCESS **H24**

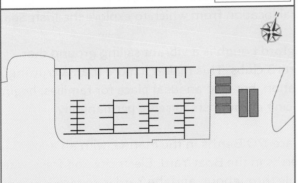

Fenit Harbour Marina is tucked away in Tralee Bay, not far south of the Shannon Estuary. Besides offering a superb cruising ground, being within a day's sail of Dingle and Kilrush, the marina also provides a convenient base from which to visit inland attractions such as the picturesque tourist towns of Tralee and Killarney. This 120-berth marina accommodates boats up to 15m LOA and benefits from deep water at all states of the tide.

The small village of Fenit incorporates a grocery shop as well a several pubs and restaurants, while among the local activities are horse riding, swimming from one of the nearby sandy beaches and golfing.

FACILITIES AT A GLANCE

Key
a Warehouse
b Marina services, harbour office, lifeboat station

KILRUSH MARINA

Kilrush Marina Ltd
Kilrush, Co. Clare, Ireland
Tel: +353 65 9052072 Mobile: +353 86 2313870
Email: info@kilrushmarina.ie

VHF **Ch 80**
ACCESS **H24**

Kilrush Marina and boatyard is well placed for exploring the unspoilt west coast of Ireland, including Galway Bay, Dingle, W Cork and Kerry. It also provides a gateway to over 150 miles of cruising on Lough Derg, the R Shannon and the Irish canal system. Accessed via lock gates, the marina lies at one end of the main street in Kilrush, the marina centre provides all the facilities for the visiting sailor. Kilrush is a vibrant market town with a long maritime history. A 15-minute ferry ride from the marina takes you to Scattery Is, once a 6th century monastic settlement but now only inhabited by wildlife. The Shannon Estuary is reputed for being the country's first marine Special Area of Conservation (SAC) and is home to Ireland's only known resident group of bottlenose dolphins.

FACILITIES AT A GLANCE

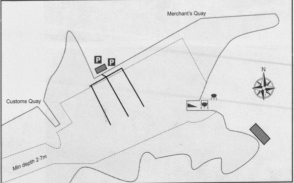

Set Sail for Carlingford Marina

Tel: +353 (0) 42 93 73 072
Email: info@carlingfordmarina.ie
Web: www.carlingfordmarina.ie

About the Marina

Carlingford Marina is located in the picturesque coastal inlet of Carlingford Lough, with the Cooley Mountains on one side, and the Mountains of Mourne on the other.

A day's sail from Dublin, Belfast, The Isle of Man, the West Coast of England and North Wales, Carlingford is an ideal location from which to explore the Irish Sea.

Carlingford Lough is a vibrant sailing ground that supports 3 clubs. This makes it more than a cruising destination, but also an ideal place for families, beginners and racing enthusiasts to settle permanently.

There are 170 Berths in the Marina, with an additional 50 Dry Berths in the Boat Yard. Electricity and fresh water is available throughout, and the Yard is serviced by a 50 tonne travel hoist.

About the Location

Carlingford is one of the best preserved medieval villages in Ireland with a number of important pre-historic and medieval sites.

The village has a deserved reputation for hospitality, with some of the finest restaurants and friendliest pubs in Ireland. Known as Ireland's best kept secret, the area has been recognized as a European Destination of Excellence, and an area of outstanding natural beauty.

Carlingford is an hour's away from both Dublin and Belfast, and the busy international airports of both cities.

Berthage Rates

Annual Berthage:	€278 per metre
Summer 4 Months:	€142 per metre
Winter 6 Months:	€126 per metre
Visitor Nightly Rate:	€2.45 per metre

Contact

+353 (0) 42 93 73072 / info@carlingfordmarina.ie

NORTH IRELAND – Liscannor Bay, clockwise to Lambay Island

Reeds PDF ebooks

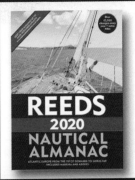

In response to popular demand, all the Reeds Almanacs are now available as searchable, highlightable PDF ebooks. (All ebooks incorporate the Marina Guide.)

Visit www.reedsnauticalalmanac.co.uk for further information

Key to Marina Plans symbols

Bottled gas		Parking
Chandler		Pub/Restaurant
Disabled facilities		Pump out
Electrical supply		Rigging service
Electrical repairs		Sail repairs
Engine repairs		Shipwright
First Aid		Shop/Supermarket
Fresh Water		Showers
Fuel - Diesel		Slipway
Fuel - Petrol		Toilets
Hardstanding/boatyard		Telephone
Internet Café		Trolleys
Laundry facilities		Visitors berths
Lift-out facilities		Wi-Fi

Area 13 - North Ireland

MARINAS
Telephone Numbers
VHF Channel
Access Times

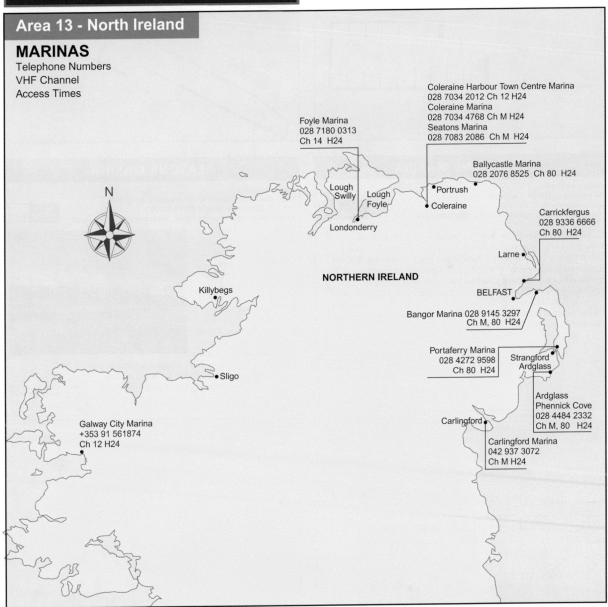

Coleraine Harbour Town Centre Marina
028 7034 2012 Ch 12 H24
Coleraine Marina
028 7034 4768 Ch M H24
Seatons Marina
028 7083 2086 Ch M H24

Ballycastle Marina
028 2076 8525 Ch 80 H24

Foyle Marina
028 7180 0313
Ch 14 H24

Lough Swilly

Lough Foyle

Portrush

Coleraine

Londonderry

Carrickfergus
028 9336 6666
Ch 80 H24

Larne

NORTHERN IRELAND

Killybegs

BELFAST

Bangor Marina 028 9145 3297
Ch M, 80 H24

Portaferry Marina
028 4272 9598
Ch 80 H24

Strangford
Ardglass

Sligo

Ardglass
Phennick Cove
028 4484 2332
Ch M, 80   H24

Galway City Marina
+353 91 561874
Ch 12 H24

Carlingford

Carlingford Marina
042 937 3072
Ch M H24

N

GALWAY CITY MARINA

Galway City Marina
Galway Harbour Co, Harbour Office, Galway, Ireland
Tel: +353 91 561874 Fax: +353 91 563738
Email: info@theportofgalway.com

VHF	Ch 12
ACCESS	HW-2 to HW

The Galway harbour Company operates a small marina in the confines of Galway Harbour with an additional 60m of pontoon-walkway. Freshwater and electrical power is available at the pontoons. Power cars can be purchased from the harbour office during the day. A number of visitors pontoons are available for hire during the summer and for winter layup. Sailors intending to call to Galway Harbour should first make contact with the Harbour office to determine if a berth is available — advisable as demand is high in this quiet and beautiful part of Ireland.

FACILITIES AT A GLANCE

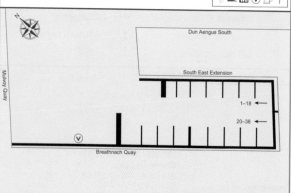

FOYLE MARINA

Foyle Marina
Londonderry Port, Lisahally, L'Derry, BT47 6FL
Tel: 02871 860555 Fax: 02871 861656
www.londonderryport.com/leisure
Email: info@londonderryport.com

VHF	Ch 14
ACCESS	H24

Foyle Marina lies in the heart of the city, 17M from the mouth of Lough Foyle, is accessible at any state of the tide and is sheltered from all directions of wind. Approach is via well-marked navigation channel with a maintained depth of 8m.

The marina has recently undergone extensive improvements with over 680m of secure pontoon mooring now available. Foyle Marina now offers full facilities to visiting vessels. Toilets and showers on site, water and electricity at each berth. Vessels up to 130m LOA can be accommodated. Craft can berth either side of the pontoons in depths of 5–7m at LW.

The pontoons are within easy walking distance of the city centre where you will find restaurants, bars, cinemas, shopping and a host of tourist attractions.

FACILITIES AT A GLANCE

Key   a   Council offices
        b   Apartments
        c   Doctor's surgery

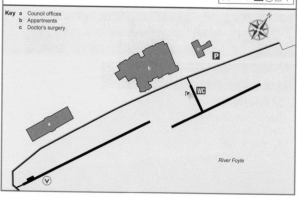

COLERAINE MARINA

Coleraine Marina
64 Portstewart Road, Coleraine,
Co Londonderry, BT52 1RR
Tel: 028 7034 4768 Email: rickiemac@talktalk.net

VHF	Ch M
ACCESS	H24

Coleraine Marina complex enjoys a superb location in sheltered waters just one mile north of the town of Coleraine and four and a half miles south of the River Bann Estuary and the open sea. Besides accommodating vessels up to 18m LOA, this modern marina with 78 berths offers hard standing, fuel and shower facilities.

Among one of the oldest known settlements in Ireland, Coleraine is renowned for its linen, whiskey and salmon. Its thriving commercial centre includes numerous shops, a four-screen cinema and a state-of-the-art leisure complex.

FACILITIES AT A GLANCE

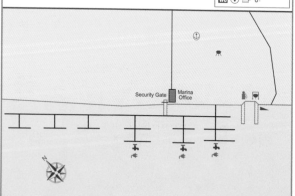

SEATONS MARINA

Seatons Marina
Drumslade Rd, Coleraine, Londonderry, BT52 1SE
Tel: 028 7083 2086 Mobile 07718 883099
Email: jill@seatonsmarina.co.uk www.seatonsmarina.co.uk

VHF	
ACCESS	H24

Seatons Marina is a privately owned business on the north coast of Ireland, which was established by Eric Seaton in 1962. It lies on the east bank of the River Bann, approximately two miles downstream from Coleraine and three miles from the sea. Long term pontoon berths are available for yachts up to 11.5 with a maximum draft of 2.4m; fore and aft moorings are available for larger vessels. Lift out and mast stepping facilities are provided by a 12 tonne trailer hoist.

FACILITIES AT A GLANCE

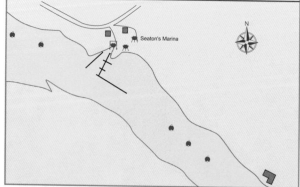

COLERAINE HARBOUR MARINA

Coleraine Harbour Town Centre Marina
Coleraine Harbour Office, 4 Riversdale Road, Coleraine, BT52 1XA
Tel: 028 7034 2012 Mobile: 07742 242788
Email: info@coleraineharbour.com
www.coleraineharbour.com

VHF Ch 12
ACCESS H24

The Marina lies upstream about five miles from the sea. Ideally situated in a sheltered location in the centre of the town, just a few minutes stroll from a selection of shops, cafes, restaurants and bars. It is the ideal location for a short or long stay.

In addition to the pontoon berths there is a 40 tonne Roodberg slipway launch/recovery trailer. Hard standing and covered storage are available.

FACILITIES AT A GLANCE

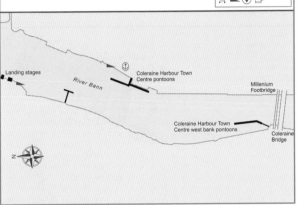

Coleraine Harbour Town Centre Marina

The ideal place to berth a yacht when visiting the River Bann.
Pontoon berths for visitors.
Situated in the centre of town.
Excellent facilities including free showers and all your marina needs.

**Access via the lifting bridge –
Telephone the Harbour Manager on
028 70 34 2012 or Channel 12 VHF**

BALLYCASTLE MARINA

Ballycastle Marina
Bayview Road, Ballycastle, Northern Ireland
Tel: 028 2076 8525/07803 505084 Fax: 028 2076 6215
Email: info@moyle-council.org

VHF Ch 80
ACCESS H24

Ballycastle is a traditional seaside town situated on Northern Ireland's North Antrim coast. The 74-berthed, sheltered marina provides a perfect base from which to explore the well known local attractions such as the Giant's Causeway world heritage site, the spectacular Nine Glens of Antrim, and Rathlin, the only inhabited island in Northern Ireland. The most northern coastal marina in Ireland, Ballycastle is accessible at all states of the tide, although yachts are required to contact the marina on VHF Ch 80 before entering the harbour. Along the seafront are a selection of restaurants, bars and shops, while the town centre is only about a five minute walk away.

FACILITIES AT A GLANCE

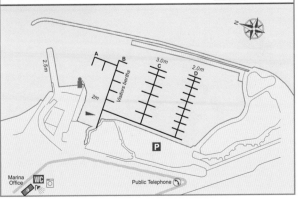

CARRICKFERGUS MARINA

Carrickferus Marina
3 Quayside, Carrickfergus, Co. Antrim, BT38 8BJ
Tel: 028 9336 6666 Fax: 028 9335 0505
Email: marina.reception@midandeastantrim.gov.uk
www.carrickfergus.org

VHF Ch 80
ACCESS H24

Carrickfergus Marina is situated on the north shore of Belfast Lough. A 300-berth, 5 Gold Anchor, fully serviced marina, renowned for our friendly reputation. Suitable for adults and families alike, with male/female facilities and a family bathroom.

A world of entertainment and things to do on your doorstep makes us an ideal destination on your travels. Choice of bars, restaurants and supermarkets within 500m. Variety of places to visit: ancient castle, museums, leisure centre, boutique shops. Family friendly choices: cinema, play parks, swimming pools and soft play centres within 10 mins walk.

FACILITIES AT A GLANCE

Key
a Apartments
b Hotel/bar/restaurant
c Marina office
d Cinema/café/restaurant
e Retail superstore

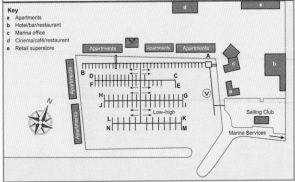

BANGOR MARINA

Quay Marinas Limited
Bangor Marina, Bangor, Co. Down, BT20 5ED
Tel: 028 9145 3297 Fax: 028 9145 3450
Email: kbaird@quaymarinas.com
www.quaymarinas.com

⚓⚓⚓⚓

VHF	Ch 11, 80
ACCESS	H24

Situated on the south shore of Belfast Lough, Bangor is located close to the Irish Sea cruising routes. The marina is right at the town's centre, within walking distance of shops, restaurants, hotels and bars. The Tourist information centre is across the road from marina reception and there are numerous visitors' attractions in the Borough. The Royal Ulster Yacht Club and the Ballyholme Yacht Club are both nearby and welcome visitors.

FACILITIES AT A GLANCE

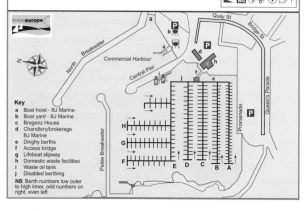

Key
a   Boat hoist - BJ Marine
b   Boat yard - BJ Marine
c   Bregenz House
d   Chandlery/brokerage BJ Marine
e   Dinghy berths
f   Access bridge
g   Lifeboat slipway
h   Domestic waste facilities
i   Waste oil tank
j   Disabled berthing
NB Berth numbers low outer to high inner, odd numbers on right, even left

CARLINGFORD MARINA

Carlingford Marina
Co. Louth, Ireland
Tel: +353 (0)42 937 3072   Fax: +353 (0)42 937 3075
Email: info@carlingfordmarina.ie
www.carlingfordmarina.ie

VHF	Ch M
ACCESS	H24

Carlingford Lough is an eight-mile sheltered haven between the Cooley Mountains to the south and the Mourne Mountains to the north. The marina is situated on the southern shore, about four miles from Haulbowline Lighthouse, and can be easily reached via a deep water shipping channel. Among the most attractive destinations in the Irish Sea, Carlingford is only 60 miles from the Isle of Man and within a day's sail from Strangford Lough and Ardglass. Full facilities in the marina include a first class bar and restaurant offering superb views across the water.

FACILITIES AT A GLANCE

Key
a   Bar and restaurant
b   Toilets, showers and laundry
c   Refuse
d   Office
e   Chandlery
f   Marina office
g   Waiting pontoon

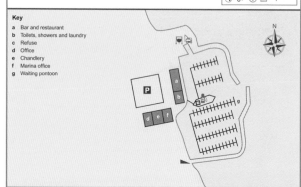

ARDGLASS MARINA

Ardglass Marina
19 Quay Street, Ardglass, BT30 7SA
Tel: 028 4484 2332
Email: infoardglassmarina@gmail.com
www.ardglassmarina.co.uk

VHF	Ch M, 80
ACCESS	H24

Situated just south of Strangford, Ardglass has the capacity to accommodate up to 22 yachts as well as space for small craft. Despite being relatively small in size, the marina boasts an extensive array of facilities, either on site or close at hand. Recent access improvements have been made for wheelchair users in the shower/WC and reception. Grocery stores, a post office, chemist and off-licence, are all within a five-minute walk from the marina. Among the local onshore activities are golf, mountain climbing in Newcastle, which is 18 miles south, as well as scenic walks at Ardglass and Delamont Park.

FACILITIES AT A GLANCE

Key
a   Administration building
b   Boat storage

Additional Facilities
Reception car park - 60 vehicles
Waste oil tanks
Local charts for Strangford Lough
Heavy duty battery charging
High pressure water washing
Internet and email access
Barbeque facilities
Car hire
Weather fax

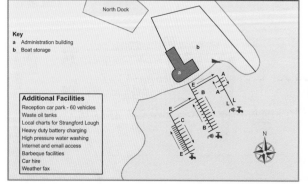

PORTAFERRY MARINA

Portaferry Marina
1 Mill View, Portaferry, BT22 1LQ
Mobile: 07703 209780 Fax: 028 4272 9784
Email: info@portaferrymarina.co.uk

VHF	Ch 80
ACCESS	H24

Portaferry Marina lies on the east shore of the Narrows, the gateway to Strangford Lough on the north east coast of Ireland. A marine nature reserve of outstanding natural beauty, the Lough offers plenty of recreational activities. The marina, which caters for draughts of up to 2.5m, is fairly small, accommodating around 30 yachts. The office is situated about 200m from the marina itself, where you will find ablution facilities along with a launderette.

Portaferry incorporates several pubs and restaurants as well as a few convenience stores, while one of its prime attractions is the Exploris Aquarium. Places of historic interest in the vicinity include Castleward, an 18th century mansion in Strangford, and Mount Stewart House & Garden in Newtownards.

FACILITIES AT A GLANCE

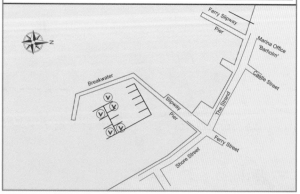

CHANNEL ISLANDS – Guernsey & Jersey

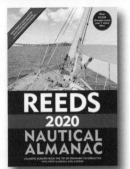
Key to Marina Plans symbols

Bottled gas		P	Parking
Chandler		✕	Pub/Restaurant
Disabled facilities		♁	Pump out
Electrical supply			Rigging service
Electrical repairs			Sail repairs
Engine repairs			Shipwright
First Aid			Shop/Supermarket
Fresh Water			Showers
Fuel - Diesel			Slipway
Fuel - Petrol		WC	Toilets
Hardstanding/boatyard			Telephone
Internet Café			Trolleys
Laundry facilities		V	Visitors berths
Lift-out facilities			Wi-Fi

Area 14 - Channel Islands

MARINAS
Telephone Numbers
VHF Channel
Access Times

ALDERNEY

Beaucette Marina
01481 245000
Ch 80 HW±3

GUERNSEY

HERM

SARK

St Peter Port
Victoria Marina
01481 725987
Ch 12, Ch 80 HW±2½

Maître Ile

N

JERSEY

St Helier Marina
01534 447730
Ch 14 HW±3

BEAUCETTE MARINA

Beaucette Marina
Vale, Guernsey, GY3 5BQ
Tel: 01481 245000 Fax: 01481 247071
Mobile: 07781 102302
Email: info@beaucettemarina.com

VHF Ch 80
ACCESS HW±3

Situated on the north east tip of Guernsey, Beaucette enjoys a peaceful, rural setting in contrast to the more vibrant atmosphere of Victoria Marina. Now owned by a private individual and offering a high standard of service, the site was originally formed from an old quarry.

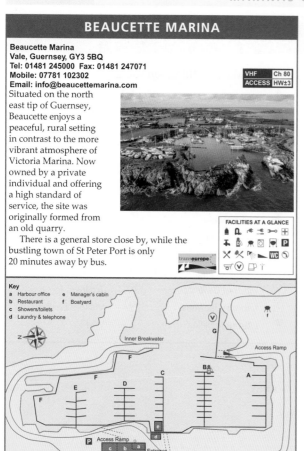

There is a general store close by, while the bustling town of St Peter Port is only 20 minutes away by bus.

transeurope

FACILITIES AT A GLANCE

Key
a Harbour office   e Manager's cabin
b Restaurant   f Boatyard
c Showers/toilets
d Laundry & telephone

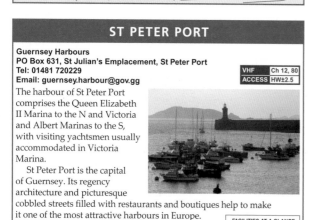

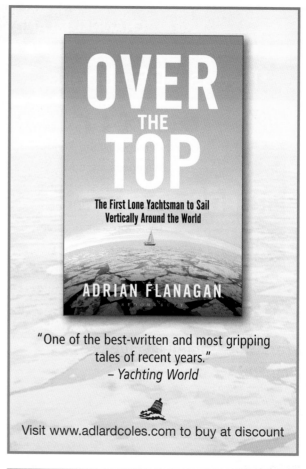
ST PETER PORT

Guernsey Harbours
PO Box 631, St Julian's Emplacement, St Peter Port
Tel: 01481 720229
Email: guernsey.harbour@gov.gg

VHF Ch 12, 80
ACCESS HW±2.5

The harbour of St Peter Port comprises the Queen Elizabeth II Marina to the N and Victoria and Albert Marinas to the S, with visiting yachtsmen usually accommodated in Victoria Marina.

St Peter Port is the capital of Guernsey. Its regency architecture and picturesque cobbled streets filled with restaurants and boutiques help to make it one of the most attractive harbours in Europe. Among the places of interest are Hauteville House, home of the writer Victor Hugo, and Castle Cornet. There are regular bus services to all parts of the island for visitors to explore a rich heritage.

FACILITIES AT A GLANCE

Key
a Customs shed
b Tourist Information
c Royal Channel Islands Yacht Club
d Toilets, showers, launderette,
   shops, pub and restaurant
e Guernsey Yacht Club
f Ferry terminal

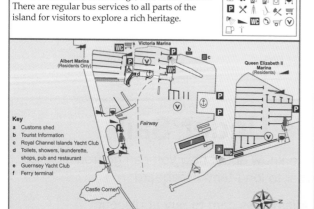

ST PETER PORT VICTORIA MARINA

Guernsey Harbours
PO Box 631, St Julian's Emplacement, St Peter Port
Tel: 01481 720229 Fax: 01481 714177
Email: guernsey.harbour@gov.gg

VHF Ch 80
ACCESS HW±2.5

Victoria Marina in St Peter Port accommodates some 300 visiting yachts. In the height of the season it gets extremely busy, but when full visitors can berth on 5 other pontoons in the Pool

or pre-arrange a berth in the QE II or Albert marinas. There are no visitor moorings in the Pool. Depending on draught, the marina is accessible approximately two and a half hours either side of HW, with yachts crossing over a sill drying to 4.2m. The marina dory will direct you to a berth on arrival or else will instruct you to moor on one of the waiting pontoons just outside.

Guernsey is well placed for exploring the rest of the Channel Islands and nearby French ports.

FACILITIES AT A GLANCE

Key
a Toilets, showers, launderette and shops
b Royal Channel Islands Yacht Club
c Refuse skip
d Marina control, port office
e Dinghy/tender landing pontoon
f Pub/restaurant
g Tourist information

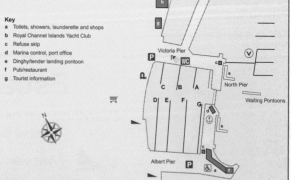

CRUISE AMONGST OVER 85
MEMBER MARINAS

Annual berth-holders based in TransEurope Marinas can benefit from a 50% visitor's berthing discount
for up to five days per year in each member marina using their TransEurope membership card.
For a current list of members and further information, please visit

www.transeuropemarinas.com

UK 🇬🇧

1. Bangor Marina
2. Rhu Marina
3. Troon Yacht Haven
4. Royal Quays Marina
5. Whitehaven Marina
6. Fleetwood Haven Marina
7. Liverpool Marina
8. Conwy Quays Marina
9. Neyland Yacht Haven
10. Penarth Quays Marina
11. Upton Marina
12. Portishead Quays Marina
13. Mylor Yacht Harbour
14. Mayflower Marina
15. Dart Marina
16. Poole Quay Boat Haven
17. Buckler's Hard Yacht Harbour
18. Town Quay Marina
19. Universal Marina
20. Cowes Yacht Haven
21. Royal Clarence Marina
22. Emsworth Yacht Harbour
23. Birdham Pool Marina
24. Dover Marina
25. Gillingham Marina
26. Fambridge Yacht Haven
27. Tollesbury Marina
28. Fox's Marina
29. Brundall Bay Marina
30. Hull Marina
31. Beaucette Marina

France 🇫🇷

1. Dunkerque
2. Saint Valery sur Somme
3. Saint Valery en Caux
4. Fécamp
5. Le Havre Plaisance
6. Dives-Cabourg-Houlgate
7. Ouistreham/Caen
8. Granville
9. Saint-Quay Port d'Armor
10. Perros-Guirec
11. Roscoff
12. Marinas de Brest
13. Douarnenez-Tréboul
14. Loctudy
15. Port la Forêt
16. Concarneau
17. Ports de Nantes
18. La Rochelle
19. Port Napoléon

Spain 🇪🇸

1. Puerto Deportivo Gijón
2. Marina Muros
3. Marina Combarro
4. Nauta Sanxenxo
5. Marina Davila Sport
6. Marina La Palma
7. Puerto Calero
8. Alcaidesa Marina
9. Pobla Marina
10. Port Ginesta

Netherlands 🇳🇱

1. Marina Den Oever
2. Jachthaven Waterland
3. Jachthaven Wetterwille
4. Marina Port Zélande
5. Jachthaven Biesbosch
6. Delta Marina Kortgene

Ireland 🇮🇪

1. Greystones Harbour Marina
2. Malahide Marina

Germany 🇩🇪

1. Sonwik Marina
2. Ancora Marina
3. Marina Boltenhagen
4. Marina Wiek auf Rügen
5. Baltic Sea Resort
6. Naturhafen Krummin
7. Lagunenstadt Ueckermünde

Portugal 🇵🇹

1. Douro Marina
2. Marina de Portimão
3. Quinta do Lorde Marina

Italy 🇮🇹

1. Porto Romano
2. Venezia Certosa Marina
3. Marina del Cavallino

Croatia 🇭🇷

1. Marina Punat

Belgium 🇧🇪

1. VNZ Blankenberge
2. VY Nieuwpoort

Greece 🇬🇷

1. Linariá Marina
2. Kos Marina

Morocco 🇲🇦

1. Marina de Saïdia

#DYK... Did you know?

Normans AUTO MARINE supply a wide range of products for all your boating & fishing needs.

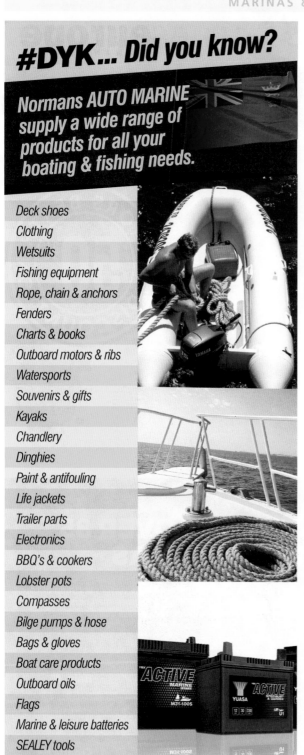

- Deck shoes
- Clothing
- Wetsuits
- Fishing equipment
- Rope, chain & anchors
- Fenders
- Charts & books
- Outboard motors & ribs
- Watersports
- Souvenirs & gifts
- Kayaks
- Chandlery
- Dinghies
- Paint & antifouling
- Life jackets
- Trailer parts
- Electronics
- BBQ's & cookers
- Lobster pots
- Compasses
- Bilge pumps & hose
- Bags & gloves
- Boat care products
- Outboard oils
- Flags
- Marine & leisure batteries
- SEALEY tools
- ...and lots more!

WHERE TO FIND US AT COMMERCIAL BUILDINGS

HEAVY BUILDING MATERIALS	HIRE	BUILDING CENTRE	HEAD OFFICE	TIMBER	AUTO MARINE	TRADE CENTRE

AUTO MARINE
Commercial Buildings
tel 01534 883377
www.normans.je

eco active

Normans *Est. Jersey 1840*

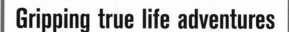

SECTION 2
MARINE SUPPLIES AND SERVICES GUIDE

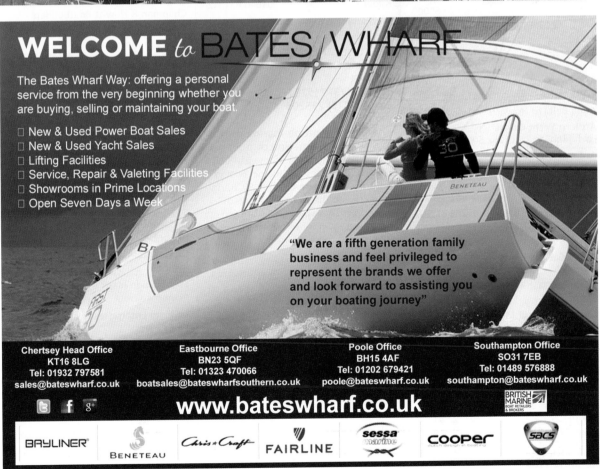

WELCOME *to* BATES WHARF

The Bates Wharf Way: offering a personal service from the very beginning whether you are buying, selling or maintaining your boat.

- New & Used Power Boat Sales
- New & Used Yacht Sales
- Lifting Facilities
- Service, Repair & Valeting Facilities
- Showrooms in Prime Locations
- Open Seven Days a Week

"We are a fifth generation family business and feel privileged to represent the brands we offer and look forward to assisting you on your boating journey"

Chertsey Head Office
KT16 8LG
Tel: 01932 797581
sales@bateswharf.co.uk

Eastbourne Office
BN23 5QF
Tel: 01323 470066
boatsales@bateswharfsouthern.co.uk

Poole Office
BH15 4AF
Tel: 01202 679421
poole@bateswharf.co.uk

Southampton Office
SO31 7EB
Tel: 01489 576888
southampton@bateswharf.co.uk

BRITISH MARINE
BOAT RETAILERS & BROKERS

www.bateswharf.co.uk

BAYLINER   BENETEAU   Chris·Craft   FAIRLINE   sessa marine   cooper   sacs

ADHESIVES

Casco Adhesives
Darwen — 07710 546899

CC Marine Services Ltd
West Mersea — 07751 734510

Industrial Self Adhesives Ltd
Nottingham — 0115 9681895

Sika Ltd Garden City — 01707 394444

Technix Rubber & Plastics Ltd
Southampton — 01489 789944

Tiflex Liskeard — 01579 320808

Trade Grade Products Ltd
Poole — 01202 820177

UK Epoxy Resins
Burscough — 01704 892364

Wessex Resins & Adhesives Ltd
Romsey — 01794 521111

3M United Kingdom plc
Bracknell — 01344 858315

ASSOCIATIONS/ AGENCIES

Cruising Association
London — 020 7537 2828

Fishermans Mutual Association (Eyemouth) Ltd
Eyemouth — 01890 750373

Maritime and Coastguard Agency
Southampton — 0870 6006505

Royal Institute of Navigation
London — 020 7591 3130

Royal National Lifeboat Institution
Poole — 01202 663000

Royal Yachting Association (RYA) Southampton — 0845 345 0400

BERTHS & MOORINGS

ABC Powermarine
Beaumaris — 01248 811413

Aqua Bell Ltd Norwich — 01603 713013

Ardfern Yacht Centre
Lochgilphead — 01852 500247/500636

Ardmair Boat Centre
Ullapool — 01854 612054

Arisaig Marine Ltd
Inverness-shire — 01687 450224

Bristol Boat Ltd Bristol — 01225 872032

British Waterways
Argyll — 01546 603210

Burgh Castle Marine
Norfolk — 01493 780331

Cambrian Marine Services Ltd
Cardiff — 029 2034 3459

Chelsea Harbour Ltd
London — 020 7225 9108

Clapson & Son (Shipbuilders) Ltd
Barton-on-Humber — 01652 635620

Crinan Boatyard, Crinan 01546 830232

Dartside Quay Brixham 01803 845445

Douglas Marine
Preston — 01772 812462

Dublin City Moorings
Dublin — +353 1 8183300

Emsworth Yacht Harbour
Emsworth — 01243 377727

Exeter Ship Canal — 01392 274306

HAFAN PWLLHELI
Glan Don, Pwllheli, Gwynedd LL53 5YT
Tel: (01758) 701219
Fax: (01758) 701443 VHF Ch80
Hafan Pwllheli has over 400 pontoon berths and offers access at virtually all states of the tide. Ashore, its modern purpose-built facilities include luxury toilets, showers, launderette, a secure boat park for winter storage, 40-ton travel hoist, mobile crane and plenty of space for car parking. Open 24-hours a day, 7 days a week.

Highway Marine
Sandwich — 01304 613925

Iron Wharf Boatyard
Faversham — 01795 536296

Jalsea Marine Services Ltd
Northwich — 01606 77870

Jersey Harbours
St Helier — 01534 447788

Jones (Boatbuilders), David
Chester — 01244 390363

Lawrenny Yacht Station
Kilgetty — 01646 651212

MacFarlane & Son
Glasgow — 01360 870214

NEPTUNE MARINA LTD
Neptune Quay, Ipswich, Suffolk IP4 1AX
Tel: (01473) 215204
Fax: (01473) 215206
e-mail:
enquiries@neptune-marina.com
www.neptune-marina.com
The quay to the heart of Ipswich! Call Ipswich lock gates on Channel 68 and Neptune Marina on Channel 80. Bring your crew to the wonderful Ipswich waterfront, with plenty of watering holes and town centre activities. You won't want to leave!

Orkney Marinas Ltd
Kirkwall — 07810 465835

V Marine
Shoreham-by-Sea — 01273 461491

Sutton Harbour Marina
Plymouth — 01752 204186

WicorMarine Fareham — 01329 237112

Winters Marine Ltd
Salcombe — 01548 843580

Yarmouth Marine Service
Yarmouth — 01983 760521

Youngboats
Faversham — 01795 536176

BOAT BUILDERS & REPAIRS

ABC Hayling Island — 023 9246 1968

ABC Powermarine
Beaumaris — 01248 811413

Advance Yacht Systems
Southampton — 023 8033 7722

Aqua-Star Ltd
St Sampsons — 01481 244550

Ardoran Marine
Oban — 01631 566123

Baumbach Bros Boatbuilders
Hayle — 01736 753228

Beacon Boatyard
Rochester — 01634 841320

Bedwell & Co
Walton on the Naze — 01255 675873

Blackwell, Craig
Co Meath — +353 87 677 9605

Boyd Boat Building
Falmouth — 07885 436722

Boatcraft
Ardrossan — 01294 603047

B+ St Peter Port — 01481 726071

Brennan, John
Dun Laoghaire — +353 1 280 5308

Burghead Boat Centre
Findhorn — 01309 690099

Carrick Marine Projects
Co Antrim — 02893 355884

Chapman & Hewitt Boatbuilders
Wadebridge — 01208 813487

Chicks Marine Ltd
Guernsey — 01481 723716

Clarence Boatyard
East Cowes — 01983 294243

Cooks Maritime Craftsmen - Poliglow
Lymington — 01590 675521

Creekside Boatyard (Old Mill Creek)
Dartmouth — 01803 832649

CTC Marine & Leisure
Middlesbrough — 01642 372600

Davies Marine Services
Ramsgate — 01843 586172

Dickie International
Bangor — 01248 363400

Dickie International
Pwllheli — 01758 701828

East Llanion Marine Ltd
Pembroke Dock — 01646 686866

Emblem Enterprises
East Cowes — 01983 294243

Fairlie Quay
Fairlie — 01475 568267

Fairweather Marine
Fareham — 01329 283500

Farrow & Chambers Yacht Builders
Humberston
www.farrowandchambers.co.uk

Fast Tack Plymouth — 01752 255171

Fergulsea Engineering
Ayr 01292 262978

Ferrypoint Boat Co
Youghal +353 24 94232

Floetree Ltd (Loch Lomond Marina)
Balloch 01389 752069

Freshwater Boatyard
Truro 01326 270443

Frogmore Boatyard
Kingsbridge 01548 531257

Furniss Boat Building
Falmouth 01326 311766

Gallichan Marine Ltd
Jersey 01534 746387

Garvel Clyde
Greenock 01475 725372

Goodchild Marine Services
Great Yarmouth 01493 782301

Gosport Boatyard
Gosport 023 9252 6534

Gweek Quay Boatyard
Helston 01326 221657

Halls
Walton on the Naze 01255 675596

Harris Pye Marine
Barry 01446 720066

Haven Boatyard
Lymington 01590 677073

Hayling Yacht Company
Hayling Island 023 9246 3592

Hoare Ltd, Bob
Poole 01202 736704

Holyhead Boatyard
Holyhead 01407 760111

Jackson Marine
Lowestoft 01502 539772

Jackson Yacht Services
Jersey 01534 743819

JEP Marine
Canterbury 01227 710102

JWS Marine Services
Southsea 023 9275 5155

Kimelford Yacht Haven
Oban 01852 200248

Kingfisher Marine
Weymouth 01305 766595

Kingfisher Ultraclean UK Ltd
Tarporley 0800 085 7039

King's Boatyard
Pin Mill 01473 780258

Kinsale Boatyard
Kinsale +353 21477 4774

Kippford Slipway Ltd
Dalbeattie 01556 620249

Lawrenny Yacht Station
Lawrenny 01646 651212

Lencraft Boats Ltd
Dungarvan +353 58 682220

Mackay Boatbuilders
Arbroath 01241 872879

Marine Blast
Holy Loch 01369 705394

Marine Services
Norwich 01692 582239

Mashford Brothers
Torpoint 01752 822232

Mayor & Co Ltd, J
Preston 01772 812250

Mears, HJ Axmouth 01297 23344

Mill, Dan, Galway +353 86 337 9304

Miller Marine
Tyne & Wear 01207 542149

Morrison, A
Killyleagh 028 44828215

Moss (Boatbuilders), David
Thornton-Cleveleys 01253 893830

Multi Marine Composites Ltd
Torpoint 01752 823513

Newing, Roy E
Canterbury 01227 860345

Noble and Sons, Alexander
Girvan 01465 712223

Northney Marine Services
Hayling Island 023 9246 9246

Northshore Sport & Leisure
King's Lynn 01485 210236

O'Sullivans Marine Ltd
Tralee +353 66 7124957

Pachol, Terry
Brighton 01273 682724

Partington Marine Ltd, William
Pwllheli 01758 612808

Pasco's Boatyard
Truro 01326 270269

Penrhos Marine
Aberdovey 01654 767478

Penzance Marine Services
Penzance 01736 361081

PJ Bespoke Boat Fitters Ltd
Crewe 01270 812244

Preston Marine Services Ltd
Preston 01772 733595

Red Bay Boats Ltd
Cushendall 028 2177 1331

Reliance Marine
Wirral 0151 625 5219

Retreat Boatyard Ltd
Exeter 01392 874720/875934

Richardson Boatbuilders, Ian
Stromness 01856 850321

Richardson Yacht Services Ltd
Newport 01983 821095

Roberts Marine Ltd, S
Liverpool 0151 707 8300

Rothman Pantall & Co
Fareham 01329 280221

Rustler Yachts
Falmouth 01326 310210

Salterns Boatyard
Poole 01202 707391

Sea & Shore Ship Chandler
Dundee 01382 450666

Seamark-Nunn & Co
Felixstowe 01394 275327

Seapower
Woolverstone 01473 780090

Slipway Cooperative Ltd
Bristol 0117 907 9938

Small, Donal
Galway +353 83 1831057

Smith, GB, & Sons
Rock 01208 862815

Spicer Boatbuilder, Nick
Weymouth Marina 01305 767118

Storrar Marine Store
Newcastle upon Tyne 0191 266 1037

TT Marine Ashwell 01462 742449

Waterfront Marine
Bangor 01248 352513

Way, A&R, Boat Building
Tarbert, Loch Fyne 01546 606657

WestCoast Marine
Troon 01292 318121

Western Marine
Dublin +353 1 280 0321

Wigmore Wright Marine Services
Penarth 029 2070 9983

Williams, Peter
Fowey 01726 870987

WQI Ltd
Bournemouth 01202 771292

Yarmouth Marine Service
01983 760521

Youngboats
Faversham 01795 536176

BOATYARD SERVICES & SUPPLIES

ABC Marine
Hayling Island 023 9246 1968

Abersoch Boatyard Services Ltd
Abersoch 01758 713900

Amble Boat Co Ltd
Amble 01665 710267

Amsbrisbeg Ltd
Port Bannatyne 01700 831215

Ardmair Boat Centre
Ullapool 01854 612054

Ardmaleish Boat Building Co Rothesay
01700 502007

www.ardoran.co.uk
W coast Scotland. All marine facilities.

Ardrishaig Boatyard Lochgilphead 01546 603280	**Coates Marine Ltd** Whitby 01947 604486	**Goodchild Marine Services** Great Yarmouth 01493 782301
Arklow Slipway Arklow +353 402 33233	**Connor, Richard** Coleraine 07712 115751	**Gosport Boatyard** Gosport 023 9252 6534
Baltic Wharf Boatyard Totnes 01803 867922	**Coombes, AA** Bembridge 01983 872296	**Gweek Quay Boatyard** Helston 01326 221657
Baltimore Boatyard Baltimore +353 28 20444	**Corpach Boatbuilding Company** Fort William 01397 772861	**Haines Boatyard** Chichester 01243 512228
Bates, Declan Kilmore Quay +353 87 252 9936	**Craobh Marina** By Lochgilphead 01852 500222	**Harbour Marine** Plymouth 01752 204691
Bedwell and Co Walton-on-the-Naze 01255 675873	**Creekside Boatyard (Old Mill Creek)** Dartmouth 01803 832649	**Harbour Marine Services Ltd** Southwold 01502 724721
Berthon Boat Co Lymington 01590 673312	**Crinan Boatyard** By Lochgilphead 01546 830232	**Harris Pye Marine** Barry 01446 720066
Birdham Shipyard Chichester 01243 512310	**Crosshaven Boatyard Co Ltd** Crosshaven +353 21 831161	**Hartlepool Marine Engineering** Hartlepool 01429 867883
BJ Marine Ltd Bangor 028 91271434	**Dale Sailing Co Ltd** Neyland 01646 603110	**Hayles, Harold** Yarmouth, IoW 01983 760373
Blagdon, A Plymouth 01752 561830	**Darthaven Marina** Kingswear 01803 752242	**Henderson, J** Shiskine 01770 860259
Boatcraft Ardrossan 01294 603047	**Dartside Quay** Brixham 01803 845445	**Heron Marine** Whitstable 01227 361255
Boatworks + Ltd St Peter Port 01481 726071	**Dauntless Boatyard Ltd** Canvey Island 01268 793782	**Hewitt, George** Binham 01328 830078
Brennan, John Dun Laoghaire +353 1 280 5308	**Davis's Boatyard** Poole 01202 674349	**Holyhead Marina & Trinity Marine Ltd** Holyhead 01407 764242
Brighton Marina Boatyard Brighton 01273 819919	**Dinas Boat Yard Ltd** Y Felinheli 01248 671642	**Instow Marine Services** Bideford 01271 861081
Bristol Marina (Yard) Bristol 0117 921 3198	**Dorset Yachts** Poole 01202 674531	**Ipswich Haven Marina** Ipswich 01473 236644
Buckie Shipyard Ltd Buckie 01542 831245	**Douglas Boatyard** Preston 01772 812462	**Iron Wharf Boatyard** Faversham 01795 536296
Bucklers Hard Boat Builders Ltd Brockenhurst 01590 616214	**Dover Yacht Co** Dover 01304 201073	**Island Boat Services** Port of St Mary 01624 832073
C & J Marine Services Newcastle Upon Tyne 0191 295 0072	**Dun Laoghaire Marina** Dun Laoghaire +353 1 2020040	**Isle of Skye Yachts** Ardvasar 01471 844216
Caley Marina Inverness 01463 236539	**Elephant Boatyard** Southampton 023 8040 3268	**Jalsea Marine Services Ltd** Weaver Shipyard, Northwich 01606 77870
Cambrian Boat Centre Swansea 01792 655925	**Elton Boatbuilding Ltd** Kirkcudbright 01557 330177	**JBS Group** Peterhead 01779 475395
Cambrian Marine Services Ltd Cardiff 029 2034 3459	**Felixstowe Ferry Boatyard** Felixstowe 01394 282173	**J B Timber Ltd** North Ferriby 01482 631765
Cantell and Son Ltd Newhaven 01273 514118	**Ferguson Engineering** Wexford +353 6568 66822133	**Jersey Harbours Dept** St Helier 01534 885588
Canvey Yacht Builders Ltd Canvey Island 01268 696094	**Ferry Marine South** Queensferry 0131 331 1233	**Kilnsale Boatyard** Kinsale +353 21 4774774
Carroll's Ballyhack Boatyard New Ross +353 51 389164	**Findhorn Boatyard** Findhorn 01309 690099	**Kingfisher Ultraclean UK Ltd** Tarporley 01928 787878
Castlepoint Boatyard Crosshaven +353 21 4832154	**Firmhelm Ltd** Pwllheli 01758 612251	**Kilrush Marina Boatyard** Kilrush +35 87 7990091
Chabot, Gary Newhaven 07702 006767	**Fowey Boatyard** Fowey 01726 832194	**Kinsale Boatyard** +353 21477 4774
Chapman & Hewitt Boatbuilders Wadebridge 01208 813487	**Fox's Marina** Ipswich 01473 689111	**KPB** Beaucette 07781 152581
Chippendale Craft Rye 01797 227707	**Frank Halls & Son** Walton on the Naze 01255 675596	**Lake Yard** Poole 01202 674531
Clapson & Son (Shipbuilders) Ltd Barton on Humber 01652 635620	**Freeport Marine** Jersey 01534 888100	**Lallow, C** Isle of Wight 01983 292112
Clarence Boatyard East Cowes 01983 294243	**Furniss Boat Building** Falmouth 01326 311766	**Latham's Boatyard** Poole 01202 748029
Coastal Marine Boatbuilders Eyemouth 01890 750328	**Garval Clyde** Greenock 01475 725372	**Laxey Towing** Douglas, Isle of Man 07624 493592
Coastcraft Ltd Cockenzie 01875 812150		**Leonard Marine, Peter** Newhaven 01273 515987
		Lincombe Marine Salcombe 01548 843580

Lomax Boatbuilders
Cliffony +353 71 66124

Lymington Yt Haven 01590 677071

MacDougalls Marine Services
Isle of Mull 01681 700294

Macduff Shipyard Ltd
Macduff 01261 832234

Madog Boatyard
Porthmadog 01766 514205/513435

Mainbrayce Marine
Alderney 01481 822772

Malakoff and Moore
Lerwick 01595 695544

Mallaig Boat Building and Engineering
Mallaig 01687 462304

Maramarine
Helensburgh 01436 810971

Marindus Engineering
Kilmore Quay +353 53 29794

Mariners Farm Boatyard
Gillingham 01634 233179

McGruar and Co Ltd
Helensburgh 01436 831313

Mevagh Boatyard
Mulroy Bay +353 74 915 4470

Mill, Dan, Galway +353 86 337 9304

Mitchell's Boatyard
Poole 01202 747857

Mooney Boats
Killybegs +353 73 31152/31388

Moore & Son, J
St Austell 01726 842964

Morrison, A Killyleagh 028 44828215

Moss (Boatbuilders), David
Thornton-Cleveleys 01253 893830

Mustang Marine
Milford Haven 01646 696320

New Horizons Rhu 01436 821555

Noble and Sons, Alexander
Girvan 01465 712223

North Pier (Oban)
Oban 01631 562892

North Wales Boat Centre
Conwy 01492 580740

Northam Marine
Brightlingsea 01206 302003

Northshore Yacht Yard
Chichester 01243 512611

Oban Yachts and Marine Services
By Oban 01631 565333

Pearn and Co, Norman
Looe 01503 262244

Penrhos Marine
Aberdovey 01654 767478

**Penzance Dry Dock and Engineering
Co Ltd** Penzance 01736 363838

Philip & Son Dartmouth 01803 833351

Phillips, HJ Rye 01797 223234

Ponsharden Boatyard
Penryn 01326 372215

Powersail and Island Chandlers Ltd
East Cowes Marina 01983 299800

Priors Boatyard
Burnham-on-Crouch 01621 782160

R K Marine Ltd
Swanwick 01489 583572

Rat Island Sailboat Company (Yard) St
Mary's 01720 423399

Rennison, Russell
Gosport 07734 688819

Retreat Boatyard Ltd
Exeter 01392 874720/875934

Rice and Cole Ltd
Burnham-on-Crouch 01621 782063

Richardson Boatbuilders, Ian Stromness
01856 850321

Richardsons Boatbuilders
Binfield 01983 821095

Riverside Yard
Shoreham Beach 01273 592456

River Yar Boatyard
Yarmouth, IoW 01983 761000

Robertsons Boatyard
Woodbridge 01394 382305

Rossbrin Boatyard
Schull +353 28 37352

Rossiter Yachts Ltd
Christchurch 01202 483250

Rossreagh Boatyard
Rathmullan +353 74 9150182

Rudders Boatyard & Moorings
Milford Haven 01646 600288

Ryan & Roberts Marine Services
Askeaton +353 61 392198

Rye Harbour Marina Rye
01797 227667

Rynn Engineering, Pat
Galway +353 91 562568

Salterns Boatyard
Poole 01202 707391

Sandbanks Yacht Company
Poole 01202 611262

Scarborough Marine Engineering Ltd
Scarborough 01723 375199

Severn Valley Cruisers Ltd (Boatyard)
Stourport-on-Severn 01299 871165

Shepards Wharf Boatyard Ltd
Cowes 01983 297821

Shipshape
King's Lynn 01553 764058

Shotley Marina Ltd
Ipswich 01473 788982

Shotley Marine Services Ltd
Ipswich 01473 788913

Silvers Marina Ltd
Helensburgh 01436 831222

Skinners Boat Yard
Baltimore +353 28 20114

Smith, GB, & Sons
Rock 01208 862815

Smith & Gibbs
Eastbourne 07802 582009

Sparkes Boatyard
Hayling Island 023 92463572

Spencer Sailing Services, Jim
Brightlingsea 01206 302911

Standard House Boatyard
Wells-next-the-Sea 01328 710593

Storrar Marine Store
Newcastle upon Tyne 0191 266 1037

Strand Shipyard Rye 01797 222070

Surry Boatyard
Shoreham-by-Sea 01273 461491

The Shipyard
Littlehampton 01903 713327

Titchmarsh Marina
Walton-on-the-Naze 01255 672185

Tollesbury Marina
Tollesbury 01621 869202

T J Rigging Conwy 07780 972411

Toms and Son Ltd, C
Fowey 01726 870232

Tony's Marine Service
Coleraine 028 7035 6422

Torquay Marina
Torquay 01803 200210

Trinity Marine & Holyhead Marina
Holyhead 01407 763855

Trouts Boatyard (River Exe)
Topsham 01392 873044

Upson and Co, RF
Aldeburgh 01728 453047

Versatility Workboats
Rye 01797 224422

Weir Quay Boatyard
Bere Alston 01822 840474

West Solent Boatbuilders
Lymington 01590 642080

WicorMarine Fareham 01329 237112

Woodrolfe Boatyard
Maldon 01621 869202

Yarmouth Marine Services
Yarmouth, IoW 01983 760521

BOAT DELIVERIES & STORAGE

ABC Marine
Hayling Island 023 9246 1968

Abersoch Boatyard Services Ltd
Pwllheli 01758 713900

Ambrisbeg Ltd
Port Bannatyne 01700 502719

Arisaig Marine
Inverness-shire 01687 450224

Bedwell and Co
Walton-on-the-Naze 01255 675873

Berthon Boat Company
Lymington 01590 673312

Boat Shifters
07733 344018/01326 210548

C & J Marine Services
Newcastle upon Tyne 0191 295 0072

Caley Marine
Inverness 01463 233437

Carrick Marine Projects
Co Antrim   02893 355884

Challenger Marine
Penryn   01326 377222

Coates Marine Ltd
Whitby   01947 604486

Convoi Exceptionnel Ltd
Hamble   023 8045 3045

Creekside Boatyard (Old Mill Creek) Dartmouth   01803 832649

Crinan Boatyard Ltd
Crinan   01546 830232

Dale Sailing Co Ltd
Neyland   01646 603110

Dart Marina Ltd
Dartmouth   01803 833351

Dartside Quay
Brixham   01803 845445

Dauntless Boatyard Ltd
Canvey Island   01268 793782

Debbage Yachting
Ipswich   01473 601169

Douglas Marine
Preston   01772 812462

East & Co, Robin
Kingsbridge   01548 531257

East Coast Offshore Yachting
                                  01480 861381

Emsworth Yacht Harbour
Emsworth   01243 377727

Exeter Ship Canal   01392 274306

Exmouth Marina   01395 269314

Firmhelm Ltd Pwllheli   01758 612244

Forrest Marine Ltd
Exeter   08452 308335

Fowey Boatyard
Fowey   01726 832194

Freshwater Boatyard
Truro   01326 270443

Hafan Pwllheli Pwllheli   01758 701219

Houghton Boat Transport
Tewkesbury   07831 486710

Gweek Quay Boatyard
Helston   01326 221657

Iron Wharf Boatyard
Faversham   01795 536296

Jalsea Marine Services Ltd
Northwich   01606 77870

KG McColl Oban   01852 200248

Latham's Boatyard
Poole   01202 748029

Lincombe Boat Yard
Salcombe   01548 843580

Marine Blast
Holy Loch   01369 705394

Marine Resource Centre Ltd
Oban   01631 720291

Marine & General Engineers
Guernsey   01481 245808

Milford Marina
Milford Haven   01646 696312/3

Moonfleet Sailing
Poole   01202 682269

Southerly Chichester   01243 512611

Pasco's Boatyard
Truro   01326 270269

Pearn and Co, Norman
Looe   01503 262244

Performance Yachting
Plymouth   01752 565023

Peters & May Ltd
Southampton   023 8048 0480

Ponsharden Boatyard
Penryn   01326 372215

Portsmouth Marine Engineering
Fareham   01329 232854

Priors Boatyard
Burnham-on-Crouch   01621 782160

Reeder School of Seamanship, Mike
Lymington   01590 674560

Rossiter Yachts
Christchurch   01202 483250

Sealand Boat Deliveries Ltd
Liverpool   01254 705225

Shearwater Sailing
Southampton   01962 775213

Shepards Wharf Boatyard Cowes Harbour Commission
Cowes   01983 297821

Silvers Marina Ltd
Helensburgh   01436 831222

Southcoasting Navigators
Devon   01626 335626

Waterfront Marine
Bangor   01248 352513

West Country Boat Transport
                                  01566 785651

WicorMarine
Fareham   01329 237112

Winters Marine Ltd
Salcombe   01548 843580

Wolff, David   07659 550131 **Yacht Solutions Ltd**
Portsmouth   023 9275 5155

Yarmouth Marine Service
Yarmouth, IoW   01983 760521

Youngboats
Faversham   01795 536176

BOOKS, CHARTS & PUBLISHERS

Adlard Coles Nautical
London   020 7631 5600

Brown Son & Ferguson Ltd
Glasgow   0141 429 1234

Cooke & Son Ltd, B Hull   01482 223454

Dubois Phillips & McCallum Ltd
Liverpool   0151 236 2776

Imray, Laurie, Norie & Wilson
Huntingdon   01480 462114

Kelvin Hughes
Southampton   023 8063 4911

Lilley & Gillie Ltd, John 0191 257 2217

Marine Chart Services
Wellingborough   01933 441629

Price & Co Ltd, WF
Bristol   0117 929 2229

QPC
Fareham   01329 287880

Stanford Charts
Bristol   0117 929 9966

Stanford Charts
London   020 7836 1321

Stanford Charts   0845 880 3730
Manchester   0870 890 3730

Wiley Nautical
Chichester   01243 779777

BOW THRUSTERS

ARS Anglian Diesels Ltd
Wakefield   01924 332492

Buckler's Hard Boat Builders Ltd
Beaulieu   01590 616214

JS Mouldings International
Bursledon   023 8063 4400

BREAKDOWN

BJ Marine Ltd
Bangor, Ireland   028 9127 1434

Seastart
National   0800 885500

CHANDLERS

ABC Powermarine
Beaumaris   01248 811413

Admiral Marine Supplies
Bootle   01469 575909

Allgadgets.co.uk
Exmouth   01395 227727

Alpine Room & Yacht Equipment
Chelmsford   01245 223563

Aquatogs Cowes   01983 295071

Arbroath Fishermen's Association
Arbroath   01241 873132

Ardfern Yacht Centre Ltd
Argyll   01852 500247

Ardoran Marine
Oban   01631 566123

Arthurs Chandlery
Gosport   023 9252 6522

Arun Canvas and Rigging Ltd
Littlehampton   01903 732561

Aruncraft Chandlers
Littlehampton   01903 713327

ASAP Supplies – Equipment & Spares Worldwide
Beccles   0845 1300870

Auto Marine
Southsea   02392 825601

Bayside Marine
Brixham   01803 856771

Bedwell and Co
Walton on the Naze   01255 675873

BJ Marine Ltd Bangor   028 9127 1434

Bluecastle Chandlers
Portland   01305 822298

Blue Water Marine Ltd
Pwllheli   01758 614600

Boatacs
Westcliffe on Sea   01702 475057

Boathouse, The
Penryn   01326 374177

Boston Marina   01205 364420

Bosun's Locker, The
Falmouth   01326 312212

Bosun's Locker, The
Ramsgate   01843 597158

Bosuns Locker, The
South Queensferry 0131 331 3875/4496

B+ St Peter Port   01481 726071

Bridger Marine, John
Exeter   01392 250970

Bristol Boat Ltd Bristol   01225 872032

Brixham Yacht Supplies Ltd
Brixham   01803 882290

Brunel Chandlery Ltd
Neyland   01646 601667

Buccaneer Ltd
Macduff   01261 835199

Bucklers Hard Boat Builders
Beaulieu   01590 616214

Burghead Boat Centre
Findhorn   01309 690099

Bussell & Co, WL
Weymouth   01305 785633

Buzzard Marine
Yarmouth   01983 760707

C & M Marine
Bridlington   01262 672212

Cabin Yacht Stores
Rochester   01634 718020

Caley Marina Inverness   01463 236539

Cambrian Boat Centre
Swansea   01792 655925

Cantell & Son Ltd
Newhaven   01273 514118

Captain Watts Plymouth 01752 927067

Carne (Sales) Ltd, David
Penryn   01326 374177

Carrickcraft
Malahide   +353 1 845 5438

Caters Carrick Ltd
Carrickfergus   028 93351919

CH Marine (Cork)   +353 21 4315700

CH Marine Skibbereen   +353 28 23190

Charity & Taylor Ltd
Lowestoft   01502 581529

Chertsey Marine Ltd
Penton Hook Marina   01932 565195

Chicks Marine Ltd
Guernsey   01481 740771

Christchurch Boat Shop
Christchurch   01202 482751

Clancy Hardware
Kilrush   +35 65 905 1085

Clapson & Son (Shipbuilders) Ltd South
Ferriby Marina   01652 635620

Clarke, Albert, Marine
Newtownards   028 9187 2325

Clyde Chandlers
Ardrossan   01294 607077

CMC Campbeltown   01586 551441

Coastal Marine Boatbuilders Ltd
(Dunbar) Eyemouth   01890 750328

Coates Marine Ltd
Whitby   01947 604486

Collins Marine St Helier   01534 732415

Compass Marine
Lancing   01903 761773

Cosalt International Ltd
Aberdeen   01224 588327

Cosalt International Ltd
Southampton   023 8063 2824

Cotter, Kieran
Baltimore   +353 28 20106

Cox Yacht Charter Ltd, Nick
Lymington   01590 673489

C Q Chandlers Ltd
Poole   01202 682095

Crinan Boats Ltd
Lochgilphead   01546 830232

CTC Marine & Leisure
Middlesbrough   01642 372600

Dale Sailing Co Ltd
Milford Haven   01646 603110

Danson Marine
Sidcup   0208 304 5678

Dartmouth Chandlery
Dartmouth   01803 839292

Dartside Quay
Brixham   01803 845445

Dauntless Boatyard Ltd
Canvey Island   01268 793782

Davis's Yacht Chandler
Littlehampton   01903 722778

Denney & Son, EL
Redcar   01642 483507

Deva Marine Conwy   01492 572777

Dickie & Sons Ltd, AM
Bangor   01248 363400

Dickie & Sons Ltd, AM
Pwllheli   01758 701828

Dinghy Supplies Ltd/Sutton Marine Ltd
Sutton   +353 1 832 2312

Diverse Yacht Services
Hamble   023 80453399

Dixon Chandlery, Peter
Exmouth   01395 273248

Doling & Son, GW
Barrow In Furness   01229 823708

Dovey Marine
Aberdovey   01654 767581

Down Marine Co Ltd
Belfast   028 9048 0247

Douglas Marine Preston 01772 812462

Dubois Phillips & McCallum Ltd
Liverpool   0151 236 2776

Duncan Ltd, JS Wick   01955 602689

Duncan Yacht Chandlers
Ely   01353 663095

East Anglian Sea School
Ipswich   01473 659992

Eccles Marine Co
Middlesbrough   01642 372600

Ely Boat Chandlers
Hayling Island   023 9246 1968

Emsworth Chandlery
Emsworth   01243 375500

Force 4 Chandlery
Stroud   0845 1300710

Exe Leisure Exeter   01392 879055

Express Marine Services
Chichester   01243 773788

Fairways Chandlery
Burnham-on-Crouch   01621 782659

Fairweather Marine
Fareham   01329 283500

Fal Chandlers
Falmouth Marina   01326 212411

Ferrypoint Boat Co
Youghal   +353 24 94232

Findhorn Marina & Boatyard
Findhorn   01309 690099

Firmhelm Ltd P
wllheli   01758 612244

Fisherman's Mutual Asssociation
(Eyemouth) Ltd
Eyemouth   01890 750373

Floetree Ltd (Loch Lomond Marina)
Balloch   01389 752069

Force 4 (Deacons)
Bursledon   023 8040 2182

Force 4 Chichester   01243 773788

Force 4 Chandlery
Mail order   0845 1300710

Force 4 Chandlery
Plymouth   01752 252489

Force 4 (Hamble Point)
Southampton   023 80455 058

Force 4 (Mercury)
Southampton   023 8045 4849

Force 4 (Port Hamble)
Southampton   023 8045 4858

Force 4 (Shamrock)
Southampton   023 8063 2725

Force 4 (Swanwick)
Swanwick   01489 881825

Freeport Marine
Jersey   01534 888100

French Marine Motors Ltd
Brightlingsea   01206 302133

Furneaux Riddall & Co Ltd
Portsmouth   023 9266 8621

Gael Force Glasgow	0141 941 1211	
Gael Force Stornoway	01851 705540	
Gallichan Marine Ltd Jersey	01534 746387	
Galway Maritime Galway	+353 91 566568	
GB Attfield & Company Dursley	01453 547185	
Gibbons Ship Chandlers Ltd Sunderland	0191 567 2101	
Goodwick Marine Fishguard	01348 873955	
Gorleston Marine Ltd Great Yarmouth	01493 661883	
GP Barnes Ltd Shoreham	01273 591705/596680	
Great Outdoors Clarenbridge, Galway	+353 87 2793821	
Green Marine, Jimmy Fore St Beer	01297 20744	
Grimsby Rigging Services Ltd Grimsby	01472 362758	
Gunn Navigation Services, Thomas Aberdeen	01224 595045	
Hale Marine, Ron Portsmouth	023 92732985	
Harbour Marine Services Ltd (HMS) Southwold	01502 724721	
Hardware & Marine Supplies Wexford	+353 53 29791	
Hartlepool Marine Supplies Hartlepool	01429 862932	
Harwoods Yarmouth	01983 760258	
Hawkins Marine Shipstores, John Rochester	01634 840812	
Hayles, Harold Yarmouth	01983 760373	
Herm Seaway Marine Ltd St Peter Port	01481 726829	
Highway Marine Sandwich	01304 613925	
Hoare Ltd, Bob, Poole	01202 736704	
Hodges, T Coleraine	028 7035 6422	
Iron Stores Marine St Helier	01534 877755	
Isles of Scilly Steamship Co St Mary's	01720 422710	
Jackson Yacht Services Jersey	01534 743819	
Jamison and Green Ltd Belfast	028 9032 2444	
Jeckells and Son Ltd Lowestoft	01502 565007	
JF Marine Chandlery Rhu	01436 820584	
JNW Services Aberdeen	01224 594050	
JNW Services Peterhead	01779 477346	
JSB Ltd Tarbert, Loch Fyne	01880 820180	

Johnston Brothers Mallaig	01687 462215
Johnstons Marine Stores Lamlash	01770 600333
Kearon Ltd, George Arklow	+353 402 32319
Kelvin Hughes Ltd Southampton	023 80634911
Kildale Marine Hull	01482 227464
Kingfisher Marine Weymouth	01305 766595
Kings Lock Chandlery Middlewich	01606 737564
Kip Chandlery Inverkip Greenock	01475 521485
Kirkcudbright Scallop Gear Ltd Kirkcudbright	01557 330399
Kyle Chandlers Troon	01292 311880
Landon Marine, Reg Truro	01872 272668
Largs Chandlers Largs	01475 686026
Lencraft Boats Ltd Dungarvan	+353 58 68220
Lincoln Marina Lincoln	01522 526896
Looe Chandlery West Looe	01503 264355
Lynch Ltd, PA Morpeth	01670 512291
Mackay Boatbuilders (Arbroath) Ltd Aberdeen	01241 872879
Mackay Marine Services Aberdeen	01224 575772
Mailspeed Marine Crawley	01273837823
Mailspeed Marine Essex Marina	01342 710618
Mailspeed Marine Warrington	01342 710618
Mainbrayce Chandlers Braye, Alderney	01481 822772
Manx Marine Ltd Douglas	01624 674842
Marine & Leisure Europe Ltd Plymouth	01752 268826
Marine MegaStore Hamble	023 8045 4400
Marine MegaStore Morpeth	01670 516151
Marine Parts Direct Swords, Co Dublin	+353 1 807 5144
Marine Scene Bridgend	01656 671822
Marine Scene Cardiff	029 2070 5780
Marine Services Jersey	01534 626930
Marine Store Wyatts West Mersea	01206 384745
Marine Store Maldon	01621 854380
Marine Store Titchmarsh Marina	01255 679028

Marine Store Walton on the Naze	01255 679028
Marine Superstore Port Solent Chandlery Portsmouth	023 9221 9843
MarineCo Torpoint	01752 816005
Maryport Harbour and Marina Maryport	01900 814431
Matthews Ltd, D Cork	+353 214 277633
McClean Greenock	01475 728234
McCready Sailboats Ltd Holywood	028 9042 1821
Moore, Kevin Cowes	01983 289699
Moore & Son, J Mevagissey	01726 842964
Morgan & Sons Marine, LH Brightlingsea	01206 302003
Mount Batten Boathouse Plymouth	01752 482666
Murphy, Nicholas Dunmore East	+353 51 383259
MUT Wick	07753 350143
Mylor Chandlery & Rigging Falmouth	01326 375482
Nautical World Bangor	028 91460330
New World Yacht Care Helensburgh	01436 820586
Newhaven Chandlery Newhaven	01273 612612
Nifpo Ardglass	028 4484 2144
Norfolk Marine Great Yarmouth	01692 670272
Norfolk Marine Chandlery Shop Norwich	01603 783150
Ocean Leisure Ltd London	020 7930 5050
One Stop Chandlery Maldon	01621 853558
O'Sullivans Marine Ltd Tralee	+353 66 7129635
Partington Marine Ltd, William Pwllheli	01758 612808
Pascall Atkey & Sons Ltd Isle of Wight	01983 292381
Pennine Marine Ltd Skipton	01756 792335
Penrhos Marine Aberdovey	01654 767478
Penzance Marine Services Penzance	01736 361081
Perry Marine, Rob Axminster	01297 631314
Pepe Boatyard Hayling Island	023 9246 1968
Performance Yachting & Chandlery Plymouth	01752 565023
Peters PLC Chichester	01243 511033

Pinnell & Bax
Northampton 01604 592808

Piplers of Poole Poole 01202 673056

Pirate's Cave, The
Rochester 01634 295233

Powersail Island Chandlers Ltd
East Cowes Marina 01983 299800

Preston Marine Services Ltd
Preston 01772 733595

Price & Co Ltd, WF
Bristol 0117 929 2229

PSM Ltd Alderney 07781 106635

Purcell Marine
Clarenbridge +353 87 279 3821

Purple Sails & Marine
Walsall 08456 435510

Quay West Marine
Poole 01202 732445

Quayside Marine
Salcombe 01548 844300

R&A Fabrication
Kirkcudbright 01557 330399

Racecourse Yacht Basin (Windsor) Ltd
Windsor 01753 851501

Rat Rigs Water Sports
Cardiff 029 2062 1309

Reliance Marine Wirral 0151 625 5219

Rigmarine Padstow 01841 532657

Riversway Marine
Preston 0844 879 4901

RHP Marine Cowes 01983 290421

RNS Marine Northam 01237 474167

Sail Loft Bideford 01271 860001

Sailaway
St Anthony 01326 231357

Salcombe Boatstore
Salcombe 01548 843708

Salterns Chandlery
Poole 01202 701556

Shipmate Salcombe 01548 844555

Sandrock Marine Rye 01797 222679

Schull Watersports Centre
Schull +353 28 28554

Sea & Shore Ship Chandler
Dundee 01382 450666

Sea Cruisers of Rye Rye 01797 222070

Sea Span Edinburgh 0131 552 2224

Sea Teach Ltd Emsworth 01243 375774

Seafare Tobermory 01688 302277

Seahog Boats Preston 01772 633016

Seamark-Nunn & Co
Felixstowe 01394 451000

Seaquest Marine Ltd
St Peter Port 01481 721773

Seaware Ltd Penryn 01326 377948

Seaway Marine Macduff 01261 832877

Sharp & Enright Dover 01304 206295

Shearwater Engineering Services Ltd
Dunoon 01369 706666

Shipshape Marine
King's Lynn 01553 764058

Ship Shape Ramsgate 01843 597000

Shorewater Sports
Chichester 01243 672315

Simpson Marine Ltd
Newhaven 01273 612612

Simpson Marine Ltd, WA
Dundee 01382 566670

Sketrick Marine Centre
Killinchy 028 9754 1400

Smith AM (Marine) Ltd
London 020 8529 6988

Solent Marine Chandlery Ltd
Gosport 023 9258 4622

South Coast Marine
Christchurch 01202 482695

South Pier Shipyard
St Helier 01534 711000

Southampton Yacht Services Ltd
Southampton 023 803 35266

Sparkes Chandlery
Hayling Island 02392 463572

S Roberts Marine Ltd
Liverpool 0151 707 8300

SSL Marine Eastbourne 01323 47900

Standard House Chandlery
Wells-next-the-Sea 01328 710593

Stornoway Fishermen's Co-op
Stornoway 01851 702563

Sunset Marine & Watersports
Sligo +353 71 9162792

Sussex Marine
St Leonards on Sea 01424 425882

Sussex Yachts Ltd
Shoreham 01273 605482

Sussex Marine Centre
Shoreham 01273 454737

Sutton Marine (Dublin)
Sutton +353 1 832 2312

SW Nets Newlyn 01736 360254

Tarbert Ltd, JSB
Tarbert 01880 820180

TCS Chandlery
Essex Marina 01702 258094
TCS Chandlery Grays 01375 374702
TCS Chandlery Southend 01702 444423

Thulecraft Ltd Lerwick 01595 693192

Tony's Marine Services
Coleraine 07866 690436

Torbay Boating Centre
Paignton 01803 558760

Torquay Chandlers
Torquay 01803 211854

Trafalgar Yacht Services
Fareham 01329 822445

Trident UK N Shields 0191 490 1736

Union Chandlery Cork +353 21 4554334

Uphill Boat Services
Weston-Super-Mare 01934 418617

Upper Deck Marine and Outriggers
Fowey 01726 832287

V Ships (Isle of Man)
Douglas 01624 688886

V F Marine Rhu 01436 820584

Viking Marine Ltd
Dun Laoghaire +353 1 280 6654

Waterfront Marine
Bangor 01248 352513

Wayne Maddox Marine
Margate 01843 297157

Western Marine
Dalkey +353 1280 0321

Wetworks, The
Burnham-on-Crouch 01621 786413

Whitstable Marine
Whitstable 01227 274168

Williams Ltd, TJ Cardiff 029 20 487676

Windjammer Marine
Milford Marina 01646 699070

Yacht & Boat Chandlery
Faversham 01795 531777

Yacht Chandlers Conwy 01492 572777

Yacht Equipment
Chelmsford 01245 223563

Yachtmail Ltd
Lymington 01590 672784

Yachtshop Conwy 01492 338505

Yachtshop Holyhead 01407 760031

You Boat Chandlery
Gosport 02392 522226

CHART AGENTS

Brown Son & Ferguson Ltd
Glasgow 0141 429 1234

Chattan Security Ltd
Edinburgh 0131 554 7527

Cooke & Son Ltd, B Hull 01482 223454

Dubois Phillips & McCallum Ltd
Liverpool 0151 236 2776

Imray Laurie Norie and Wilson Ltd
Huntingdon 01480 462114

Kelvin Hughes
Southampton 023 8063 4911

Lilley & Gillie Ltd, John
North Shields 0191 257 2217

MARINE CHART SERVICES
Maritime House, 32 Denington Rd,
Wellingborough NN8 2QH
Tel: 01933 441629
Fax: 01933 442662
www.chartsales.co.uk
Access to many thousands of
Navigation Charts & publications in
different format.

MARINE SUPPLIES AND SERVICES GUIDE

CHANDLERS

Price & Co, WF
Bristol 0117 929 2229

Sea Chest Nautical Bookshop
Plymouth 01752 222012

Seath Instruments (1992) Ltd
Lowestoft 01502 573811

Small Craft Deliveries
Woodbridge 01394 382655

Smith (Marine) Ltd, AM
London 020 8529 6988

South Bank Marine Charts Ltd Grimsby
01472 361137

Stanford Charts Bristol 0117 929 9966

Stanford Charts
London 020 7836 1321

Todd Chart Agency Ltd
County Down 028 9146 6640

UK Hydrographics Office
Taunton 01823 337900

Warsash Nautical Bookshop
Warsash 01489 572384

CLOTHING

Absolute
Gorleston on Sea 01493 442259

Aquatogs Cowes 01983 245892

Crew Clothing
London 020 8875 2300

Crewsaver
Gosport 01329 820000

Douglas Gill
Nottingham 0115 9460844

Fat Face fatface.com

Gul International Ltd
Bodmin 01208 262400

Guy Cotten UK Ltd
Liskeard 01579 347115

Harwoods
Yarmouth 01983 760258

Helly Hansen
Nottingham 0115 979 5997

Henri Lloyd
Manchester 0161 799 1212

Joules 0845 6066871

Mad Cowes Clothing Co
Cowes 0845 456 5158

Matthews Ltd, D
Cork +353 214 277633

Mountain & Marine
Poynton 01625 859863

Musto Ltd Laindon 01268 491555

Purple Sails & Marine
Walsall 0845 6435510

Quba Sails
Lymington 01590 689362

Quba Sails
Salcombe 01548 844599

Yacht Parts
Plymouth 01752 252489

CODE OF PRACTICE EXAMINERS

Booth Marine Surveys, Graham
Birchington-on-Sea 01843 843793

Cannell & Associates, David M
Wivenhoe 01206 823337

COMPUTERS & SOFTWARE

Dolphin Maritime Software
White Cross 01524 841946

Forum Software Ltd
Nr Haverfordwest 01646 636363

Kelvin Hughes Ltd
Southampton 023 8063 4911

Memory-Map
Aldermaston 0844 8110950

PC Maritime Plymouth 01752 254205

DECK EQUIPMENT

Aries Van Gear Spares
Penryn 01326 377467

Ronstan Gosport 023 9252 5377

Harken UK Lymington 01590 689122

IMP Royston 01763 241300

Kearon Ltd George +353 402 32319

Pro-Boat Ltd
Burnham-on-Crouch 01621 785455

Ryland, Kenneth
Stanton 01386 584270

Timage & Co Ltd
Braintree 01376 343087

DIESEL MARINE/ FUEL ADDITIVES

Corralls Poole 01202 674551

Cotters Marine & General Supplies
Baltimore +353 28 20106

Expresslube
Henfield 01444 254115

Gorey Marine Fuel Supplies
Gorey 07797 742384

Hammond Motorboats
Dover 01304 206809

Iron Wharf Boatyard
Faversham 01795 536296

Lallow, Clare Cowes 01983 760707

Marine Support & Towage
Cowes 01983 200716/07860 297633

Quayside Fuel
Weymouth 07747 182181

Rossiter Yachts
Christchurch 01202 483250

Sleeman & Hawken
Shaldon 01626 778266

DIVERS

Abco Divers Belfast 028 90610492

Andark Diving
Burseldon 01489 581755

Argonaut Marine
Aberdeen 01224 706526

Baltimore Diving and Watersports Centre West Cork +353 28 20300

C & C Marine Services
Largs 01475 687180

Cardiff Commercial Boat Operators Ltd
Cardiff 029 2037 7872

Clyde Diving Centre
Inverkip 01475 521281

Divetech UK King's Lynn 01485 572323

Diving & Marine Engineering
Barry 01446 721553

Donnelly, R
South Shields 07973 119455

DV Diving 028 9146 4671

Falmouth Divers Ltd
Penryn 01326 374736

Fathoms Ltd Wick 01955 605956

Felixarc Marine Ltd
Lowestoft 01502 509215

Grampian Diving Services
New Deer 01771 644206

Higgins, Noel +353 872027650

Hudson, Dave
Trearddur Bay 01407 860628

Hunt, Kevin Tralee +353 6671 25979

Kaymac Diving Services
Swansea 08431 165523

Keller, Hilary Buncrana +353 77 62146

Kilkee Diving Centre
Kilkee +353 6590 56707

Leask Marine Kirkwall 01856 874725

Looe Divers Hannafore 01503 262727

MacDonald, D Nairn 01667 455661

Medway Diving Contractors Ltd
Gillingham 01634 851902

MMC Diving Services
Lake, Isle of Wight 07966 579965

Mojo Maritime
Penzance 01736 762771

Murray, Alex
Stornoway 01851 704978

New Dawn Dive Centre
Lymington 01590 675656

Northern Divers (Engineering) Ltd
Hull 01482 227276

Offshore Marine Services Ltd
Bembridge 01983 873125

Parkinson (Sinbad Marine Services), J
Killybegs +353 73 31417

Port of London Authority
Gravesend 01474 560311

Purcell, D – Crouch Sailing School
Burnham 01621 784140/0585 33

Salvesen UK Ltd
Liverpool   0151 933 6038

Sea-Lift Diving
Dover   01304 829956

Southern Cylinder Services
Fareham   01329 221125

Sub Aqua Services
North Ormesby   01642 230209

Teign Diving Centre
Teignmouth   01626 773965

Tuskar Rock Marine
Rosslare   +353 53 33376

Underwater Services
Dyffryn Arbwy   01341 247702

Wilson Alan c/o Portrush Yacht Club
Portrush   028 2076 2225

Woolford, William
Bridlington   01262 671710

ELECTRICAL AND ELECTRONIC ENGINEERS

AAS Marine
Aberystwyth   01970 631090

Allworth Riverside Services, Adrian
Chelsea Harbour Marina
                             07831 574774

ASL Auto Services
Boston   01205 761560

Auto Marine Electrics
Holy Loch   01369 701555

Baker, Keith Brentford   07792 937790

Belson Design Ltd, Nick
Southampton   077 6835 1330

Biggs, John Weymouth Marina,
Weymouth   01305 778445

BJ Marine Ltd Bangor   028 9127 1434

BM Electrical
Kirkcudbright   07584 657192

Boat Electrics Troon   01292 315355

Buccaneer Ltd
Macduff   01261 835199

Calibra Marine
Dartmouth   01803 833094

Campbell & McHardy Lossiemouth
Marina, Lossiemouth   01343 812137

CES Sandown Sparkes Marina,
Hayling Island   023 9246 6005

Colin Coady Marine
Malahide   +353 87 265 6496

Contact Electrical
Arbroath   01241 874528

DDZ Marine Ardossan   01294 607077

EC Leisure Craft
Essex Marina   01702 568482

Energy Solutions
Rochester   01634 290772

Enterprise Marine Electronic & Technical Services Ltd
Aberdeen   01224 593281

Eurotek Marine
Eastbourne   01323 479144

Evans, Lyndon
Brentford   07795 218704

Floetree Ltd (Loch Lomond Marina)
Balloch   01389 752069

Hamble Marine
Hamble   02380 001088

HNP Engineers (Lerwick) Ltd
Lerwick   01595 692493

Jackson Yacht Services
Jersey   01534 743819

Jedynak, A Salcombe   01548 843321

Kippford Slipway Ltd
Dalbeattie   01556 620249

Lynch Ltd, PA Morpeth   01670 512291

Lynch, John Tralee   +353 87 992 3102

Mackay Boatbuilders (Arbroath) Ltd
Aberdeen   01241 872879

Marine, AW Gosport   023 9250 1207

Marine Electrical Repair Service
London   020 7228 1336

Maxfield Electrical
Doncaster   07976 825349

MB Marine Troon   01292 311944

McMillan, Peter
Kilrush   +35 86 8388617

MES Falmouth Marina,
Falmouth   01326 378497

Mount Batten Boathouse
Plymouth   01752 482666

New World Yacht Care
Rhu   01436 820586

Neyland Marine Services Ltd
Milford Haven   01646 600358

Powell, Martin Shamrock Quay,
Southampton   023 8033 2123

PR Systems
Plymouth   01752 936145

Radio & Electronic Services Beaucette Marina,
Guernsey   01481 728837

RHP Marine Cowes   01983 290421

Rothwell, Chris
Torquay Marina   01803 850960

Ruddy Marine
Galway   +353 87 742 7439

Rutherford, Jeff Largs   01475 568026

SM International
Plymouth   01752 662129

Sussex Fishing Services
Rye   01797 223895

Tony's Marine Services
Coleraine   07866 690436

Ultra Marine Systems
Mayflower International Marina,
Plymouth   07989 941020

Upham, Roger
Chichester   01243 514511

Volspec Ipswich   01473 780144

Weyland Marine Services
Milford Haven   01646 600358

ELECTRONIC DEVICES AND EQUIPMENT

Anchorwatch UK
Edinburgh   0131 447 5057

Aquascan International Ltd
Newport   01633 841117

Atlantis Marine Power Ltd
Plymouth   01752 208810

Autosound Marine
Bradford   01274 688990

B&G Romsey   01794 518448

Brookes & Gatehouse
Romsey   01794 518448

Boat Electrics & Electronics Ltd
Troon   01292 315355

Cactus Navigation & Communication
London   020 7833 3435

CDL Aberdeen   01224 706655

Charity & Taylor Ltd
Lowestoft   01502 581529

Diverse Yacht Services
Hamble   023 8045 3399

Dyfed Electronics Ltd
Milford Haven   01646 694572

Echopilot Marine Electronics Ltd
Ringwood   01425 476211

Enterprise Marine
Aberdeen   01224 593281

Euronav Ltd
Portsmouth   023 9298 8806

Exposure Lights
Pulborough   01798 83930

Furuno UK
Fraserburgh   01346 518300
Havant   023 9244 1000

Garmin (Europe) Ltd
Romsey   0870 850 1242

Golden Arrow Marine Ltd
Southampton   023 8071 0371

Greenham Regis Marine Electronics
Lymington   01590 671144

Greenham Regis Marine Electronics
Poole   01202 676363

Greenham Regis Marine Electronics
Southampton   023 8063 6555

ICS Electronics
Arundel   01903 731101

JG Technologies Ltd
Weymouth   0845 458 9616

KM Electronics Lowestoft	01502 569079
Kongsberg Simrad Ltd Aberdeen	01224 226500
Kongsberg Simrad Ltd Wick	01955 603606
Landau UK Ltd Hamble	02380 454040
Enterprise Marine Aberdeen	01224 593281
Marathon Leisure Hayling Island	023 9263 7711
Marine Instruments Falmouth	01326 375483
MB Marine Troon	01292 311944
Microcustom Ltd Ipswich	01473 215777
Nasa Marine Instruments Stevenage	01438 354033
Navionics UK Plymouth	01752 204735
Ocean Leisure Ltd London	020 7930 5050
Plymouth Marine Electronics Plymouth	01752 227711
Radio & Electronic Services Ltd St Peter Port	01481 728837
Raymarine Ltd Portsmouth	02392 714700
Redfish Car Company Stockton-on-Tees	01642 633638
Robertson, MK Oban	01631 563836
Satcom Distribution Ltd Salisbury	01722 410800
Seaquest Marine Ltd Guernsey	01481 721773
Seatronics Aberdeen	01224 853100
Selex Communications Aberdeen	01224 890316
Selex Communications Bristol	0117 931 3550
Selex Communications Brixham	01803 882716
Selex Communications Fraserburgh	01346 518187
Selex Communications Glasgow	0141 882 6909
Selex Communications Hull	01482 326144
Selex Communications Kilkeel	028 4176 9009
Selex Communications Liverpool	01268 823400
Selex Communications Lowestoft	01502 572365
Selex Communications Newcastle upon Tyne	0191 265 0374
Selex Communications Newlyn	01736 361320

Selex Communications Penryn	01326 378031
Selex Communications Plymouth	01752 222878
Selex Communications Rosyth	01383 419606
Selex Communications Southampton	023 8051 1868
Silva Ltd Livingston	01506 419555
SM International Plymouth	01752 662129
Sperry Marine Ltd Peterhead	01779 473475
Stenmar Ltd Aberdeen	01224 827288
Transas Nautic Portsmouth	023 9267 4016
Veripos Precise Navigation Aberdeen	01224 965800
Wema (UK) Honiton	01404 881810
Wilson & Co Ltd, DB Glasgow	0141 647 0161
Woodsons of Aberdeen Ltd Aberdeen	01224 722884

ENGINES AND ACCESSORIES

Airylea Motors Aberdeen	01224 872891
Amble Boat Co Ltd Amble	01665 710267
Anchor Marine Products Benfleet	01268 566666
Aquafac Ltd Luton	01582 568700
Barrus Ltd, EP Bicester	01869 363636
British Polar Engines Ltd Glasgow	0141 445 2455
Bukh Diesel UK Ltd Poole	01202 668840
CJ Marine Mechanical Troon	01292 313400
Cleghorn Waring Ltd Letchworth	01462 480380
Cook's Diesel Service Ltd Faversham	01795 538553
Southern Shipwright (SSL) Brighton	01273 601779
Southern Shipwright (SSL) Eastbourne	01323 479000
Fender-Fix Maidstone	01622 751518
Fettes & Rankine Engineering Aberdeen	01224 573343
Fleetwood & Sons Ltd, Henry Lossiemouth	01343 813015
Gorleston Marine Ltd Great Yarmouth	01493 661883
Halyard Salisbury	01722 710922
Interseals (Guernsey) Ltd Guernsey	01481 246364

Kelpie Boats Pembroke Dock	01646 683661
Keypart Watford	01923 330570
Lancing Marine Brighton	01273 410025
Lencraft Boats Ltd Dungarvan	+353 58 68220
Lewmar Ltd Havant	023 9247 1841
Liverpool Power Boats Bootle	0151 944 1163
Lynch Ltd, PA Morpeth	01670 512291
MacDonald & Co Ltd, JN Glasgow	0141 810 3400
Mariners Weigh Shaldon	01626 873698
MMS Ardrossan	01294 604831
Mooring Mate Ltd Bournemouth	01202 421199
Newens Marine, Chas Putney	020 8788 4587
Ocean Safety Southampton	023 8072 0800
RK Marine Ltd Hamble	01489 583585
Swanwick	01489 583572
Sillette Sonic Ltd Sutton	020 8337 7543
Sowester Simpson-Lawrence Ltd Poole	01202 667700
Timage & Co Ltd Braintree	01376 343087
Thorne Boat Services Thorne	01405 814197
Vetus Den Ouden Ltd Totton	023 8045 4507
Western Marine Dublin	+353 1 280 0321
Whitstable Marine Whitstable	01227 262525
Yates Marine, Martin Galgate	01524 751750
Ynys Marine Cardigan	01239 613179

FOUL-WEATHER GEAR

Aquatogs Cowes	01983 295071
Crew Clothing London	020 8875 2300
Century Finchampstead	0118 9731616
Crewsaver Gosport	01329 820000
Douglas Gill Nottingham	0115 946 0844
FBI Leeds	0113 270 7000
Gul International Ltd Bodmin	01208 262400

Helly Hansen
Nottingham   0115 979 5997

Henri Lloyd
Manchester   0161 799 1212

Musto Ltd Laindon   01268 491555

Pro Rainer Windsor   07752 903882

GENERAL MARINE EQUIPMENT & SPARES

Ampair Ringwood   01425 480780

Aries Vane Gear Spares
Penryn   01326 377467

Arthurs Chandlery, R
Gosport   023 9252 6522

Atlantis Marine Power Ltd
Plymouth   01752 208810

Barden UK Ltd Fareham 01489 570770

Calibra Marine International Ltd
Southampton   08702 400358

CH Marine (Cork)   +353 21 4315700

Chris Hornsey (Chandlery) Ltd
Southsea   023 9273 4728

Compass Marine (Dartmouth) Dartmouth 01803 835915

Cox Yacht Charter Ltd, Nick
Lymington   01590 673489

CTC Marine & Leisure
Middlesbrough   01642 372600

Exposure Lights
Pulborough   01798 83930

Frederiksen Boat Fittings (UK) Ltd
Gosport   023 9252 5377

Furneaux Riddall & Co Ltd
Portsmouth   023 9266 8621

Hardware & Marine Supplies
Co Wexford   +353 (53) 29791

Index Marine
Bournemouth   01202 470149

Kearon Ltd, George
Arklow   +353 402 32319

Marathon Leisure
Hayling Island   023 9263 7711

Pro-Boat Ltd
Burnham-on-Crouch   01621 785455

Pump International Ltd
Cornwall   01209 831937

Quay West Marine
Poole   01202 732445

Rogers, Angie Bristol   0117 973 8276

Ryland, Kenneth
Stanton   01386 584270

Tiflex
Liskeard   01579 320808

Vetus Boating Equipment
Southampton   02380 454507

Whitstable Marine
Whitstable   01227 262525

Yacht Parts
Plymouth   01752 252489

HARBOUR MASTERS

Aberaeron	01545 571645
Aberdeen	01224 597000
Aberdovey	01654 767626
Aberystwyth	01970 611433
Alderney & Burhou	01481 822620
Amble	01665 710306
Anstruther	01333 310836
Appledore	01237 474569
Arbroath	01241 872166
Ardglass	028 4484 1291
Ardrossan Control Tower	01294 463972
Arinagour Piermaster	01879 230347
Arklow	+353 402 32466
Baltimore	+353 28 22145
Banff	01261 815544
Bantry Bay	+353 27 53277
Barmouth	01341 280671
Barry	01446 732665
Beaucette	01481 245000
Beaulieu River	01590 616200
Belfast Lough	028 90 553012
Belfast River Manager	028 90 328507
Bembridge	01983 872828
Berwick-upon-Tweed	01289 307404
Bideford	01237 346131
Blyth	01670 352678
Boston	01205 362328
Bridlington	01262 670148/9
Bridport	01308 423222
Brighton	01273 819919
Bristol	0117 926 4797
Brixham	01803 853321
Buckie	01542 831700
Bude	01288 353111
Burghead	01542 831700
Burnham-on-Crouch	01621 783602
Burnham-on-Sea	0300 303 7799
Burtonport	+353 075 42155
Caernarfon	01286 672118
Caernarfon	07786 730865
Camber Berthing Offices – Portsmouth	023 92297395
Campbeltown	01586 552552
	07825 732862
Caledonian Canal Off. (Inverness)	01463 725500
Cardiff	029 20400500

Carnlough Harbour	07703 606763
Castletown Bay	01624 823549
Charlestown	01726 67526
Chichester Harbour	01243 512301
Clovelly	01273 431549
	07975 501380
Conwy	01492 596253
Cork	+353 21 4273125
Corpach Canal Sea Lock	01397 772249
Courtmacsherry	+353 8673 94299
	+353 23 46311/46600
Coverack	01326 380679
Cowes	01983 293952
Crail	01333 450820
Craobh Haven	01852 502222
Crinan Canal Office	01546 603210
Cromarty Firth	01381 600479
Cromarty Harbour	01381 600493
Crookhaven	+353 28 35319
Cullen	01542 831700
Dingle	+353 66 9151629
Douglas	01624 686628
Dover	01304 240400 Ext 4520
Dublin	+353 1 874871
Dun Laoghaire	+353 1 280 1130/8074
Dunbar	07958 754858
Dundee	01382 224121
East Loch Tarbert	01859 502444
Eastbourne	01323 470099
Eigg Harbour	01687 482428
Elie	01333 330051
Estuary Control - Dumbarton	01389 726211
Exe	01392 274306
Exeter	01392 265791
Eyemouth	01890 750223
	07885 742505
Felixstowe	07803 476621
Findochty	01542 831700
Fisherrow	0131 665 5900
Fishguard (Lower Harbour)	01348 874726
Fishguard	01348 404425
Fleetwood	01253 872323
Flotta	01856 701411
Folkestone	01303 715354
Fowey	01726 832471/2.
Fraserburgh	01346 515858

Galway Bay	+353 91 561874	Milford Haven	01646 696100	River Blackwater	01621 856487
Garlieston	01988 600274	Minehead (Mon-Fri)	01643 702566	River Colne (Brightlingsea)	01206 302200
Glasson Dock	07910 315606	Montrose	01674 672302	River Dart	01803 832337
Gorey Port Control	01534 447788	Mousehole	01736 731511	River Deben	01473 736257
Gourdon	01569 762741	Mullion Cove	01326 240222	River Exe Dockmaster	01392 274306
Great Yarmouth	01493 335501	Nairn Harbour Office	01667 452453	River Humber	01482 327171
Grimsby Dockmaster	01472 359181	Newhaven Harbour Admin		River Medway	01795 596593
Groomsport Bay	028 91 278040		01273 612872/612926	River Orwell	01473 231010
Hamble River	01489 576387	Newlyn	01736 731897	River Roach	01621 783602
Hayle	07500 993867	Newquay	07737 387217	River Stour	01255 243000
Helford River	01326 732544	Newport Harbour Office		River Tyne/North Shields	0191 257 2080
Helmsdale	01431 821692		01983 525994		
Holy Island	01289 389217	North Berwick	00776 467373	River Yealm	01752 872533
Holyhead	01407 763071	Oban	01631 562892	Rivers Alde & Ore	07528 092635
Hopeman	01542 831700	Padstow	01841 532239	Rosslare Europort	+353 53 915 7921
Howth	+353 1 832 2252	Peel	01624 842338	Rothesay	01700 503842
Ilfracombe	01271 862108	Penrhyn Bangor	01248 352525		07799 724225
Inverness	01463 715715	Penzance	01736 366113	Ryde	01983 613879
Ipswich	01473 211771	Peterhead	01779 483630	Salcombe	01548 843791
Irvine	01294 487286	Pierowall	01857 677216	Sark	01481 832323
Johnshaven	01561 362262	Pittenweem	01333 312591	Scalloway	01595 880574
Kettletoft Bay	01857 600227	Plockton	01599 534589	Schull	+353 27 28136
Killybegs	+353 73 31032	Polperro	01503 272634	Scarborough	01723 373530
Kilmore Quay	+353 53 912 9955		07966 528045	Scrabster	01847 892779
Kinlochbervie	01971 521235	Poole	01202 440233	Seaham	07786 565205
	07901 514350	Port Ellen Harbour Association		Sharpness, Gloucester Harbour Trustees	01453 811913
Kinsale	+353 21 4772503		01496 302458		
Kirkcudbright	01557 331135	Port Isaac	01208 880321	Shoreham	01273 598100
Kirkwall	01856 872292		07855 429422	Silloth	016973 31358
Langstone Harbour	023 9246 3419	Port St Mary	01624 833205	Sligo	+353 91 53819
Larne	02828 872100	Porth Dinllaen	01758 720276	Southampton	023 8033 9733
Lerwick	01595 692991	Porthleven	01326 574207	Southend-on-Sea	01702 611889
Littlehampton	01903 721215	Porthmadog	01766 512927	Southwold	01502 724712
Liverpool	0151 949 6134/5	Portknockie	01542 831700	St Helier	01534 447788
Loch Gairloch	01445 712140	Portland	01305 824044	St Ives	07793 515460
Loch Inver	01571 844267	Portpatrick	01776 810355	St Margaret's Hope	01856 831454
	07958 734610	Portree	01478 612926	St Mary's	01720 422768
Looe	01503 262839	Portrush	028 70822307	St Michael's Mount	07870 400282
	07918 728955	Portsmouth Harbour Commercial Docks	023 92297395	St Monans (part-time)	07930 869538
Lossiemouth (Marina)	07969 213513			St Peter Port	01481 720229
	07969 213521	Portsmouth Harbour Control		Stonehaven	01569 762741
Lough Foyle	028 7186 0555		023 92723694	Stornoway	01851 702688
Lowestoft	01502 572286	Portsmouth Harbour	023 92723124	Strangford Lough	028 44 881637
Lyme Regis	01297 442137	Preston	01772 726711	Stranraer	07734 073421
Lymington	01590 672014	Pwllheli	01758 701219	Stromness	07810 465825
Lyness	01856 791387	Queenborough	01795 662051	Stronsay	01857 616317
Macduff	01261 832236	Queens Gareloch/Rhu	01436 674321	Sullom Voe	01806 242551
Maryport	01900 814431	Ramsey	01624 812245	Sunderland	0191 567 2626
Menai Strait	01248 712312	Ramsgate	01843 572100		
Methil	01333 462725	River Bann & Coleraine			
Mevagissey	01726 843305		028 7034 2012		

Swale	01795 561234
Swansea	01792 653787
Tayport Hbr Trust	01382 553799
Tees & Hartlepool Port Authority	01429 277205
Teignmouth	01626 773165
Tenby	01834 842717
Thames Estuary	01474 562200
Tobermory Moorings Officer	07917 832497
Torquay	01803 292429
Troon	01292 281687
Truro	01872 272130
Ullapool	01854 612091
Waldringfield	01394 736291
Walton-on-the-Naze	01255 851899
Watchet	01643 703704
Waterford	+353 51 899801
Wells-next-the-Sea	01328 711646
West Bay (Bridport)	01308 423222
	07870 240636
Wexford	+353 53 912 2039
Weymouth	01305 206423
Whitby	01947 602354
Whitehaven	01946 692435
Whitehills	01261 861291
Whitstable	01227 274086
Wick	01955 602030
Wicklow	+353 404 67455
Workington	01900 602301
Yarmouth	01983 760321
Youghal	+353 24 92626
	+353 86 780 0878

HARBOURS

Bristol Harbour	0117 903 1484
Clyde Marina – Ardrossan	01294 607077
Jersey Hbrs St Helier	01534 885588
Maryport Harbour and Marina Maryport	01900 818447/4431
Peterhead Bay Authority Peterhead	01779 474020
Sark Moorings – Channel Islands	01481 832260

INSURANCE/FINANCE

Admiral Marine Ltd Salisbury	01722 416106
Bishop Skinner Boat Insurance London	0800 7838057
Bluefin London	0800 074 5200
Castlemain Ltd St Peter Port	01481 721319
Craven Hodgson Associates Leeds	0113 243 8443
Giles Insurance Brokers Irvine	01294 315481
GJW Direct Liverpool	0151 473 8000
Haven Knox-Johnston West Malling	01732 223600
Lombard Southampton	023 8024 2171
Mercia Marine Malvern	01684 564457
Nautical Insurance Services Ltd Leigh-on-Sea	01702 470811
Navigators & General Brighton	01273 863400
Pantaenius UK Ltd Plymouth	01752 223656
Porthcawl Insurance Consultants Porthcawl	01656 784866
Saga Boat Insurance Folkestone	01303 771135
St Margarets Insurances London	020 8778 6161
Towergate Insurance Shrewsbury	0344 892 1987

LIFERAFTS & INFLATABLES

Adec Marine Ltd Croydon	020 8686 9717
Avon Inflatables Llanelli	01554 882000
Cosalt International Ltd Aberdeen	01224 826662
Glaslyn Marine Supplies Ltd Porthmadog	01766 513545
Hale Marine, Ron Portsmouth	023 9273 2985
Guernsey Yacht Club St Peter Port	01481 722838
IBS Boats South Woodham Ferrers	01245 323211/425551
KTS Seasafety Kilkeel	028 918 28405
Nationwide Marine Hire Warrington	01925 245788
Norwest Marine Ltd Liverpool	0151 207 2860
Ocean Safety Southampton	023 8072 0800
Polymarine Ltd Conwy	01492 583322
Premium Liferaft Services Burnham-on-Crouch	0800 243673
Ribeye Dartmouth	01803 832060
South Eastern Marine Services Ltd Basildon	01268 534427
Suffolk Marine Safety Ipswich	01473 833010

Whitstable Marine Whitstable	01227 262525

MARINAS

Aberystwyth Marina	01970 611422
Amble Marina	01665 712168
Arbroath Harbour	01241 872166
Ardfern Yacht Centre Ltd	01852 500247
Ardglass Marina	028 44842332
Arklow Marina	+353 87 258 8078
Ballycastle Marina	028 2076 8525
Banff Harbour Marina	01261 815544
Bangor Marina	028 91 453297
Beaucette Marina	01481 245000
Bembridge Harbour Authority	01983 872828
Berthon Lymington Marina	01590 647405
Birdham Pool Marina	01243 512310
Blackwater Marina	01621 740264
Boston Gateway Marina	07480 525230
Bradwell Marina	01621 776235
Bray Marina	01628 623654
Brentford Dock Marina	020 8232 8941
Bridgemarsh Marine	01621 740414
Brighton Marina	01273 819919
Bristol Marina	0117 921 3198
Brixham Marina	01803 882929
Bucklers Hard Marina	01590 616200
Burnham Yacht Harbour Marina Ltd	01621 782150
BWML Glasson Basin	01524 751491
BWML Limehouse Marina	020 7308 9930
Cahersiveen Marina	+353 66 947 2777
Caley Marina	01463 236539
Campbeltown Marina	07798 524821
Cardiff Marina	02920 396078
Carlingford Marina	+353 42 9373072
Carrickfergus Marina	**028 9336 6666**
Castlepark Marina	+353 21 477 4959
Chatham Maritime Marina	01634 899200
Chelsea Harbour Marina	07770 542783
Chichester Marina	01243 512731
Clyde Marina Ltd	01294 607077
Cobbs Quay Marina	01202 674299
Coleraine Harbour Town Centre Marina	028 7034 2012
Coleraine Marina	028 703 44768
Conwy Quays Marina	01492 593000
Cork Harbour Marina	+353 87 3669009

Cowes Harbour Shepards Marina	Hythe Marina Village 02380 207073	Parkstone Yacht Club Haven
01983 297821	Inverness Marina 01463 220501	01202 738824
Cowes Yacht Haven 01983 299975	Ipswich Haven Marina 01473 236644	Peel Marina 01624 842338
Craobh Marina 01852 500222	Island Harbour Marina 01983 539994	Penarth Quays Marina 02920 705021
Crinan Boatyard 01546 830232	James Watt Dock Marina	Penton Hook 01932 568681
Crosshaven Boatyard Marina	01475 729838	Peterhead Bay Marina 01779 477868
+353 21 483 1161	Kemps Quay 023 8063 2323	Plymouth Yacht Haven 01752 404231
Dart Marina Yacht Harbour	Kilmore Quay Marina	Poolbeg YBC & Marina
01803 837161	+353 53 91 29955	+353 1 668 9983
Darthaven Marina 01803 752242	Kilrush Marina +353 65 9052072	Poole Quay Boat Haven 01202 649488
Dartside Quay 01803 845445	Kinsale Yacht Club Marina	Poplar Dock Marina 0207 308 9930
Deganwy Marina 01492 576888	+353 21 477 2196	Port Bannatyne Marina 01700 503116
Dingle Marina +353 (0)87 925 4115	Kip Marina 01475 521485	Port Edgar Marina 0131 331 3330
Douglas Marina 01624 686627	Kirkcudbright Marina 01557 331135	Port Ellen Marina 07464 151200
Dover Marina 01304 241663	Kirkwall Marina 01856 871313	Port Hamble Marina 023 8045 2741
Dun Laoghaire Marina	La Collette Yacht Basin 01534 885588	Port of Poole Marina 01202 649488
+353 1 202 0040	Lady Bee Marina 01273 593801	Port Pendennis Marina 01326 211211
Dunstaffnage Marina Ltd	Lake Yard Marina 01202 674531	Port Solent Marina 02392 210765
01631 566555	Largs Yacht Haven 01475 675333	Port Werburgh 01634 252107
East Cowes Marina 01983 293983	Lawrence Cove Marina +353 27 75044	Portaferry Marina 07703 209780
East Ferry Marina +353 21 483 3390	Littlehampton Marina 01903 713553	Portavadie Marina 01700 811075
Emsworth Yacht Harbour	Liverpool Marina Bar & Grill	Portishead Quays Marina
01243 377727	0151 707 6777	01275 841941
Endeavour Quay 02392 584200	Lossiemouth Marina 01343 813066	Portland Marina 0345 430 2012
Essex Marina 01702 258531	Lowestoft Cruising Club	Preston Marina 01772 733595
Falmouth Haven Marina 01326 310991	07810 522515	Quay Marinas Rhu 01436 820238
Falmouth Marina 01326 316620	Lowestoft Haven Marina	Queen Anne's Battery 01752 671142
Fambridge Yacht Haven	01502 580300	Ridge Wharf Yacht Centre
01621 740370	Lymington Harbour Commission	01929 552650
Fambridge Yacht Station	01590 672014	Royal Clarence Marina 02392 523523
01621 742911	Lymington Yacht Haven 01590 677071	Royal Cork Yacht Club Marina
Fenit Harbour & Marina	Malahide Marina +353 1 845 4129	+353 21 483 1023
+353 66 7136231	Mallaig Marina 01687 462406	Royal Harbour Marina, Ramsgate
Fleetwood Haven Marina	Maryport Harbour and Marina	01843 572100
01253 879062	01900 814431	Royal Harwich Yacht Club Marina
Fox's Marina & Boatyard	Mayflower International Marina	01473 780319
01473 689111	01752 556633	Royal Norfolk and Suffolk YC
Foyle Port Marina 02871 860555	Melfort Pier & Harbour 01852 200333	01502 566726
Gallions Point Marina 0207 476 7054	Mercury Yacht Harbour 023 8045 5994	Royal Northumberland YC
Galway Harbour Marina	Milford Marina 01646 696312	01670 353636
+353 91 561874	Millbay Marina Village 01752 226785	Royal Quays Marina 0191 272 8282
Gillingham Marina 01634 280022	Multihull Centre 01752 823900	Ryde Leisure Harbour 01983 613879
Gosport Marina 023 9252 4811	Mylor Yacht Harbour 01326 372121	Salterns Marina Ltd 01202 709971
Hafan Pwllheli 01758 701219	Nairn Marina 01667 456008	Salve Engineering Marina
Hamble Point Marina 02380 452464	Neptune Marina Ltd 01473 215204	+353 21 483 1145
Harbour of Rye 01797 225225	Newhaven Marina 01273 513881	Sandpoint Marina (Dumbarton)
Hartlepool Marina 01429 865744	Neyland Yacht Haven 01646 601601	01389 762396
Haslar Marina 023 9260 1201	Northney Marina 02392 466321	Saxon Wharf 023 8033 9490
Heybridge Basin 07712 079764	Noss Marina 01803 839087	Seaport Marina 01463 725500
Holy Loch Marina 01369 701800	Oban Marina & Yacht Services Ltd	Seaton's Marina 028 703 832086
Holyhead Marina 01407 764242	01631 565333	Shamrock Quay 023 8022 9461
Howth Marina +353 1839 2777	Ocean Village Marina 023 8022 9385	Sharpness Marine 01453 811476
Hull Marina 01482 609960	Padstow Harbour 01841 532239	Shotley Marina 01473 788982
Humber Cruising Association	Parkstone Bay Marina 01202 747857	South Dock Marina 020 7252 2244
01472 268424		South Ferriby Marina 01652 635620

Southdown Marina	01752 823084
Southsea Marina	02392 822719
Sovereign Harbour Marina	
	01323 470099
Sparkes Marina	023 92463572
St Helier Marina	01534 447708
St Katharine Marina	0207 264 5312
St Peter Port Marinas	01481 720229
St Peter's Marina	0191 265 4472
Stornoway Marina	01851 702688
Stranraer Marina	01776 706565
Stromness Marina	01856 871313
Suffolk Yacht Harbour Ltd	
	01473 659240
Sunderland Marina	0191 514 4721
Sunseeker Marina	01202 381111
Sutton Harbour	01752 204702
Swansea Marina	01792 470310
Swanwick Marina	01489 884081
Tarbert Harbour	01880 820344
The Shipyard	01903 713327
Titchmarsh Marina	01255 672185
Tobermory Harbour Authority	
	01688 302876
Tollesbury Marina	01621 869202
Torpoint Yacht Harbour	01752 813658
Torquay Marina	01803 200210
Town Quay Marina	02380 234397
Troon Yacht Haven	01292 315553
Universal Marina	01489 574272
Victoria Dock Marina	01286 672346
Victoria Marina	01481 725987
Walton & Frinton Yacht Trust Limited	
	01255 675873
Waterford City Marina	
	+353 87 238 4944
Weymouth Harbour	01305 838386
Weymouth Marina	01305 767576
Whitby Marina	01947 602354
Whitehaven Marina	01946 692435
Whitehills Marina	01261 861427
Wick Marina	01955 602030
WicorMarine Yacht Haven	
	01329 237112
Windsor Marina	01753 853911
Wisbech Yacht Harbour	01945 588059
Woolverstone Marina	**01473 780206**
Yarmouth Harbour	01983 760321

MARINE ENGINEERS

AAS Marine
Aberystwyth 01970 631090

Allerton Engineering
Lowestoft 01502 537870

APAS Engineering Ltd
Southampton 023 8063 2558

Ardmair Boat Centre
Ullapool 01854 612054

Arisaig Marine
Inverness-shire 01687 450224

Arun Craft
Littlehampton 01903 723667

ASL Auto Services
Boston 01205 761560

Atlantis Marine Power Ltd
Plymouth 01752 208810

Attrill & Sons, H
Bembridge 01983 872319

Auto & Marine Services
Botley 07836 507000

Auto Marine Southsea 023 9282 5601

Baker, Keith
Brentford 07792 937790

BJ Marine Ltd Bangor 028 9127 1434

Bristol Boat Ltd
Bristol 01225 872032

Browne, Jimmy
Tralee +353 87 262 7158

Buccaneer Ltd
Macduff 01261 835199

Buzzard Marine Engineering
Yarmouth 01983 760707

C & B Marine Ltd
Chichester Marina 01243 511273

Caddy, Simon
Falmouth Marina
Falmouth 01326 372682

Caledonian Marine
Rhu Marina 01436 821184

Cardigan Outboards
Cardigan 01239 613966

Channel Islands Marine Ltd
Guernsey 01481 716880

Channel Islands Marine Ltd
Jersey 01534 767595

Cook's Diesel Service Ltd
Faversham 01795 538553

Cragie Engineering
Kirkwall 01856 874680

Wartsila Havant 023 9240 0121

Crinan Boatyard Ltd
Crinan 01546 830232

Cutler Marine Engineering, John
Emsworth 01243 375014

Dale Sailing Co Ltd
Milford Haven 01646 603110

Davis Marine Services
Ramsgate 01843 586172

Denney & Son, EL
Redcar 01642 483507

DH Marine (Shetland) Ltd
Shetland 01595 690618

Emark Marine Ltd
Emsworth 01243 375383

Evans, Lyndon
Brentford 07795 218704

Evans Marine Engineering, Tony
Pwllheli 01758 703070

Ferrypoint Boat Co
Youghal +353 24 94232

Fettes & Rankine Engineering
Aberdeen 01224 573343

Floetree Ltd
Loch Lomond Marina
Balloch 01389 752069

Fowey Harbour Marine Engineers
Fowey 01726 832806

Fox Marine Services Ltd
Jersey 01534 721312

Freeport Marine
Jersey 01534 888100

French Marine Motors Ltd
Colchester 01206 302133

French Marine Motors Ltd
Titchmarsh Marina 01255 850303

GH Douglas Marine Services
Fleetwood Harbour Village Marina,
Fleetwood 01253 877200

Golden Arrow Marine
Southampton 023 8071 0371

Goodchild Marine Services
Great Yarmouth 01493 782301

Goodwick Marine
Fishguard 01348 873955

Gosport Marina 023 9252 4811

Griffins Garage Dingle Marina,
Co Kerry +353 66 91 51178

Hale Marine, Ron
Portsmouth 023 9273 2985

Hamnavoe Engineering
Stromness 01856 850576

Harbour Engineering
Itchenor 01243 513454

Hartlepool Marine Engineering
Hartlepool 01429 867883

Hayles, Harold
Yarmouth 01983 760373

Herm Seaway Marine Ltd
St Peter Port 01481 726829

HNP Engineers (Lerwick Ltd)
Lerwick 01595 692493

Hodges, T Coleraine   028 7035 6422

Home Marine Emsworth Yacht
Harbour, Emsworth   01243 374125

Hook Marine Ltd Troon   01292 679500

Humphrey, Chris
Teignmouth   01626 772324

Instow Marine Services
Bideford   01271 861081

Jones (Boatbuilders), David
Chester   01244 390363

Keating Marine Engineering Ltd, Bill
Jersey   01534 733977

Kingston Marine Services
Cowes   01983 299385

Kippford Slipway Ltd
Dalbeattie   01556 620249

Lansdale Pannell Marine
Chichester   01243 550042

Lencraft Boats Ltd
Dungarvan   +353 58 68220

Llyn Marine Services
Pwllheli   01758 612606

Lynx Engineering
St Helens, Isle of Wight   01983 873711

M&G Marine Services
Mayflower International Marina,
Plymouth   01752 563345

MacDonald & Co Ltd, JN
Glasgow   0141 810 3400

Mackay Marine Services
Aberdeen   01224 575772

Mainbrayce Marine
Alderney   01481 722772

Malakoff and Moore
Lerwick   01595 695544

Marine Blast
Holy Loch   01369 705394

Mallaig Boat Building and Engineering
Mallaig   01687 462304

Marindus Engineering
Kilmore Quay   +353 53 29794

Marine Engineering Looe
Brixham   01803 844777

Marine Engineering Looe
Looe   01503 263009

Marine Engineering Services
Port Dinorwic   01248 671215

Marine General Engineers Beaucette
Marina, Guernsey   01481 245808

Marine Propulsion
Hayling Island   07836 737488

Marine & General Engineers
St. Sampsons Harbour, Guernsey
01481 245808

Marine Servicing
Eastbourne   07932 318414

Marine-Trak Engineering
Mylor Yacht Harbour
Falmouth   01326 376588

Marine Warehouse
Gosport   023 9258 0420

Marlec Marine
Ramsgate   01843 592176

Martin Outboards
Galgate   01524 751750

McQueen, Michael
Kilrush   +35 87 2574623

Meiher, Denis
Fenit   +353 87 958 4744

MES Marine Greenock   01475 744655

MMS Ardrossan   01294 604831/
07836 342332

Mobile Marine Engineering Liverpool
Marina, Liverpool   01565 733553

Mount's Bay Engineering
Newlyn   01736 363095

MP Marine Maryport   01900 810299

New World Yacht Care
Helensburgh   01436 820586

North Western Automarine Engineers
Largs   01475 687139

Noss Marine Services Dart Marina,
Dartmouth   01803 833343

Owen Marine, Robert
Porthmadog   01766 513435

Pace, Andy
Newhaven   01273 516010

**Penzance Dry Dock and Engineering
Co Ltd** Penzance   01736 363838

Pirie & Co, John S
Fraserburgh   01346 513314

Portavon Marine
Keynsham   01225 424301

Power Afloat, Elkins Boatyard
Christchurch   01202 489555

Powerplus Marine Cowes Yacht Haven,
Cowes   01983 290421

Pro-Marine Queen Anne's Battery
Marina, Plymouth   01752 267984

PT Marine Engineering
Hayling Island   023 9246 9332

R & M Marine
Portsmouth   023 9273 7555

R & S Engineering
Dingle Marina   +353 66 915 1189

Reddish Marine
Salcombe   01548 844094

RHP Marine Cowes   01983 290421

RK Marine Ltd
Hamble   01489 583585

RK Marine Ltd
Swanwick   01489 583572

Rossiter Yachts Ltd
Christchurch   01202 483250

Ryan & Roberts Marine Services
Askeaton   +353 61 392198

Salve Marine Ltd
Crosshaven   +353 21 4831145

Seamark-Nunn & Co
Felixstowe   01394 275327

Seapower Ipswich   01473 780090

Seaward Engineering
Glasgow   0141 632 4910

Seaway Marine
Gosport   023 9260 2722

Shearwater Engineering Services Ltd
Dunoon   01369 706666

Silvers Marina Ltd
Helensburgh   01436 831222

Starey Marine
Salcombe   01548 843655

Swordfish Marine Engineering
Holy Loch   01369 701905

Tarbert Marine
Arbroath   01241 872879

Thorne Boat Services
Thorne   01405 814197

Tollesbury Marine Engineering
Tollesbury Marina   01621 869919

Tony's Marine Services
Coleraine   07866 690436

TOR (Gerald Hales)
Stornoway   01851 871025

Vasey Marine Engineering, Gordon
Fareham   07798 638625

Volspec Ltd
Tollesbury   01621 869756

Wallis, Peter Torquay Marina,
Torquay   01803 844777

WB Marine Chichester   01243 512857

West Coast Marine
Troon   01292 318121

West Marine
Brighton   01273 626656

Weymouth Marina Mechanical Services
Weymouth   01305 779379

Whittington, G Lady Bee Marine,
Shoreham   01273 593801

Whitewater Marine
Malahide   +353 1 816 8473

Wigmore Wright Marine Services
Penarth Marina   029 2070 9983

Wright, M Manaccan   01326 231502

Wyko Industrial Services
Aberdeen   01224 246560

Ynys Marine
Cardigan   01239 613179

Youngboats
Faversham   01795 536176

1° West Marine Ltd
Portsmouth   023 9283 8335

MASTS, SPARS & RIGGING

JWS Marine Services
Portsmouth   02392 755155

A2 Rigging
Falmouth   01326 312209

Allspars Plymouth   01752 266766

Amble Boat Co Ltd
Morpeth   01665 710267

Arun Canvas & Rigging
Littlehampton   01903 732561

B+ St Peter Port   01481 726071

Buchanan, Keith
St Mary's   01720 422037

Bussell & Co, WL
Weymouth   01305 785633

Carbospars Ltd
Hamble   023 8045 6736

Cable & Rope Works
Bexhill-on-Sea   01424 220112

Clarke Rigging, Niall
Coleraine   07916 083858

Clyde Rigging
Ardrossan   07773 244821

Coates Marine Ltd
Whitby   01947 604486

Dauntless Boatyard Ltd
Canvey Island   01268 793782

Davies Marine Services
Ramsgate   01843 586172

Eurospars Ltd
Plymouth   01752 550550

Exe Leisure
Exeter   01392 879055

Fox's Marine Ipswich Ltd
Ipswich   01473 689111

Freeland Yacht Spars Ltd
Dorchester on Thames   01865 341277

Gordon, AD Portland   01305 821569

Hamble Custom Rigging Centre
Hamble   023 8045 2000

Harris Rigging Totnes 01803 840160

Heyn Engineering
Belfast   028 9035 0022

Holman Rigging
Chichester   01243 514000

Irish Spars and Rigging
Malahide   +353 86 209 5996

JWS Marine Services
Portsmouth   02392 755155

Kildale Marine Hull   01482 227464

Kilrush Marina Boatyard
Kilrush   +35 87 7990091

Lowestoft Yacht Services
Lowestoft   01502 585535

Laverty, Billy Galway +353 86 3892614

Leitch, WB
Tarbert, Loch Fyne   01880 820287

Lewis, Harry
Kinsale   +353 87 266 7127

Marine Resource Centre
Oban   01631 720291

Martin Leaning Masts & Rigging
Hayling   023 9237 1157

Mast & Rigging
Crosshaven   +353 21 483 3878

Mast & Rigging Services
Largs   01475 670110

Mast & Rigging Services
Inverkip   01475 522700

MP Marine Maryport   01900 810299

Ocean Rigging
Lymington   01590 676292

Owen Sails Oban   01631 720485

Pro Rig S Ireland   +353 87 298 3333

Ratsey, Stephen
Milford Haven   01646 601561

Riglt Ardrossan   07593 220213

Rig Magic Ipswich   01473 655089

Rig Shop
Southampton   023 8033 8341

Ronstan Gosport   023 9252 5377

Salcombe Boatstore
Salcombe   01548 843708

Seldén Mast Ltd
Gosport   01329 504000

Silvers Marina Ltd
Helensburgh   01436 831222

Silverwood Yacht Services Ltd
Portsmouth   023 9232 7067

Spencer Rigging
Cowes   01983 292022

Storrar Marine Store
Newcastle upon Tyne   0191 266 1037

Tedfords Rigging & Rafts
Belfast   028 9032 6763

TJ Rigging Conwy   07780 972411

TS Rigging Malden   01621 874861

Windjammer Marine
Milford Marina   01646 699070

Yacht Rigging Services
Plymouth   01752 226609

Z Spars UK Hadleigh   01473 822130

NAVIGATION EQUIPMENT – GENERAL

Belson Design Ltd, Nick
Southampton   077 6835 1330

Brown Son & Ferguson Ltd
Glasgow   0141 429 1234

Cooke & Son Ltd, B
Hull   01482 223454

Diverse Yacht Services
Hamble   023 8045 3399

Dolphin Maritime Software Ltd
Lancaster   01524 841946

Dubois Phillips & McCallum Ltd
Liverpool   0151 236 2776

Garmin Southampton   02380 524000

Geonav UK Ltd
Poole   0870 240 4575

Imray Laurie Norie and Wilson Ltd
St Ives, Cambs   01480 462114

Kelvin Hughes
Southampton   023 8063 4911

Lilley & Gillie Ltd, John
North Shields   0191 257 2217

Marine Chart Services
Wellingborough   01933 441629

Navico UK
Romsey   01794 510010

PC Maritime
Plymouth   01752 254205

Price & Co, WF Bristol 0117 929 2229

Raymarine Ltd
Portsmouth   023 9269 3611

Royal Institute of Navigation
London   020 7591 3130

Sea Chest Nautical Bookshop
Plymouth   01752 222012

Seath Instruments (1992) Ltd
Lowestoft   01502 573811

Smith (Marine) Ltd, AM
London   020 8529 6988

South Bank Marine Charts Ltd
Grimsby   01472 361137

Southcoasting Navigators
Devon   01626 335626

Stanford Charts
Bristol   0117 929 9966
London   020 7836 1321
Manchester   0870 890 3730

Todd Chart Agency Ltd
County Down   028 9146 6640

UK Hydrographic Office
Taunton   01823 337900

Warsash Nautical Bookshop
Warsash   01489 572384

Yachting Instruments Ltd
Sturminster Newton   01258 817662

PAINT & OSMOSIS

Advanced Blast Cleaning Paint
Tavistock   01822 617192
                             07970 407911

Herm Seaway Marine Ltd
St Peter Port   01481 726829

Gillingham Marina   01634 280022

Hempel Paints
Southampton   02380 232000

International Coatings Ltd
Southampton   023 8022 6722

Marineware Ltd
Southampton   023 8033 0208

NLB Marine
Ardrossan   01563 521509

Pro-Boat Ltd
Burnham on Crouch   01621 785455

Rustbuster Ltd
Peterborough   01775 761222

SP Systems
Isle of Wight   01983 828000

PROPELLERS & STERGEAR/REPAIRS

CJR Propulsion Ltd
Southampton   023 8063 9366

Darglow Engineering Ltd
Wareham   01929 556512

Propeller Revolutions
Poole   01202 671226

Sillette – Sonic Ltd
Sutton   020 8337 7543

Vetus Den Ouden Ltd
Southampton   02380 454507

RADIO COURSES / SCHOOLS

**Bisham Abbey Sailing
& Navigation School**
Bisham   01628 474960

**East Coast Offshore Yachting –
Les Rant** Perry   01480 861381

Hamble School of Yachting
Hamble   023 8045 6687

Pembrokeshire Cruising
Neyland   01646 602500

Plymouth Sailing School
Plymouth   01752 493377

Start Point Sailing
Kingsbridge   01548 810917

REEFING SYSTEMS

Atlantic Spars Ltd
Brixham   01803 843322

Calibra Marine International Ltd
Southampton   08702 400358

Eurospars Ltd
Plymouth   01752 550550

Holman Rigging
Chichester   01243 514000

Sea Teach Ltd
Emsworth   01243 375774

Southern Spar Services
Northam   023 8033 1714

Wragg, Chris
Lymington   01590 677052

Z Spars UK Hadleigh   01473 822130

REPAIR MATERIALS & ACCESSORIES

Akeron Ltd
Southend on Sea   01702 297101

Howells & Son, KJ
Poole   01202 665724

JB Timber Ltd
North Ferriby   01482 631765

Robbins Timber Bristol   0117 9633136

Sika Ltd
Welwyn Garden City   01707 394444

Solent Composite Systems
East Cowes   01983 292602

Technix Rubber & Plastics Ltd
Southampton   01489 789944

Tiflex Liskeard   01579 320808

Timage & Co Ltd
Braintree   01376 343087

Trade Grade Products Ltd
Poole   01202 820177

Wessex Resins & Adhesives Ltd
Romsey   01794 521111

ROPE & WIRE

Cable & Rope Works
Bexhill-on-Sea   01424 220112

Euro Rope Ltd
Scunthorpe   01724 280480

Marlow Ropes
Hailsham   01323 444444

Mr Splice Leicester   0800 1697178

Spinlock Ltd Cowes   01983 295555

TJ Rigging Conwy   07780 972411

SAFETY EQUIPMENT

AB Marine Ltd
St Peter Port   01481 722378

Adec Marine Ltd
Croydon   020 8686 9717

Anchorwatch UK
Edinburgh   0131 447 5057

Avon Inflatables
Llanelli   01554 882000

Cosalt International Ltd
Aberdeen   01224 588327

Crewsaver Gosport   01329 820000

Glaslyn Marine Supplies Ltd
Porthmadog   01766 513545

Exposure Lights
Pulborough   01798 839300

Guardian Fire Protection
Manchester   0800 358 7522

Hale Marine, Ron
Portsmouth   023 9273 2985

Herm Seaway Marine Ltd
St Peter Port   01481 722838

KTS Seasafety Kilkeel   028 41762655

McMurdo Pains Wessex
Portsmouth   023 9262 3900

Met Office Bracknell   0845 300 0300

Nationwide Marine Hire
Warrington   01925 245788

Norwest Marine Ltd
Liverpool   0151 207 2860

Ocean Safety
Southampton   023 8072 0800

Polymarine Ltd
Conwy   01492 583322

Premium Liferaft Services
Burnham-on-Crouch   0800 243673

Ribeye Dartmouth   01803 832060

South Eastern Marine Services Ltd
Basildon   01268 534427

Suffolk Sailing
Ipswich   01473 604678

Whitstable Marine
Whitstable   01227 262525

Winters Marine Ltd
Salcombe   01548 843580

SAILMAKERS & REPAIRS

Allison-Gray
Dundee   01382 505888

Alsop Sailmakers, John
Salcombe   01548 843702

AM Trimming Windsor   01932 821090

Arun Canvas & Rigging
Littlehampton   01903 732561

Arun Sails Chichester   01243 573185

Bank Sails, Bruce
Southampton   01489 582444

Barrett, Katy
St Peter Port   07781 404299

Batt Sails Bosham   01243 575505

Bissett and Ross
Aberdeen   01224 580659

Boatshed, The
Felinheli, Bangor   01248 679939

Breaksea Sails Barry   01446 730785

Bristol Sails Bristol   0117 922 5080

Buchanan, Keith
St Mary's   01720 422037

C&J Marine Textiles
Chichester   01243 782629

Calibra Sails
Dartmouth   01803 833094

Clarke Rigging, Niall
Coleraine   07916 083858

Coastal Covers
Portsmouth   023 9252 0200

Covercare Fareham   01329 311878

Covers + Stuff
Douglas, Isle of Man   07624 400037

Crawford, Margaret
Kirkwall   01856 875692

Crusader Sails Poole   01202 670580

Crystal Covers
Portsmouth   023 9238 0143

Cullen Sailmakers
Galway   +353 91 771991

Dolphin Sails Harwich   01255 243366

Doyle Sails
Southampton   023 8033 2622

Downer International Sails & Chandlery
Dun Laoghaire   +353 1 280 0231

Duthie Marine Safety, Arthur
Glasgow   0141 429 4553

Dynamic Sails
Emsworth   01243 374495

Flew Sailmakers
Portchester   01329 822676

Fylde Coast Sailmaking Co
Fleetwood   01253 873476

Freeman Sails
Padstow   07771 610053

Garland Sails Bristol   01275 393473

Goacher Sails
Cumbria   01539 488686

Gowen Ocean Sailmakers
West Mersea   01206 384412

Green Sailmakers, Paul
Plymouth   01752 660317

Henderson Sails & Covers
Southsea   023 9229 4700

Hood Sailmakers UK
Wareham   0844 209 4789

Hooper, A Plymouth   01752 830411

Hyde Sails
Southampton   0845 543 8945

Jackson Yacht Services
Jersey   01534 743819

Jeckells and Son Ltd (Wroxham)
Wroxham   01603 782223

Jessail Ardrossan   01294 467311

JKA Sailmakers
Pwllheli   01758 613266

Kemp Sails Ltd
Wareham   01929 554308/554378

Kildale Marine Hull   01482 227464

Lawrence Sailmakers, J
Brightlingsea   01206 302863

Leitch, WB
Tarbert, Loch Fyne   01880 820287

Leith UK
Berwick on Tweed   01289 307264

Le Monnier, Yannick
Galway   +353 87 628 9854

Lodey Sails Newlyn   01736 719359

Lossie Sails
Lossiemouth   07989 956698

Lucas Sails Portchester   023 9237 3699

Malakoff and Moore
Lerwick   01595 695544

McCready and Co Ltd, J
Belfast   028 90232842

McKillop Sails, John
Kingsbridge   01548 852343

McNamara Sails, Michael
Great Yarmouth   01692 584186

McWilliam Sailmaker (Crosshaven)
Crosshaven   +353 21 4831505

Sail Shape
Fowey   01726 833731

Montrose Rope and Sails
Montrose   01674 672657

Mountfield Sails
Hayling Island   023 9246 3720

Mouse Sails Holyhead   01407 763636

Nicholson Hughes Sails
Rosneath   01436 831356

North Sea Sails
Tollesbury   01621 869367

North West Sails
Keighley   01535 652949

Northrop Sails
Ramsgate   01843 851665

O'Mahony Sailmakers
Kinsale   +353 86 326 0018

O'Sullivans Marine Ltd
Tralee   +353 66 7129635

Owen Sails Benderloch   01631 720485

Parker & Kay Sailmakers –
East Ipswich   01473 659878

Parker & Kay Sailmakers –
South Hamble   023 8045 8213

Penrose Sailmakers
Falmouth   01326 312705

Pinnell & Bax
Northampton   01604 592808

Pollard Marine
Port St Mary   01624 835831

Quantum Sails
Ipswich Haven Marina   01473 659878

Quantum-Parker & Kay Sailmakers
Hamble   023 8045 8213

Quay Sails (Poole) Ltd
Poole   01202 681128

Ratsey & Lapthorn
Isle of Wight   01983 294051

Ratsey Sailmakers, Stephen
Milford Haven   01646 601561

Relling One Design
Portland   01305 826555

SO31 Bags
Southampton   023 8045 5106

Rig Shop, The	
Southampton	023 8033 8341
Rockall Sails	
Chichester	01243 573185
Sail Locker	
Woolverstone Marina	01473 780206
Sail Style	
Hayling Island	023 9246 3720
Sails & Canvas Exeter	01392 877527
Sail Register Ulceby	01469 589444
Saltern Sail Co	
West Cowes	01983 280014
Saltern Sail Company	
Yarmouth	01983 760120
Sanders Sails	
Lymington	01590 673981
Saturn Sails Largs	01475 689933
Scott & Co, Graham	
St Peter Port	01481 259380
Shore Sailmakers	
Swanwick	01489 589450
SKB Sails Falmouth	01326 372107
Sketrick Sailmakers Ltd	
Killinchy	028 9754 1400
Solo Sails Penzance	01736 366004
Storrar Marine Store	
Newcastle upon Tyne	0191 266 1037
Suffolk Sails	
Woodbridge	01394 386323
Sunset Sails Sligo	+353 71 62792
Torquay Marina Sails and Canvas	
Exeter	01392 877527
Trident UK Gateshead	0191 490 1736
Sailcare (UK) Ltd	
Cowes	01983 248589
Underwood Sails	
Queen Anne's Battery	
Plymouth	01752 229661
W Sails Leigh-on-Sea	01702 714550
Warren Hall	
Beaucette, Guernsey	07781 444280
Watson Sails Dublin	+353 1 846 2206
WB Leitch and Son	
Tarbert	01880 820287
Westaway Sails	
Plymouth Yacht Haven	01752 892560
Westsails.ie Kilrush	+35 876289854

Wilkinson Sails	
Burnham-on-Crouch	01621 786770
Wilkinson Sails	
Teynham	01795 521503
Yacht Shop, The	
Fleetwood	01253 879238

SOLAR POWER

Ampair Ringwood	01425 480780
Barden UK Ltd Fareham	01489 570770
Marlec Engineering Co Ltd	
Corby	01536 201588

SPRAYHOODS & DODGERS

A & B Textiles	
Gillingham	01634 579686
Allison–Gray Dundee	01382 505888
Arton, Charles	
Milford-on-Sea	01590 644682
Arun Canvas and Rigging Ltd	
Littlehampton	01903 732561
Boatshed, The	
Felinheli, Bangor	01248 679939
Buchanan, Keith	
St Mary's	01720 422037
C & J Marine Textiles	
Chichester	01243 785485
Covercare Fareham	01329 311878
Covercraft	
Southampton	023 8033 8286
Crystal Covers	
Portsmouth	023 9238 0143
Forth Marine Textiles	
Holy Loch	01383 622444
Jeckells and Son Ltd	
Wroxham	01603 782223
Jessail Ardrossan	01294 467311
Lomond Boat Covers	
Alexandria	01389 602734
Lucas Sails Portchester	023 9237 3699
Poole Canvas Co Ltd	
Poole	01202 677477
Sail Register Ulceby	01469 589444
Saundersfoot Auto Marine	
Saundersfoot	01834 812115
Trident UK Gateshead	0191 490 1736

SURVEYORS AND NAVAL ARCHITECTS

Amble Boat Company Ltd	
Amble	01665 710267

Ark Surveys East Anglia/South Coast	
	01621 857065/01794 521957
Atkin & Associates	
Lymington	01590 688633
Barbican Yacht Agency Ltd	
Plymouth	01752 228855
Battick, Lee St Helier	01534 611143
Booth Marine Surveys, Graham	
Birchington-on-Sea	01843 843793
Byrde & Associates	
Kimmeridge	01929 480064
Bureau Maritime Ltd	
Maldon	01621 859181
Byrde & Associates	
Kimmeridge	01929 480064
Cannell & Associates, David M	
Wivenhoe	01206 823337
Cardiff Commercial Boat Operators Ltd	
Cardiff	029 2037 7872
Clarke Designs LLP, Owen	
Dartmouth	01803 770495
Connor, Richard	
Coleraine	07712 115751
Cox, David Penryn	01326 340808
Davies, Peter N	
Wivenhoe	01206 823289
Down Marine Co Ltd	
Belfast	028 90480247
Evans, Martin	
Kirby le Soken	07887 724055
Goodall, JL Whitby	01947 604791
Green, James Plymouth	01752 660516
Greening Naval Architect Ltd, David	
Salcombe	01548 842000
Hansing & Associates	
North Wales/Midlands	01248 671291
JP Services – Marine Safety & Training	
Chichester	01243 537552
MacGregor, WA	
Felixstowe	01394 676034
Mahoney & Co, KPO	
Co Cork	+353 21 477 6150
Marinte Surveys UK	
Emsworth	07798 554535
Marintec Lymington	01590 683414
Norwood Marine	
Margate	01843 835711
Quay Consultants Ltd	
West Wittering	01243 673056
Scott Marine Surveyors & Consultants	
Conwy	01492 573001

S Roberts Marine Ltd
Liverpool 0151 707 8300

Staton-Bevan, Tony
Lymington 01590 645755/
07850 315744

Thomas, Stephen
Southampton 023 8048 6273

Towler, Perrin
Lymington 01590 718087

Victoria Yacht Surveys
Cornwall 0800 083 2113

Ward & McKenzie
Woodbridge 01394 383222

Ward & McKenzie (North East)
Pocklington 01759 304322

YDSA Yacht Designers & Surveyors Association Bordon 0845 0900162

TAPE TECHNOLOGY

CC Marine Services (Rubbaweld) Ltd
London 020 7402 4009

Trade Grade Products Ltd
Poole 01202 820177

UK Epoxy Resins
Burscough 01704 892364

3M United Kingdom plc
Bracknell 0870 5360036

TRANSPORT/YACHT DELIVERIES

Boat Shifters
07733 344018/01326 210548

Convoi Exceptionnel Ltd
Hamble 023 8045 3045

Debbage Yachting
Ipswich 01473 601169

East Coast Offshore Yachting
01480 861381

Hainsworth's UK and Continental
Bingley 01274 565925

Houghton Boat Transport
Tewkesbury 07831 486710

MCL Transboat 08455 201900

MJS Boat Transport
Alexandria, Scotland 01389 755047

Moonfleet Sailing Poole 01202 682269

Performance Yachting
Plymouth 01752 565023

Peters & May Ltd
Southampton 023 8048 0480

Reeder School of Seamanship, Mike
Lymington 01590 674560

Seafix Boat Transfer
North Wales 01766 514507

Sealand Boat Deliveries Ltd
Liverpool 01254 705225

Shearwater Sailing
Southampton 01962 775213

Southcoasting Navigators
Devon 01626 335626

West Country Boat Transport
01566 785651

Wolff, David 07659 550131

TUITION/SAILING SCHOOLS

Association of Scottish Yacht Charterers Argyll 07787 363562
01852 200258

Bisham Abbey Sailing & Navigation School Bisham 01628 474960

Blue Baker Yachts
Ipswich 01473 780008

British Offshore Sailing School
Hamble 023 8045 7733

Coastal Sea School
Weymouth 0870 321 3271

Dart Harbour Sea School
Dartmouth 01803 839339

Dartmouth Sailing
Dartmouth 01803 833399

Drake Sailing School
Plymouth 01635 253009

East Anglian Sea School
Ipswich 01473 659992

**East Coast Offshore Yachting
– Les Rant** Perry 01480 861381

Gibraltar Sailing Centre
Gibraltar +350 78554

Glenans Irish Sailing School
Baltimore +353 28 20154

Hamble School of Yachting
Hamble 023 8045 6687

Haslar Sea School
Gosport 023 9260 2708

Hobo Yachting
Southampton 023 8033 4574

Hoylake Sailing School
Wirral 0151 632 4664

Ibiza Sailing School 07092 235 853

International Yachtmaster Academy
Southampton 0800 515439

JP Services – Marine Safety & Training
Chichester 01243 537552

Lymington Cruising School
Lymington 01590 677478

Marine Leisure Association (MLA)
Southampton 023 8029 3822

Menorca Cruising School
01995 679240

Moonfleet Sailing
Poole 01202 682269

National Marine Correspondence School Macclesfield 01625 262365

Pembrokeshire Cruising
Neyland 01646 602500

Performance Yachting & Chandlery
Plymouth 01752 565023

Plain Sailing
Dartmouth 01803 853843

Plymouth Sailing School
Plymouth 01752 493377

Port Edgar Marina & Sailing School
Port Edgar 0131 331 3330

Portsmouth Outdoor Centre
Portsmouth 023 9266 3873

Portugal Sail & Power 01473 833001

Safe Water Training Sea School Ltd
Wirral 0151 630 0466

Sail East
Felixstowe 01255 502887

Sail East
River Crouch 07860 271954

Sail East
River Medway 07932 157027

Sail East Harwich 01473 689344

Sally Water Training
East Cowes 01983 299033

Sea-N-Shore
Salcombe 01548 842276

Seafever East Grinstead 01342 316293

Solaris Mediterranean Sea School
01925 642909

Solent School of Yachting
Southampton 023 8045 7733

Southcoasting Navigators
Devon 01626 335626

Southern Sailing
Southampton 01489 575511

Start Point Sailing
Dartmouth 01548 810917

Sunsail
Port Solent/Largs 0870 770 6314

Team Sailing Gosport 023 9252 4370

Workman Marine School
Portishead 01275 845844

Wride School of Sailing, Bob
North Ferriby 01482 635623

WATERSIDE ACCOMMODATION & RESTAURANTS

51st State Bar & Grill
Dunoon 01369 703595

Abbey, The Penzance 01736 366906

Al Porto
Hull Marina 01482 238889

Arun View Inn, The
Littlehampton 01903 722335

Baywatch on the Beach
Bembridge 01983 873259

Beaucette Marina Restaurant
Guernsey 01481 247066

Bella Napoli
Brighton Marina 01273 818577

Bembridge Coast Hotel
Bembridge 01983 873931

Budock Vean Hotel
Porth Navas Creek 01326 252100

Café Mozart Cowes 01983 293681

Caffé Uno Port Solent 023 9237 5227

Chandlers Bar & Bistro
Queen Anne's Battery Marina
Plymouth 01752 257772

Chiquito Port Solent 02392 205070

Cruzzo Malahide Marina
Co Dublin +353 1 845 0599

Cullins Yard Bistro
Dover 01304 211666

Custom House, The
Poole 01202 676767

Dart Marina River Lounge
Dartmouth 01803 832580

Doghouse Swanwick Marina,
Hamble 01489 571602

Dolphin Restaurant
Gorey 01534 853370

Doune Knoydart 01687 462667

El Puertos
Penarth Marina 029 2070 5551

Falmouth Marina
Marine Bar and Restaurant
Falmouth 01326 313481

Ferry Boat Inn West Wick Marina
Nr Chelmsford 01621 740208

Ferry Inn, The (restaurant)
Pembroke Dock 01646 682947

Fisherman's Wharf
Sandwich 01304 613636

Folly Inn Cowes 01983 297171

Gaffs Restaurant
Fenit, County Kerry +353 66 71 36666

Godleys Hotel Fenit
County Kerry +353 66 71 36108

Harbour Lights Restaurant
Walton on the Naze 01255 851887

Haven Bar and Bistro, The
Lymington Yacht Haven 01590 679971

Haven Hotel Poole 08453 371550

HMS Ganges Restaurant
Mylor Yacht Harbour 01326 374320

Holy Loch Inn
Holy Loch 01369 706903

Hunters Bar & Grill
Holy Loch 01369 707772

Jolly Sailor, The
Bursledon 023 8040 5557

Kames Hotel Argyll 01700 811489

Ketch Rigger, The Hamble Point
Marina Hamble 023 8045 5601

Kings Arms Stoborough 01929 552705

Kota Restaurant
Porthleven 01326 562407

La Cala Lady Bee Marina
Shoreham 01273 597422

La Cantina Restaurant
Dunoon 01369 703595

Le Nautique
St Peter Port 01481 721714

Lighter Inn, The
Topsham 01392 875439

Mariners Bistro Sparkes Marina,
Hayling Island 023 9246 9459

Mary Mouse II Haslar Marina,
Gosport 023 9252 5200

Martha's Vineyard
Milford Haven 01646 697083

Master Builder's House Hotel
Buckler's Hard 01590 616253

Millstream Hotel
Bosham 01243 573234

Montagu Arms Hotel
Beaulieu 01590 612324

Oyster Quay
Mercury Yacht Harbour,
Hamble 023 8045 7220

Paris Hotel Coverack 01326 280258

Pebble Beach, The
Gosport 023 9251 0789

Philip Leisure Group
Dartmouth 01803 833351

Priory Bay Hotel
Seaview, Isle of Wight 01983 613146

Quayside Hotel Brixham 01803 855751

Queen's Hotel Kirkwall 01856 872200

Sails Dartmouth 01803 839281

Shell Bay Seafood Restaurant
Poole Harbour 01929 450363

Simply Italian Sovereign Harbour,
Eastbourne 01323 470911

Spinnaker, The
Chichester Marina 01243 511032

Spit Sand Fort
The Solent 01329 242077

Steamboat Inn
Lossiemouth 01343 812066

Tayvallich Inn, The
Argyll 01546 870282

Villa Adriana Newhaven Marina
Newhaven 01273 513976

Warehouse Brasserie, The
Poole 01202 677238

36 on the Quay
Emsworth 01243 375592

WEATHER INFORMATION

Met Office Exeter 0870 900 0100

WOOD FITTINGS

Howells & Son, KJ
Poole 01202 665724

Onward Trading Co Ltd
Southampton 01489 885250

Robbins Timber
Bristol 0117 963 3136

Sheraton Marine Cabinet
Witney 01993 868275

YACHT BROKERS

ABC Powermarine
Beaumaris 01248 811413

ABYA Association of
Brokers & Yacht Agents
Bordon 0845 0900162

Adur Boat Sales
Southwick 01273 596680

Ancasta International Boat Sales
Southampton 023 8045 0000

Anglia Yacht Brokerage
Bury St Edmunds 01359 271747

Ardmair Boat Centre
Ullapool 01854 612054

Barbican Yacht Agency, The
Plymouth 01752 228855

Bates Wharf Marine Sales Ltd
01932 571141

BJ Marine Bangor 028 9127 1434

Boatworks + Ltd
St Peter Port 01481 726071

Caley Marina Inverness 01463 236539

Calibra Marine International Ltd
Southampton 08702 400358

Camper & Nicholsons International
London 020 7009 1950

Clarke & Carter Interyacht Ltd
Ipswich/Burnham on Crouch
01473 659681/01621 785600

Coastal Leisure Ltd
Southampton 023 8033 2222

Dale Sailing Brokerage
Neyland 01646 603105

Deacons Southampton 023 8040 2253

Exe Leisure Topsham 001392 879055

Ferrypoint Boat Co
Youghal +353 24 94232

Gweek Quay Boatyard
Helston 01326 221657

**International Barge
& Yacht Brokers**
Southampton 023 8045 5205

Iron Wharf Boatyard
Faversham 01795 536296

Jackson Yacht Services
Jersey 01534 743819

Kings Yacht Agency
Beaulieu 01590 616316

Kippford Slipway Ltd
Dalbeattie 01556 620249

Lencraft Boats Ltd
Dungarvan +353 58 68220

Liberty Yachts Ltd
Plymouth 01752 227911

Lucas Yachting, Mike
Torquay 01803 212840

Network Yacht Brokers
Dartmouth 01803 834864

Network Yacht Brokers
Plymouth 01752 605377

New Horizon Yacht Agency
Guernsey 01481 726335

Oyster Brokerage Ltd
Southampton 02380 831011

Pearn and Co, Norman
(Looe Boatyard) Looe 01503 262244

Performance Boat Company
Maidenhead 07768 464717

Peters Chandlery
Chichester 01243 511033

Portavon Marina
Keynsham 0117 986 1626

Retreat BY Topsham 01392 874720

SD Marine Ltd
Southampton 023 8045 7278

Sea & Shore Ship Chandler
Dundee 01382 202666

South Pier Shipyard
St Helier 01534 711000

South West Yacht Brokers Group
Plymouth 01752 401421

Sunbird Marine Services
Fareham 01329 842613

Swordfish Marine Brokerage
Holy Loch 01369 701905

Trafalgar Yacht Services
Fareham 01329 823577

Transworld Yachts
Hamble 023 8045 7704

Walton Marine Sales
Brighton 01273 670707
Portishead 01275 840132

Walton Marine Sales
Wroxham 01603 781178

Watson Marine, Charles
Hamble 023 8045 6505

Western Marine
Dublin +353 1280 0321

Woodrolfe Brokerage
Maldon 01621 868494

Youngboats Faversham 01795 536176

YACHT CHARTERS & HOLIDAYS

Ardmair Boat Centre
Ullapool 01854 612054

**Association of Scottish Yacht
Charterers** Argyll 01880 820012

Camper & Nicholsons International
London 020 7009 1950

Coastal Leisure Ltd
Southampton 023 8033 2222

Crusader Yachting
Turkey 01732 867321

Dartmouth Sailing
Dartmouth 01803 833399

Dartmouth Yacht Charters
Kingswear 01803 883501

Doune Marine Mallaig 01687 462667

Four Seasons Yacht Charter
Gosport 023 9251 1789

Golden Black Sailing
Cornwall 01209 715757

Hamble Point Yacht Charters
Hamble 023 8045 7110

Haslar Marina & Victory Yacht Charters
Gosport 023 9252 0099

Indulgence Yacht Charters
Padstow 01841 719090

Liberty Yachts West Country, Greece,
Mallorca & Italy 01752 227911

Nautilus Yachting
Mediterranean & Caribbean
01732 867445

On Deck Sailing
Southampton 023 8063 9997

Patriot Charters & Sail School
Milford Haven 01437 741202

West Country Yachts
Plymouth 01752 606999
Falmouth 01326 212320

Puffin Yachts
Port Solent 01483 420728

Sailing Holidays Ltd
Mediterranean 020 8459 8787

Sailing Holidays in Ireland
Kinsale +353 21 477 2927

Setsail Holidays
Greece, Turkey,
Croatia, Majorca 01787 310445

Shannon Sailing Ltd
Tipperary +353 67 24499

Sleat Marine Services
Isle of Skye 01471 844216

Smart Yachts
Mediterranean 01425 614804

South West Marine Training
Dartmouth 01803 853843

Sovereign Sailingl
Kinsale +353 87 6172555

Sunsail
Worldwide 0870 770 0102

Templecraft Yacht Charters
Lewes 01273 812333

TJ Sailing Gosport 07803 499691

Top Yacht Sailing Ltd
Havant 02392 347655

Victory Yacht Charters
Gosport 023 9252 0099

West Wales Yacht Charter
Pwllheli 07748 634869

39 North (Mediterranean)
Kingskerwell 07071 393939

YACHT CLUBS

Aberaeron YC
Aberdovey 01545 570077

Aberdeen and Stonehaven SC
Nr Inverurie 01569 764006

Aberdour BC 01383 860029

Abersoch Power BC
Abersoch 01758 712027

Aberystwyth BC
Aberystwyth 01970 624575

Aldeburgh YC 01728 452562

Alderney SC 01481 822959

Alexandra YC
Southend-on-Sea 01702 340363

Arklow SC +353 402 33100

Arun YC Littlehampton 01903 716016

Axe YC Axemouth 01297 20043

Ayr Yacht and CC 01292 476034

Ballyholme YC Bangor 028 91271467

Baltimore SC +353 28 20426

Banff SC 01464 820308

Bantry Bay SC +353 27 51724

Barry YC 01446 735511

Beaulieu River SC
Brockenhurst 01590 616273

Bembridge SC
Isle of Wight 01983 872237

Benfleet YC
Canvey Island 01268 792278

**Blackpool and
Fleetwood YC** 01253 884205

Blackwater SC Maldon 01621 853923

Blundellsands SC 0151 929 2101

Bosham SC Chichester 01243 572341

Brading Haven YC
Isle of Wight 01983 872289

Bradwell CC 01621 892970

Bradwell Quay YC
Wickford 01268 890173

Brancaster Staithe SC 01485 210249

Brandy Hole YC
Hullbridge 01702 230320

Brightlingsea SC 01206 303275

Brighton Marina YC
Peacehaven 01273 818711

Bristol Avon SC 01225 873472

Bristol Channel YC
Swansea 01792 366000

Bristol Corinthian YC
Axbridge 01934 732033

Brixham YC 01803 853332

**Burnham Overy
Staithe SC** 01328 730961

Burnham-on-Crouch SC
01621 782812

Burnham-on-Sea SC
Bridgwater 01278 792911

Burry Port YC 01554 833635

Cabot CC 01275 855207

Caernarfon SC (Menai Strait)
Caernarfon 01286 672861

Campbeltown SC 01586 552488

Island YC Canvey Island 01702 510360

Cardiff YC 029 2046 3697

Cardiff Bay YC 029 20226575

Carlingford Lough YC
Rostrevor 028 4173 8604

Carrickfergus SC
Whitehead 028 93 351402

Castle Cove SC
Weymouth 01305 783708

Castlegate Marine Club
Stockton on Tees 01642 583299

Chanonry SC Fortrose 01463 221415

Chichester Cruiser and Racing Club
01483 770391

Chichester YC 01243 512918

Christchurch SC 01202 483150

Clyde CC Glasgow 0141 221 2774

Co Antrim YC
Carrickfergus 028 9337 2322

Cobnor Activities Centre Trust
01243 572791

Coleraine YC 028 703 44503

Colne YC Brightlingsea 01206 302594

Conwy YC Deganwy 01492 583690

Coquet YC 01665 710367

Corrib Rowing & YC
Galway City +353 91 564560

Cowes Combined Clubs
01983 295744

Cowes Corinthian YC
Isle of Wight 01983 296333

Cowes Yachting 01983 280770

Cramond BC 0131 336 1356

Creeksea SC
Burnham-on-Crouch 01245 320578

Crookhaven SC +353 87 2379997

Crouch YC
Burnham-on-Crouch 01621 782252

Dale YC 01646 636362

Dartmouth YC 01803 832305

Deben YC Woodbridge 01394 384440

Dell Quay SC Chichester 01243 514639

Dingle SC +353 66 51984

Douglas Bay YC 01624 673965

Dovey YC
Aberdovey 01213 600008

Dun Laoghaire MYC +353 1 288 938

Dunbar SC
Cockburnspath 01368 86287

East Antrim BC 028 28 277204

East Belfast YC 028 9065 6283

East Cowes SC 01983 531687

East Dorset SC Poole 01202 706111

East Lothian YC 01620 892698

Eastney Cruising Association
Portsmouth 023 92734103

Eling SC 023 80863987

Emsworth SC 01243 372850

Emsworth Slipper SC 01243 372523

Essex YC Southend 01702 478404

Exe SC (River Exe)
Exmouth 01395 264607

Eyott SC Mayland 01245 320703

Fairlie YC 01294 213940

Falmouth Town SC 01326 373915

Falmouth Watersports Association
Falmouth 01326 211223

Fareham Sailing & Motor BC
Fareham 01329 280738

Felixstowe Ferry SC 01394 283785

Findhorn YC Findhorn 01309 690247

Fishguard Bay YC
Lower Fishguard 01348 872866

Flushing SC Falmouth 01326 374043

Folkestone Yacht and Motor BC
Folkestone 01303 251574

Forth Corinthian YC
Haddington 0131 552 5939

Forth YCs Association
Edinburgh 0131 552 3006

Fowey Gallants SC 01726 832335

Foynes YC Foynes +353 69 91201

Galway Bay SC +353 91 794527

Glasson SC Lancaster 01524 751089

Glenans Irish Sailing School
+353 1 6611481

Glenans Irish SC (Westport)
+353 98 26046

Gosport CC Gosport 02392 586838

Gravesend SC 07538 326623

Greenwich YC London 020 8858 7339

Grimsby and Cleethorpes YC
Grimsby 01472 356678

Guernsey YC
St Peter Port 01481 725342

Hamble River SC
Southampton 023 80452070

Hampton Pier YC
Herne Bay 01227 364749

Hardway SC Gosport 023 9258 1875

Hartlepool YC 01429 233423

Harwich Town SC 01255 503200

Hastings and St Leonards YC
Hastings 01424 420656

Haven Ports YC
Woodbridge 01473 659658

Hayling Ferry SC; Locks SC
Hayling Island 07870 367571

Hayling Island SC 023 92463768

Helensburgh SC Rhu 01436 672778

Helensburgh 01436 821234

Helford River SC
Helston 01326 231006

Herne Bay SC 01227 375650

Highcliffe SC
Christchurch 01425 274874

Holyhead SC 01407 762526

Holywood YC 028 90423355

Hoo Ness YC Sidcup 01634 250052

Hornet SC Gosport 023 9258 0403

Howth YC +353 1 832 2141

Hoylake SC Wirral	0151 632 2616
Hullbridge YC	01702 231797
Humber Yawl Club	01482 667224
Hundred of Hoo SC	01634 250102
Hurlingham YC London	020 8788 5547
Hurst Castle SC	01590 645589
Hythe SC Southampton	02380 846563
Hythe & Saltwood SC	01303 265178
Ilfracombe YC	01271 863969
Iniscealtra SC	
Limerick	+353 61 338347
Invergordon BC	01349 893772
Irish CC	+353 214870031
Island CC Salcombe	01548 844631
Island SC Isle of Wight	01983 296621
Island YC	
Canvey Island	01268 510360
Isle of Bute SC	
Rothesay	01700 502819
Isle of Man YC	
Port St Mary	01624 832088
Itchenor SC Chichester	01243 512400
Keyhaven YC	01590 642165
Killyleagh YC	028 4482 8250
Kircubbin SC	028 4273 8422
Kirkcudbright SC	01557 331727
Langstone SC Havant	023 9248 4577
Largs SC Largs	01475 670000
Larne Rowing & SC	028 2827 4573
Lawrenny YC	01646 651212
Leigh-on-Sea SC	01702 476788
Lerwick BC	01595 696954
Lilliput SC Poole	01202 740319
Littlehampton Yacht Club	
Littlehampton	01903 713990
Loch Ryan SC Stranraer	01776 706322
Lochaber YC	
Fort William	01397 772361
Locks SC Portsmouth	07980 856267
Looe SC	01503 262559
Lossiemouth CC	
Fochabers	01348 812121
Lough Swilly YC Fahn	+353 74 22377
Lowestoft CC	07810 522515
Lyme Regis Power BC	01297 443788
Lyme Regis SC	01297 442373
Lymington Town SC	0159 674514
Lympstone SC Exeter	01395 278792
Madoc YC Porthmadog	01766 512976
Malahide YC	+353 1 845 3372

Maldon Little Ship Club	
	01621 854139
Manx Sailing & CC	
Ramsey	01624 813494
Marchwood YC	023 80666141
Margate YC	01843 292602
Marina BC Pwllheli	01758 612271
Maryport YC	01228 560865
Mayflower SC Plymouth	01752 662526
Mayo SC (Rosmoney)	
Rosmoney	+353 98 27772
Medway YC Rochester	01634 718399
Menai Bridge BC	
Beaumaris	01248 810583
Mengham Rythe SC	
Hayling Island	023 92463337
Merioneth YC Barmouth	01341 280000
Monkstone Cruising and SC	
Swansea	01792 812229
Montrose SC Montrose	01674 672554
Mumbles YC Swansea	01792 369321
Mylor YC Falmouth	01326 374391
Nairn SC	01667 453897
National YC	
Dun Laoghaire	+353 1 280 5725
Netley SC Netley	023 80454272
New Quay YC	
Aberdovey	01545 560516
Newhaven & Seaford SC	
Seaford	01323 890077
Newport and Uskmouth SC	
Cardiff	01633 271417
Newtownards SC	028 9181 3426
Neyland YC	01646 600267
North Devon YC	
Bideford	01271 861390
North Fambridge Yacht Centre	
	01621 740370
North Haven YC Poole	01202 708830
North of England Yachting Association	
Kirkwall	01856 872331
North Sunderland Marine Club	
Sunderland	01665 721231
North Wales CC	
Conwy	01492 593481
North West Venturers YC (Beaumaris)	
Beaumaris	0161 2921943
Oban SC Ledaig by Oban	
	01631 563999
Orford SC Woodbridge	01394 450997
Orkney SC Kirkwall	01856 872331
Orwell YC Ipswich	01473 602288

Oulton Broad Yacht Station	
	01502 574946
Ouse Amateur SC	
Kings Lynn	01553 772239
Paignton SC Paignton	01803 525817
Parkstone YC Poole	01202 743610
Peel Sailing and CC Peel	01624 842390
Pembroke Haven YC	01646 684403
Pembrokeshire YC	
Milford Haven	01646 692799
Penarth YC	029 20708196
Pentland Firth YC	
Thurso	01847 891803
Penzance YC	01736 364989
Peterhead SC Ellon	01779 75527
Pin Mill SC	
Woodbridge	01394 780271
Plym YC Plymouth	01752 404991
Poolbeg YC	+353 1 660 4681
Poole YC	01202 672687
Porlock Weir SC	
Watchet	01643 862702
Port Edgar YC Penicuik	0131 657 2854
Port Navas YC Falmouth	01326 340065
Port of Falmouth Sailing Association	
Falmouth	01326 372927
Portchester SC	
Portchester	023 9237 6375
Porthcawl Harbour BC	
Swansea	01656 655935
Porthmadog SC	
Porthmadog	01766 513546
Portrush YC Portrush	028 7082 3932
Portsmouth SC	02392 820596
Prestwick SC Prestwick	01292 671117
Pwllheli SC Pwllhelli	01758 613343
Queenborough YC	
Queenborough	01795 663955
Quoile YC	
Downpatrick	028 44 612266
River Towy BC	
Tenby	01267 241755
RAFYC	023 80452208
Redclyffe YC Poole	01929 557227
Restronguet SC	
Falmouth	01326 374536
Ribble CC	
Lytham St Anne's	01253 739983
River Wyre YC	01253 811948
RNSA (Plymouth)	01752 55123/83
Rochester CC	01634 841350

Rock Sailing and Water Ski Club
Wadebridge　　　　01208 862431

Royal Dart YC
Dartmouth　　　　01803 752496

Royal Motor YC Poole　01202 707227

Royal Anglesey YC (Beaumaris)
Anglesey　　　　01248 810295

Royal Burnham YC
Burnham-on-Crouch　01621 782044

Royal Channel Islands YC (Jersey)
St Aubin　　　　01534 745783

Royal Cinque Ports YC
Dover　　　　01304 206262

**Royal Corinthian YC
(Burnham-on-Crouch)**
Burnham-on-Crouch　01621 782105

Royal Corinthian YC (Cowes)
Cowes　　　　01983 293581

Royal Cork YC
Crosshaven　　+353 214 831023

Royal Cornwall YC (RCYC)
Falmouth　　　　01326 312126

Royal Dorset YC
Weymouth　　　　01305 786258

Royal Forth YC
Edinburgh　　　　0131 552 3006

Royal Fowey YC Fowey　01726 833573

Royal Gourock YC　01475 632983

Royal Highland YC
Nairn　　　　01667 493855

Royal Irish YC
Dun Laoghaire　+353 1 280 9452

Royal London YC
Isle of Wight　　　019 83299727

Royal Lymington YC　01590 672677

Royal Mersey YC
Birkenhead　　　　0151 645 3204

Royal Motor YC Poole　01202 707227

Royal Naval Club and Royal Albert YC
Portsmouth　　　023 9282 5924

Royal Naval Sailing Association
Gosport　　　　023 9252 1100

Royal Norfolk & Suffolk YC
Lowestoft　　　　01502 566726

Royal North of Ireland YC
　　　　　028 90 428041

Royal Northern and Clyde YC
Rhu　　　　01436 820322

Royal Northumberland YC
Blyth　　　　01670 353636

Royal Plymouth Corinthian YC
Plymouth　　　　01752 664327

Royal Scottish Motor YC
　　　　　0141 881 1024

Royal Solent YC
Yarmouth　　　　01983 760256

Royal Southampton YC
Southampton　　　023 8022 3352

Royal Southern YC
Southampton　　　023 8045 0300

Royal St George YC
Dun Laoghaire　+353 1 280 1811

Royal Tay YC
Dundee　　　　01382 477133

Royal Temple YC
Ramsgate　　　　01843 591766

Royal Torbay YC
Torquay　　　　01803 292006

Royal Ulster YC
Bangor　　　　028 91 270568

Royal Victoria YC
Fishbourne　　　01983 882325

Royal Welsh YC (Caernarfon)
Caernarfon　　　01286 672599

Royal Welsh YC
Aernarfon　　　　01286 672599

Royal Western YC
Plymouth　　　　01752 226299

Royal Yacht Squadron
Isle of Wight　　　01983 292191

Royal Yorkshire YC
Bridlington　　　01262 672041

Rye Harbour SC　01797 223136

Salcombe YC　　01548 842593

Saltash SC　　01752 845988

Scalloway BC
Lerwick　　　　01595 880409

Scarborough YC　01723 373821

Schull SC　　+353 28 37352

Scillonian Sailing and BC
St Mary's　　　01720 277229

Seasalter SC Whitstable　07773 189943

Seaview YC
Isle of Wight　　01983 613268

Shoreham SC Henfield　01273 453078

Skerries SC
Carlingdford Lough　+353 1 849 1233

Slaughden SC
Duxford　　　　01728 689036

Sligo YC Sligo　　+353 71 77168

Solva Boat Owners Association
Fishguard　　　01437 721538

Solway YC
Kirkdudbright　　01556 620312

South Caernavonshire YC
Abersoch　　　01758 712338

South Cork SC　+353 28 36383

South Devon Sailing School
Newton Abbot　　01626 52352

South Gare Marine Club - Sail Section
Middlesbrough　　01642 505630

South Shields SC　0191 456 5821

South Woodham Ferrers YC
Chelmsford　　　01245 325391

Southampton SC　023 8044 6575

Southwold SC　01986 784225

Sovereign Harbour YC
Eastbourne　　　01323 470888

St Helier YC　01534 721307/32229

St Mawes SC　01326 270686

Starcross Fishing & CC (River Exe)
Starcross　　　01626 891996

Starcross YC Exeter　01626 890470

Stoke SC Ipswich　01473 624989

Stornoway SC　01851 705412

Stour SC　　01206 393924

Strangford Lough YC
Newtownards　　028 97 541202

Strangford SC
Downpatrick　　028 4488 1404

Strood YC Aylesford　01634 718261

Sunderland YC　0191 567 5133

Sunsail Portsmouth　023 92222224

Sussex YC
Shoreham-by-Sea　01273 464868

Swanage SC　01929 422987

Swansea Yacht & Sub-Aqua Club
Swansea　　　01792 469096

Tamar River SC
Plymouth　　　01752 362741

Tarbert Lochfyne YC　01880 820376

Tay Corinthian BC
Dundee　　　　01382 553534

Tay YCs Association　01738 621860

Tees & Hartlepool YC　01429 233423

Tees SC
Aycliffe Village　01429 265400

Teifi BC - Cardigan Bay
Fishguard　　　01239 613846

Teign Corinthian YC
Teignmouth　　01626 777699

Tenby SC　01834 842762

Tenby YC　01834 842762

Thames Estuary YC　01702 345967

Thorney Island SC　01243 371731

Thorpe Bay YC　01702 587563

Thurrock YC Grays　01375 373720

Tollesbury CC　01621 869561

Topsham SC		01392 877524
Torpoint Mosquito SC -		
Plymouth		01752 812508
Tralee SC		+353 66 7136119
Troon CC		01292 311190
Troon YC		01292 315315
Tudor SC Portsmouth		02392 662002
Tynemouth SC		
Newcastle upon Tyne		0191 2572167
Up River YC		
Hullbridge		01702 231654
Upnor SC		01634 718043
Vanguard SC		
Workington		01228 674238
Wakering YC Rochford		01702 530926
Waldringfield SC		
Woodbridge		01394 283347
Walls Regatta Club		
Lerwick		01595 809273
Walton & Frinton YC		
Walton-on-the-Naze		01255 675526
Warrenpoint BC		028 4175 2137
Warsash SC Soton		01489 583575
Watchet Boat Owner Association		
Watchet		01984 633736
Waterford Harbour SC		
Dunmore East		+353 51 383389
Watermouth YC		
Watchet		01271 865048
Wear Boating Association		
		0191 567 5313
Wells SC		
Wells-next-the-sea		01328 711190

West Kirby SC	0151 625 5579
West Mersea YC	
Colchester	01206 382947
Western Isles YC	01688 302371
Western YC Kilrush	+353 87 2262885
Weston Bay YC	
Portishead	07867 966429
Weston CC Soton	02380 466790
Weston SC Soton	02380 452527
Wexford HBC	+353 53 22039
Weymouth SC	01305 785481
Whitby YC	07786 289393
Whitstable YC	01227 272942
Wicklow SC	+353 404 67526
Witham SC Boston	01205 363598
Wivenhoe SC Colchester	01206 822132
Woodbridge CC	01394 386737
Wormit BC	01382 553878
Yarmouth SC	01983 760270
Yealm YC	
Newton Ferrers	01752 872291
Youghal Sailing Club	+353 24 92447

YACHT DESIGNERS

Cannell & Associates, David M	
Wivenhoe	01206 823337
Clarke Designs LLP, Owen	
Dartmouth	01803 770495
Giles Naval Architects, Laurent	
Lymington	01590 641777
Harvey Design, Ray	
Barton on Sea	01425 613492
Jones Yacht Design, Stephen	
Warsash	01489 576439

Wharram Designs, James	
Truro	01872 864792
Wolstenholme Yacht Design	
Coltishall	01603 737024

YACHT MANAGEMENT

Barbican Yacht Agency Ltd	
Plymouth	01752 228855
Coastal Leisure Ltd	
Southampton	023 8033 2222
O'Sullivan Boat Management	
Dun Laoghaire	+353 86 829 6625
Swanwick Yacht Surveyors	
Swanwick	01489 564822
Amble Boat Company Ltd	
Amble	01665 710267

YACHT VALETING

Autogleam	
Lymington	0800 074 4672
Blackwell, Craig	
Co Meath	+353 87 677 9605
Bright 'N' Clean	
South Coast	01273 604080
Clean It All	
Nr Brixham	01803 844564
Kip Marina Inverkip	01475 521485
Mainstay Yacht Maintenance	
Dartmouth	01803 839076
Mobile Yacht Maintenance	
	07900 148806
Shipshape Hayling Is	023 9232 4500